Edward B. Cowell

The Kusumanjali:

Or, Hindu proof of the existence of a supreme being

Edward B. Cowell

The Kusumanjali:
Or, Hindu proof of the existence of a supreme being

ISBN/EAN: 9783337731168

Printed in Europe, USA, Canada, Australia, Japan

Cover: Foto ©ninafisch / pixelio.de

More available books at **www.hansebooks.com**

THE KUSUMÁNJALI,

OR

HINDU PROOF OF THE EXISTENCE OF A SUPREME BEING,

BY

UDAYANA ÁCHÁRYA,

WITH THE

COMMENTARY OF HARI DÁSA BHAṬṬÁCHÁRYA,

EDITED AND TRANSLATED BY

E. B. COWELL, M. A.,

ASSISTED BY

PAṆḌITA MAHE'SA CHANDRA NYÁYARATNA.

CALCUTTA:
PRINTED AT THE BAPTIST MISSION PRESS, CIRCULAR ROAD.
1864.

TO

PROFESSOR MAX MÜLLER,

IN MEMORY OF

OLD OXFORD DAYS.

PREFACE.

THE following treatise is very celebrated amongst Hindu logicians, and, however little it may be calculated to interest the general English reader, it will certainly not be without a use and interest to those Europeans whose studies are directed to the higher branches of Sanskrit literature. They will hardly fail to be attracted by a work which, though obscure and technical, professes to grapple, from a Hindu standing-point, with the world-old problem, how the existence of the Supreme Being is to be proved; and perhaps those who are interested in the history of philosophy may turn over some of the pages with curiosity, especially when they occasionally recognise old familiar arguments and objections in their quaint Oriental disguise. The Kusumánjali is as much inferior to the tenth book of Plato's Laws or the twelfth of Aristotle's Metaphysics, as Hindu philosophy itself is to that of Greece; but nothing can rob India of the merit of an original system of logic and metaphysics, unborrowed from any other land. It has been said that the past history of philosophy is the record of glorious failures in the attempt to solve an insuperable problem; and it cannot be uninteresting to trace the brave efforts of a Hindu thinker, far away from the circle of Christianity, who, perplexed by the doubts or open disbelief taught in many of the systems current in his day, endeavoured, however vainly, to build for his countrymen the first truth of Theology on a firm logical foundation.

——— Audacia certè
Laus erit; in magnis et voluisse sat est.

Udayana A'chárya, like nearly every old Hindu writer, is a *name* and nothing more. He shines like one of the fixed stars in India's literary firmament, but no telescope can discover any appreciable diameter; his name is a *point* of light, but we can detect therein nothing that belongs to our earth or material existence. The details of his life are a blank,* and the very century in which he flourished is an unsettled question in Hindu literary history.

Dr. Hall, in his valuable 'Index to the Bibliography of the Hindu philosophical systems,' (p. 20,) has endeavoured to identify Udayana with Uddyotakara, (whom he places not later than the seventh century,†) but this is untenable, as will be proved, I think, in the sequel.

The first point to settle is the *order* of the series of ancient Nyáya works, ' the sútras of Gotama and Kanáda having been explained and annotated by a triple [or rather quadruple] set of commentaries.‡' The order which I venture to propose is as follows,

I.—The original *Sútras* or Aphorisms ascribed to the Ṛishi Gotama or Akshapáda.

II.—The *Nyáya-bháshya,*—a commentary on No. I. by Pakshila Swámin, sometimes called Vátsyáyana.

III.—The *Nyáya-vártika,*—a commentary on No. II. by Uddyotakara Áchárya. I procured lately, from a pandit of Nuddea, a fragment of this work containing a portion of the first book.§

IV.—The *Nyáya-vártika-tátparya-ṭíká*—a commentary on No. III. by Váchaspati Mis'ra.

V.—The *Nyáya vártika-tátparya-paris'uddhi*—a commentary on No. IV. by Udayana Áchárya.

My reasons for this arrangement are the following.

---

* The only incident I have met with, is the dubious tradition given in the 'Rational Refutation of Hindu philosophical systems,' p. 6, *note*.

† Uddyotakara is mentioned in Subandhu's Vásavadattá, which Dr. Hall has proved to be fully 1200 years old.

‡ Colebrooke.

§ There is an incomplete MS. in the Asiatic Society's Library, which professes to contain the third and fourth adhyáyas (*ity auddyotakariye nyáyavártake*, &c.,) but it is only Váchaspati Mis'ra's ṭíká.—The Nuddea fragment contains only the vártika to the first three sútras,—its colophon is

इति श्रीपरमर्षिभारद्वाजश्रीमदुद्द्योतकरन्यायाचार्यप्रणीतन्यायवि-
द्ध्योवार्तिकं सम्पूर्णं ॥

In the Calcutta Sanskrit College Library there is a MS. of the *Nyáya-vártika-tátparya-ṭíká,* the opening lines of which I subjoin.

विश्वव्यापी विश्वशक्तिः पिनाकी विश्वेश्वानो विश्वकृद् विश्वमूर्तिः ।
विश्वत्राता विश्वसंचारकारी विश्वाराध्यो राधयत्वीप्सितं नः ॥ १ ॥
नमामि धर्मविज्ञानवैराग्यैश्वर्यशालिनं ।
निधये वाग्विशुद्धीनामक्षपादाय तायिने ॥ २ ॥
यस्यव्याख्याच्छलेनैव निरस्ताखिलदूषणा ।
न्यायवार्तिकतात्पर्यटीकाऽक्षाभिर्विधास्यते ॥ ३ ॥
इच्छामः किमपि पुरूयं दुस्तरकुनिबन्धपङ्कमग्नानां ।
उद्योतकरगवीनामतिजरतीनां समुद्धरणात् ॥ ४ ॥

अथ भगवताऽक्षपादेन निःश्रेयसहेतौ शास्त्रे प्रणीते, व्युत्पादिते च भगवता पक्षिलस्वामिना, किमपरमवशिष्यते यदर्थं वार्त्तिकारम्भ इति शङ्कां निराचिकीर्षुः सूत्रकारोक्तप्रयोजनानुवादपूर्वकं वार्त्तिकारम्भप्रयोजनं दर्शयति 'यदक्षपादः' इति । यद्यपि भाष्यकृता कृतव्युत्पादनमेतत् तथापि दिङ्नागप्रभृतिभिरर्वाचीनैः कुहेतुसन्तमसमुत्थापनेन आच्छादितं शास्त्रं न तत्त्वनिर्णयाय पर्याप्तमित्युद्योतकरेण स्वनिबन्धोद्योतेन तदपनीयत इति प्रयोजनवानयमारम्भः ।

This passage is evidently a commentary on the work of Uddyotakara Áchárya, whose opening words (*yad Akshapádah,*) the author professes to quote and explain; and he states that the Nyáya 'Sástra was originally delivered by Akshapáda or Gotama and completed by Pakshila Swámin, and that Uddyotakara compiled his Vártika or 'annotations' in order to clear away the erroneous interpretations of Diṇnága and others. The Sanskrit College has also a MS. of the Tátparya paris'uddhi of Udayanáchárya, which is undoubtedly a commentary on No. IV. Thus it commences with an invocation to Saraswatí, वाक्चेतसोर्मम तथा भव सावधाना वाचस्पतेर्वचसि न स्खलतो यथेते। and it then proceeds to comment on the first 'Sloka quoted above—विश्वाराध्य इत्यत्र विश्वपदेन &c.

Now if Váchaspati Mi'sra commented on a work of Uddyotakara, and Udayana again on the work of Váchaspati Mi'sra, Uddyotakara and Udayana must be different persons.

A second question however now arises,—who is the Pakshila Swámin, to illustrate whose work Uddyotakara compiled his Vártika?

The only *Nyáya-bháshya* now known to exist is that which bears the name of Vátsyáyana. By the kindness of Professor Griffith, I have procured a MS. of it from the Benares College Library,* and, on comparing this work with the quotations from Pakshila Swámin's *bháshya* which are frequently given in the fragment of the *Vártika* and in Váchaspati's *Tátparya-ṭíká*, I have discovered that the two works are *the same*. A few extracts will make this evident.

The *Nyáya bháshya* of Vátsyáyana thus commences, प्रमाणतोऽर्थप्रतिपत्तौ प्रवृत्तिसामर्थ्यादर्थवत् प्रमाणम् प्रमाणमन्तरेण नार्थप्रतिपत्तिः । Now the fragment of the *Vártika* commences,

यदच्चपादः प्रवरो मुनीनां प्रमाय शास्त्रं जगतो जगाद ।
कुतार्किताज्ञाननिवृत्तिहेतुः करिष्यते तस्य मया निबन्धः ॥

प्रमाणादिपदार्थतत्त्वज्ञानान्निःश्रेयसाधिगम इत्येतच्छास्त्रादिमं सूत्रं । तस्याभिसम्बन्धवाक्यं प्रमाणतोऽर्थप्रतिपत्ताविळ्वमादि, तस्यानुसन्धानवाक्यं ।

Similarly in the third leaf of the *Tátparya-ṭíká* we read, तदेवं प्रथमसूत्रतात्पर्यमुक्त्वा भाष्यस्यादिवाक्यतात्पर्यमाह 'प्रमाणतोऽर्थप्रतिपत्ताविद्यादि तस्यानुसन्धानं' । तस्य शास्त्रस्य निःश्रेयसाधिगमेन सह सूचेन घटितस्य कुतश्चिन्निमित्तात् विघटनाशङ्कायां अनु सूत्रघटनायाः पश्चात् सन्धानं घटनं अनुसन्धानं । तस्य वाक्यमनुसन्धानवाक्यं ।

The words of the *vártika*, with their enclosed quotation from the *bháshya*, are thus quoted and explained in the *ṭíká*. After discussing some doubts, it goes on,

सेयमाशङ्का प्रमाण्यज्ञानोपायकथनेनादिवाक्येन भाष्यकृता निराकृता, तथा हि 'प्रमाणमर्थवत्' इति । नित्ययोगेन मतुप् । नित्यता चाव्यभिचारिता, तेनार्थाव्यभिचारीत्यर्थः ।...... अत्र हेतुः 'प्रवृत्तिसामर्थ्यात्' समर्थप्रवृत्तिजनकत्वात् । प्रवृत्तिजनकत्वं तु प्रमाणस्य न साक्षात् किन्त्वर्थप्रतिपत्तिजननद्वारेणेत्याह 'प्रमाणतोऽर्थप्रतिपत्तौ' इति । सर्वस्य वाक्यस्योपपत्तिं वार्तिकव्याख्यानावसरे निवेदयिष्यामः ॥

* It contains 123 leaves, and its colophon is इति वात्स्यायनीये न्यायभाष्ये पञ्चमोऽध्यायः ।

The third Adhyáya of Vátsyáyana's *Nyáyabháshya* opens with परीक्षितानि प्रमाणानि प्रमेयमिदानीं परीक्ष्यते तचात्मादीत्या- त्मा विविच्यते । and similarly the third adhyáya of the *Tátparya țíká* commences, अत्र भाष्यं 'परीक्षितानि प्रमाणानि प्रमेयमिदानीं परीक्ष्यते' इति वृत्तानुकीर्तनम् Then again, a few lines after, कस्मात् प्रथमत आत्मैव परीक्ष्यते न प्रमेयान्तरमित्यत आह 'तचा- त्मादीनि' इति । Shortly afterwards it adds तदेतद् वार्तिक- कारो व्याचष्टे ।*

There can, therefore, be hardly a doubt as to the Nyáya-bháshya of Pakshila Swámin and that of Vátsyáyana being the same work.† The latter name seems to imply that the author wrote the book while his father or elder brother (compare Pánini 4. 1. 105 with 4. 1. 94, 101, 163 and 164,) was alive. Pakshila was his private, Vátsyáyana was his generic, name. Swámin may imply his becoming an *udásina*, or it may have been merely an honorary title. The Pandits similarly have a tradition that a Nyáya-vártika was written by Bháradwája. Dr. Hall mentions in his Catalogue that Uddyotakara belonged to the *gotra* of Bharadwája, and the same thing is stated in the colophon to the Nuddea fragment; and thus the two appellations, Vátsyáyana and Bháradwája, will mutually illustrate each other.

We may thus consider it as proved that Udayana Áchárya is the *fifth*, not the *third*, in the series of Naiyáyika authorities; but are we able to determine anything as to the time in which he flourished? We can hardly hope to fix it with precision, but we are not left wholly to conjecture, as we have, I think, a *terminus à quo* as well as a *terminus ad quem* to limit our chronological uncertainty.

We must here again have recourse to our former expedient of arranging the different authors by their respective quotations,—

---

* Similarly the lines quoted from Pakshila Swámin in the Sarva D. Sangraha, p. 115, are found in Vátsyáyana, (MS. fol. 4.)
† I hope that the Asiatic Society will publish the Nyáyabháshya in the Biliotheca Indica, as a second MS. has been just procured from Nuddea. No work could be of greater importance for giving an insight into the older Nyáya.

the only data which the total absence of literary history in India allows us to use. In this way we can establish a second series of writers, viz. S'ankara A´chárya, Váchaspati Mis'ra, Udayana A´chárya and Mádhava A´chárya; and, as in this series the dates of the first and last are known, we can approximately determine the dates of the intermediate pair. We cannot be far wrong in assigning S'ankara A´chárya to the beginning of the ninth century of our era,* and we know by the testimony of copper land-grants as well as tradition that Mádhava A´chárya and his patron Vírabukka flourished in the earlier half of the fourteenth century.† Now Váchaspati Mis'ra, the fourth in our previous series of Naiyáyika authors, wrote one of the most celebrated glosses (the *Bhámatí*) on S'ankara A´chárya's commentary on the Vedánta Sútras.‡ We have seen that Udayana A´chárya commented in turn on Váchaspati; and his own work, now presented to the reader, is several times quoted by Mádhava in his Sarva Dars'ana Sangraha.§ Now in India a writer must have long ceased to have any visible connection with the present before a Pandit would trouble himself to write commentaries on his works or quote from them as a well-accepted authority; and perhaps therefore we may, without fear of much error, fix Váchaspati Mis'ra in the tenth, and Udayanáchárya in the twelfth century. It is something to think that the author of the Kusumánjali may have been an unknown contemporary of Abelard.

The Kusumánjali consists of seventy-two *kárikás* or memorial couplets, divided into five chapters; and as the author's aim was to pack his arguments into the smallest possible compass, the book is of course unintelligible without a commentary. It is not generally known that the author himself compiled such a commentary; and in fact it is not improbable

---

* Colebrooke's Essays, vol. I. p. 332. Wilson's Sanskrit Dict. preface, 1st ed.
† Wilson's Mackenzie Cat. vol. I. p. cxl. Colebrooke's Essays, vol. I. p. 301.
‡ Both the *Bhámatí* and the *Nyáya-vártika-tátparya-ṭíká* are mentioned in Váchaspati's own list of his works, see Dr. Hall's Catalogue, p. 87.
§ As *e. g.* p. 7, l. 18; p. 113, l. 6; p. 120, l. 13; p. 133, l. 4.

that the work, as it originally appeared, was in verse and prose,—the latter portion consisting of detached passages of varying length, introduced between the stanzas to supply the necessary links for understanding the argument. There is an imperfect MS. of this description in the Sanskrit Coll. Library. It is called the Kusumánjali, and contains the first chapter in 24 foll.; but it unfortunately ends abruptly at the beginning of the second. It is remarkable that there is no sign of division between the two chapters,—the discussion of the second objection goes on in unbroken continuity with that of the first. As the work is very rare and Dr. Hall does not notice it in his very copious Catalogue, I subjoin a few more details.*

It commences with the first Káriká *(satpratipaksha,)* as the opening invocation; then follows the second *(swargápavargayoh.)* Then follows the long prose passage (beginning with *iha yadyapi*, and ending with *abhávácchcheti,*) which is always given as supplying the place of the third káriká. This is followed by the first additional remark.

तच्च न प्रथमः कस्यः, यतः, सापेच्चत्वादित्यादि (here follows s'l. 4.)। न ह्ययं संसारोऽनेकविधदुःखमयो निरपेच्चो भवितुमर्हति, तदा हि स्यादेव, न स्यादेव वा, न तु कदाचित् स्यात्। अकस्मादेव भवतीति चेन्न "हेतुभूतिनिषेधो न खानुपाख्यविधिनं च । खभाववर्णना नैवमवधेर्नियतत्वतः"। हेतुनिषेधे भवनस्थानपेच्चत्वेन सर्वदाऽविशेषात्, भवनप्रतिषेधे प्रागिव पश्चादप्यभवनं अविशेषात्। उत्पत्तेः पूर्वं खयमसतः खोत्पत्तावप्रभुत्वेन खस्मादिति पच्चानुपपत्तेः, पौर्वापर्यनियमश्च कार्यकारणभावः, न चैकं पूर्वमपरञ्चेति तच्चस्य भेदाधिष्ठानत्वात्। अनुपाख्यस्य हेतुत्वे प्रागपि सत्त्वप्रसङ्गो पुनः सदात्मनत्वापत्तेः। 'स्यादेतत् नाकस्मादिति कारणनिषेधमात्रं भवननिषेधो वा खात्महेतुलं वा निरपेख्यहेतुकत्वं वाऽभिधित्सितं, अपि तु अनपेच्च एव कस्मिन्नियतदेशवनियतकाल इति खभाव इति क्रमः'।

---

* Udayana is not specified as the author of the commentary, but it seems to belong to the same author as the kárikás, since there is only one *mangalácharaṇa* for both, and the prose and verse follow each other as from the same pen. Unfortunately the MS. is carelessly transcribed and full of blunders. My extract contains many conjectural emendations.

न, निरवधित्वेऽनियतावधिकत्वे वा कादाचित्कत्व्याघातात् । न ह्युत्तरकाले संसर्गित्वमात्रं कादाचित्कत्वं किन्तु प्रागसति, सावधित्वे स एव प्राच्यो हेतुरित्युच्यते । अस्तु प्रागभाव एव अवधिरिति चेन्न अन्येषामपि तत्काले सत्त्वात् अन्यथा तस्यैव तत्काले निरूपणानुप-पत्तेः । तथा च न तदेकावधिकत्वमविप्रघात् । इतरनिरपेक्षस्य प्रागभावस्यावधित्वे प्राग्पि तदवधेः कार्यस्य सत्त्वप्रसङ्गात् । 'सन्तु ये केचिदवधयो न तु तेऽपेक्ष्यन्ते इति स्वभावार्थः' इति चेन्न अपेक्ष्यन्त इति कोऽर्थः । किं न नियता आहोस्विन्नियता अप्यनुपकारकाः । प्रथमे धर्मो दहनवद्दूरभमप्यवधीकुर्यात् नियामकाभावात् द्वितीये तु किमुपकारान्तरेण निरमस्यैवापेक्षार्थत्वात् तस्यैव च कारणार्थ-त्वात्, इष्टस्य च स्वभावस्येष्टत्वात् ।

Besides this commentary of the original author's, various pandits have written commentaries to illustrate the work,—for an account of these and the secondary glosses which these have in turn elicited, I refer the reader to Dr. Hall's Catalogue, pp. 82-84.

The Kusumánjali was first printed in Calcutta in the 'Saka year 1769, with the commentary of Haridása Bhaṭṭáchárya,—and it was subsequently reprinted in Bengali letters in the Samvat year 1916. For the present edition, two old MSS. have been collated,* which have been long in the possession of Naiyáyika families ; and from these I have introduced several emendations into the old text of the commentary.

I have endeavoured to make my translation as accurate as I could, but I cannot fail to have left inadvertencies, for which I must plead in excuse the thorny nature of the subject. I have consulted pandits in all difficulties, but, as their explanations are necessarily given in Sanskrit or Bengali, it is not always easy to detect the frequent subtil distinctions of Hindu metaphysics. The translation is as literal as I could make it so as to be intelligible, and I have every where endeavoured to supplement it by copious notes. But I cannot hope that the general reader

---

* Lent to me by Paṇḍita Jayanáráyaṇa Tarkapanchánana and Paṇḍita Mahes'a-chandra Nyáyaratna.

will be much interested in the major part of the treatise. Hindu philosophers reject all attempt to mix the *dulce* with the *utile*; and, as Dr. Röer has well observed,* " the punishment of this mystery and exclusion is the want of interest felt in the study of their works." I have subjoined a short synopsis of the whole argument, which will shew the ground over which our author professes to travel; and I hope that any one interested in the subject will be able with a little attention to master most of it. The only really abstruse portions are the latter half of the first and third chapters, and the discussion on the meaning of *vidhi* in the fifth; and these will certainly not repay an English reader for the trouble of understanding them.

In my translation I have frequently borrowed Dr. Hall's terminology, as found in his admirable translation of Paṇḍita Nehemiah Nílakaṇṭha 'Sástrí Gore's 'Rational Refutation of the Hindu Philosophical systems,' and I beg to express my continual obligations to the pandit and his translator.

But my acknowledgments are especially due to the Professors of the Sanskrit College, without whose assistance hardly one page of my translation could have been made. I have associated the name of Paṇḍita Mahes'achandra Nyáyaratna with my own on the title page, as I read the original with him; he has also helped me in the collation of the MSS., and his short gloss on the more difficult passages will be of great service to the Sanskrit student. But I must not omit to express my many obligations to Paṇḍita Jayanáráyaṇa Tarkapanchánana and Paṇḍita Táránátha Tarkaváchaspati, the Professors of Philosophy and Grammar,—the two most learned Hindus I have met during my residence in India, and whose names, I hope, will be not wholly unknown in Europe from their respective editions of the Vais'eshika Sútras and the Siddhánta Kaumudí.

E. B. C.

Calcutta, March, 1864.

---

* Categories of Nyáya Philosophy, Introd. p. v.

SYNOPSIS OF THE KUSUMÁNJALI.

First Cluster.

The contemplation of God produces liberation ; but the doubt arises,—is there a God for us to contemplate ? the universal practical consent of mankind is conceded, but a fivefold theoretic objection is raised against His existence, i.—iii.

A. There is no such supernatural cause of another world as *adrishṭa* or desert.

This leads to a discussion on the relation of cause and effect, iv., v., the Mímánsaka notion of a distinct category, called capacity, and the Vedantist and Sánkhya tenet of one common material cause, vi.—xiii. ; the Sánkhya system is discussed, xiv. ; the materialist, xv. ; the Bauddha, xvi., xvii. Objections against causality answered in xviii., xix. Adrishṭa being unintelligent, its acceptance involves the concession of a Supreme Being to direct it, xix., xx.

Second Cluster.

B. Sacrifices &c. are a sufficient cause of another world, and we need not assume any Supreme Being.

This is met by arguments drawn from the need of an external authority, and the fact of successive creations and destructions of the world, which involve the destruction of the Veda from æon to æon, i.—iv.

Third Cluster.

C. There are arguments to prove God's non-existence, as drawn from the six current proofs *(pramáṇas),*—

α, from perception *(pratyaksha,)* as He is not perceived. This is met by a discussion on the nature of non-perception, i.—iii.

β. From inference *(anumána)* iv.—vii.

γ. From comparison *(upamána,)* viii.—xii.

δ. From testimony *(s'abda)* xiii.—xvii.

ε. From presumption *(arthápatti)* xviii., xix.

ζ. From non-perception *(anupalabdhi)* xx.—xxiii.

The two last are denied to be proofs,—the four first are shewn to be silent against Theism.

Fourth Cluster.

D. Some of the Mímánsakas hold that even if God did exist He could not be an authority *(pramáṇa)* to us.

The Mímánsaka definition of *pramá* is shewn to be erroneous, i.—iv., and its true definition given in v., vi.

Fifth Cluster.

E. There is an absence of any positive argument for God's existence.

To meet this, eight separate arguments are given in i. These are discussed, ii.—v.

A new interpretation of i. is then suggested which would give eight vaidic arguments. This is interrupted by a discussion on the true meaning of *vidhi* or 'command,' vi.—xiv. The second interpretation of i. is resumed, xv., xvi. The subject is summed up, xvii.—xix.

कुसुमाञ्जलिः ।

श्रीमदुदयनाचार्यविरचितः ।

श्रीहरिदासभट्टाचार्यकृतव्याख्यानसहितः ।

श्रीमद्येमचन्द्रन्यायरत्नसङ्कलिततात्पर्यविवरणान्वितः ।

तत्सङ्कलितेन तु संस्कृतविद्यालयाध्यक्षेण

श्रीमता इ॰ बि॰ काउएलसाहेबेन

संशोधितः ।

कलिकाता-राजधान्यां

व्याप्टिष्ट-मिसन्-यन्त्रे मुद्रितः ।

शकाब्दाः १७८५ ॥ ख्रीष्टाब्दाः १८६४ ॥

कुसुमाञ्जलिः।

प्रथमः स्तवकः।

ईषद्दीर्घदनधीतविद्यया तातमाह्लादमाविवर्धयन् ।
द्वेषघाय भवत्कर्मजन्मनां कोऽपि गोपतनयो नमस्ते ॥

दृष्टदेवतासङ्कीर्तनं ब्रह्मप्रतिपादकसच्छब्दप्रयोगात्मकञ्च
मङ्गलं कुर्वन् ग्रन्थनामाह

सत्यचत्प्रसरः सतां परिमलप्रोद्बोधबद्धोत्सवो
विद्वानो न विमर्दनेऽत्तरसप्रस्यन्दमाधीकभूः ।
ईशस्यैष निवेशितः पदयुगे भृङ्गायमाणं भ्रम-
च्चेतो मे रमयत्वविघ्नमनघायप्रसूनाञ्चलिः ॥ १ ॥

एषोऽनघो निर्दोषः, न्यायः समस्तरूपोपपन्नलिङ्गप्रतिपा-
दकं वाक्यं, स एव कुसुमाञ्जलिः मे मम चित्तं रमयतु दुःख-
सामग्रीविहीनं करोतु । अनघं शब्ददोषरहितं, विषया-
न्तरशुद्धेः पूर्वार्धेनैव निरासाभिधानादिति प्रकाशः । अविघ्नं यथा
स्यात्, ईशस्य पदयुगे, पद्यतेऽनेनेतिव्युत्पत्त्या पदं प्रत्यायकं, तद्युगं
प्रमाणतर्करूपं, तत्र निवेशितः तद्विषयतया उत्पादितः । चेतः
कीदृशं, भृङ्गायमाणं भृङ्ग इव मकरन्दे दुःखविगमोपाये सहृष्णं,
भ्रमत् दुःखविगमोपायमनुसन्दधत् । प्रसूनाञ्चलिसाम्यमाह

सदित्यादि । सता समीचीनेन, पक्षेणानुकूलेन रविकिरणादिना प्रसरो विकाशो यस्य स तथा, सतां पक्षाणां दलानां विकाशो यच्च स तथेति वा । सतामनुपहतघ्राणानां परिमलस्य गन्धविशेषस्य प्रबोधेन साक्षात्कारेण बह्वुत्सव आनन्दो येन सः । विमर्दने करण्टविमर्दने न विज्ञानः नान्यथाभूतसंस्थानः । अमृततुल्यं रसं प्रस्यन्दते इति प्रस्यन्दः, एतादृशं माध्वीकं मधु, तस्य भूरत्युत्तिस्थानम् ॥ न्यायपक्षे, सति प्रामाणिके पक्षतावच्छेदकविशिष्टे इति यावत्, पक्षे विषाधर्म्यविशिष्टसाध्यधर्मके धर्मिणि, प्रसरः प्रकर्षेण सरो ज्ञानं यस्मात्, एतेनाश्रयासिद्धिस्वरूपासिद्धिबाधनिरासः । सतां विवेचकानां, परि सर्वतोभावेन, मनः सम्बन्धो व्याप्तिः, तस्याः प्रबोधेन प्रमया बह्वुत्सव आनन्दो येन, एतेन व्यभिचारव्याप्यत्वासिद्धिविरोधानां निरासः । विमर्दने विरोधिप्रमाणचिन्तायां न विज्ञानः न कार्योच्चमः, तेन सत्प्रतिपक्षराहित्यम् । अमृतं मोक्षः, रस इत्युमानं 'इदि-चितः' इति* न्यायात्, प्रस्यन्द उत्पद्यमानं तेन मोक्षस्यासाध्यता निराकृता, तदेव माध्वीकं, तस्य भूरत्युत्तिस्थानम् ॥ १ ॥

'नन्वीश्वरपदयुग्मनिवेशितस्य न्यायस्य मोक्षरूपफलसम्बन्धे मानाभावः, तत्त्वज्ञानविषयात्मबोधकस्वात्मशब्दस्य† संसारनिदानमिथ्याज्ञानविषयस्वात्ममात्रपरत्वात् तन्मननादेव मोक्षोपायत्वात्' इतिशङ्कायामाह

---

* 'इदिचितो भावो द्र्व्यवत् प्रकाश्यते' इति संक्षिप्तसारे ।
† "आत्मा वा अरे द्रष्टव्यः श्रोतव्यो मन्तव्यो निदिध्यासितव्यः" इति ऋग्वेदा० ।

स्वर्गापवर्गयोर्मार्गमामनन्ति मनीषिणः ।
यदुपास्तिमसावच्च परमात्मा निरूप्यते ॥ २ ॥

स्वर्गापवर्गयोः स्वर्गतुल्ययोः अपवर्गयोर्जीवन्मुक्तिपरममुक्त्योः । ईश्वरमननाद्दृष्टद्वारा खात्मसाचात्कारद्वारा वा मुक्तौ हेतुः, "तमेव विदित्वाऽतिमृत्युमेति नान्यः पन्था विद्यतेऽयनाय" (श्वेता॰ उ॰) इति श्रुतिस्तत्कारणत्वे मानम् । खात्मसाचात्कारस्य मोचहेतुत्वे मानञ्च "यदात्मानं विजानीयादहमस्मीति पूरुषः । किमिच्छन् कस्य कामाय शरीरमनुसंसरेत्" (वृहदा॰) इति ॥२॥

इह यद्यपि यं कमपि पुरुषार्थमर्थयमानाः, शुद्धबुद्धस्वभाव इत्यौपनिषदाः, आदिविद्वान् सिद्ध इति कापिलाः, क्लेशकर्मविपाकाशयैरपरामृष्टो निर्माणकायमधिष्ठाय सम्प्रदायप्रद्योतकोऽनुग्राहकश्चेति पातञ्जलाः, लोकवेदविरुद्धैरपि निर्लेपः स्वतन्त्र इति माहापाशुपताः, शिव इति शैवाः, पुरुषोत्तम इति वैष्णवाः, पितामह इति पौराणिकाः, यज्ञपुरुष इति याज्ञिकाः, सर्वज्ञ इति सौगताः, निरावरण इति दिगम्बराः, उपाश्रयेन देशित इति मीमांसकाः, लोकव्यवहारसिद्ध इति चार्वाकाः, यावदुक्तोपपन्न इति नैयायिकाः, किं बहुना, यं कारवोऽपि विश्वकर्मेत्युपासते, तस्मिन्नेवं जातिगोत्रप्रवरचरणकुलधर्मादिवदसंसारं सुप्रसिद्धानुभवे भगवति भवे तत्त्वसन्देह एव कुतः, किं निरूपणीयम् । तथापि, न्यायचर्चैयमीशस्य मननव्यपदेशभाक् । उपासनैव क्रियते श्रवणानन्तरागता । श्रुतो हि भगवान् ब्रह्म श्रुतिस्मृतीतिहासपुराणादिषु,

इदानीं मन्तव्यो भवति "श्रोतव्यो मन्तव्यः" इति श्रुतेः "आगमे-
नानुमानेन ध्यानाभ्यासरसेन च। त्रिधा प्रकल्पयन् प्रज्ञां लभते
योगमुत्तमं" इतिस्मृतेश्व। तदिह सङ्क्षेपतः पञ्चधी विप्रति-
पत्तिः,—अलौकिकस्य परलोकसाधनस्याभावात्, अन्यथापि
परलोकसाधनानुष्ठानसम्भवात्, तदभावावेदकप्रमाणसद्भावात्,
सत्त्वेऽपि तस्याप्रमाणत्वात्, तत्साधकप्रमाणाभावाच्चेति ॥ ३ ॥

शुद्धो द्वितीयरचितः, बुद्धो बोधस्वरूपः, आदौ सर्गादौ
विद्वान् चित्रूपः, सिद्धः अष्टविधैश्वर्यवान्, अविद्यास्मितराग-
द्वेषाभिनिवेशाः पञ्च क्लेशाः, कर्म धर्माधर्मं हेतुर्योगहिंसादिः,
विपाका जात्यायुर्भोगाः, आम्नाया धर्माधर्माः, निर्माणार्थं कायो
निर्माणकायः, सम्प्रदायो वेदः, प्रद्योतकः प्रकाशकः, वेदस्य
नित्यत्वात्, घटादौ कर्तव्येऽनुग्राहकः त्रिश्वयिता, त्रिभो निस्त्रै-
गुण्यः, पितामहो जनकस्याऽपि जनकः, इज्यते इति यज्ञः, सर्वज्ञः
त्रैणिकसर्वज्ञः, आवरणमविद्यारागद्वेषमोहाभिनिवेशाः, उपा-
स्खलेन देशितो मन्त्रादिः, यावत्क्लेशेषु यदुपपन्नं तेनोपपन्नः, चरणं
शाखा । शब्दसिद्धत्वादयन्निमित्त्याऽनुमितेन संशयासक्तं दोषाय।
'तुष्यतु दुर्जनः' इति न्यायेन संशयमात्र तदिदंत्यादि ॥ ३ ॥

धर्माधर्मात्मकालौकिकपरलोकसाधने विप्रतिपन्नं प्रति तत्सा-
धनं, सिद्धे च तस्मिन् तदधिष्ठातृतया ईश्वरसिद्धिः, अचेतनस्य
कारणस्य सचेतनाधिष्ठानेनैव कार्यजनकत्वात्। तत्साधनायाह

सापेक्षत्वादनादिलादैचिच्यादिस्ववृत्तितः ।
प्रत्यात्मनियमाङ्कुरेरस्ति हेतुरलौकिकः ॥ ४ ॥

अलौकिकोऽतीन्द्रियः परलोकहेतुरस्तीति प्रतिज्ञा । तच्च प्रथमतः कारणसामान्यसाधनाच्च सापेक्षत्वादिति । सापेक्षत्वं कादाचित्कत्वं, तथा च कार्यं सहेतुकं कादाचित्कत्वात् भोजनजन्यत्वस्निवत् । 'ननु घटादिहेतोः सदातनत्वे घटादेरपि सदातनत्वापत्तिः, तथा च तस्य कादाचित्कत्वं वाच्यम्, एवं तत्कारणपरम्परापि कादाचित्की सहेतुका वाच्या' इत्यनवस्थायामुत्तरमनादित्वादिति, बीजाङ्कुरवत् प्रामाणिकीयमनवस्था न दोषायेत्यर्थः । 'ननु ब्रह्मैव कारणमस्तु, किं वा नानाबुद्ध्यात्मिका प्रकृतिरेव तथाऽस्तु' इत्यत्राह वैचित्र्यादिति । कार्यं विचित्रकारणवत् विचित्रकार्यत्वात् । 'ननु दृष्टं यागादेव कारणमस्तु किमदृष्टेन' इत्यत्राह विश्ववृत्तित इति । विश्वेषां परलोकार्थिनां वृत्तितः यागादौ प्रवृत्तितः, स्वर्गादिफलकत्वज्ञानमेव यागादिप्रवृत्तिजनकं, यागादेश्च तज्जनकत्वं तत्कालावस्थायिव्यापारं विना न सम्भवतीति अदृष्टसिद्धिः । 'नन्वदृष्टं न भोगसमानाधिकरणं किन्तु भोग्यादिनिष्ठत्वेनैव भोगजनकं' इत्यत्राह प्रत्यात्मनियमादिति । भुक्तेर्भोगस्य प्रतिनियतात्मवृत्तित्वात्, व्यधिकरणादृष्टस्य भोगजनकत्वेऽतिप्रसङ्गात् ॥ ४ ॥

'अकस्मादेव भवति, न किञ्चिदपेक्ष्यं कार्यमिति, अत एव "अनिमित्ततो भावोत्पत्तिः कण्टकतैक्ष्ण्यादिदर्शनात्" इति पूर्वपक्षसूत्रं (न्यायसू० ४।२२)' तत्राह

हेतुभ्रतिनिषेधो न खानुपाख्यविधिर्न च ।
स्वभाववर्णना नैवमवधेर्नियतत्वतः ॥ ५ ॥

अकस्मादिति* किं हेतुनिषेधपरं भवननिषेधपरं वा, व्यतिरिक्तहेतुनिषेधपरं पारमार्थिकहेतुनिषेधपरं वा, अनेकभयद्वाहेतुकत्वमन्येऽलौकिकहेतुकत्वञ्च पर्य्यवस्यति, स्वभाववादित्यर्थपरं वा । खं कार्य्यम्, अनुपाख्यमलीकम्। अवधेर्नियतत्वः नियतावधिककार्य्यदर्शनात्, अनियतावधिकत्वे च कादाचित्कत्वव्याकोप इति भावः ॥ ५ ॥

'नन्वनादिश्चेत् कार्य्यकारणप्रवाहः कादाचित्कत्वान्यथानुपपत्त्या कल्प्यः, तदा वह्निलावच्छिन्नस्य धूमादिव्यभिचारितया धूमाद्यकारणत्वे कादाचित्कत्वस्वभावव्याकोपः, कारणान्तरस्य च वक्तुमशक्यत्वात्'। अत्र वह्न्यनुकूलैकशक्तिमत्त्वेन कारणता, शक्तिश्च पदार्थान्तरं प्रतिव्यक्ति नाना अनित्येऽनित्या "नित्ये नित्यैव सा शक्तिरनित्ये भावहेतुजा" इति तत्सिद्धान्तात्। 'वह्न्यनुकूला धूमारणिमणिनिष्ठा शक्तिर्नित्या' इति तु मतान्तरम्। न्यायमतं तु धूमादिजन्यतावच्छेदकं वैजात्यमेव, विजातीयेऽेकजातीयकार्य्यानुकूलशक्तिकल्पने धूमादिना वह्न्यनुमानं न स्यात्, न

---

* अकस्मादित्यत्र किंशब्दस्य हेतुपरत्वे तेनैव नञोऽन्वयात् तदभावे कार्य्यस्य भवनं लभ्यते, पञ्चम्यर्थभवनेनान्वये भवननिषेधो लभ्यते। उभयविधञ्चैतत् प्रत्येकं नञोऽन्वयेन निष्पद्यत इति प्रत्येकान्वयरूप एकः पक्षः। अथ कस्मादिति समुदितस्य विशिष्टार्थे हेतुप्रयोज्यभवने नञोऽन्वये विशिष्टाभावो लभ्यते। तथा च एकविशेषनिषेधस्य विशेषान्तराभ्यनुज्ञाफलकत्वात् पर्य्युदासञ्ज्ञा वाऽहेतोर्भवनं लभ्यते। अहेतुश्च हेतुभिन्नं कार्य्यमलीकञ्च सम्भवतीति विशिष्टान्वयपक्षे तदुभयरूपं पक्षान्तरं निरस्यति खानुपाख्य इत्यादिना।

स्याच्च हणफुत्कारसमवधानस्य निर्मन्थनारणिसमवधानस्य प्रति-
फलितरविकिरणमणिसमवधानस्य च प्रतिनियमः, कारण-
तावच्छेदकावच्छिन्नस्यैव कारणतावच्छेदकान्तरावच्छिन्नसम-
वधाने कार्यजनस्य दृष्टत्वात्, फुत्कारमणिसम्बन्ध्यादितोऽपि
वह्न्यापत्तेः । यदि च हणफुत्कारादिसम्बन्ध्यादिषु वह्न्यनुकूलैका
शक्तिः कल्प्यते तदा नैतत् समाधानं, परन्तु तार्णवह्न्यादिनिष्ठं
वैजात्यं प्रत्यक्षसिद्धं दीपत्वादिवदिति न पदार्थान्तरशक्ति-
कल्पनम् । अमुमर्थमाह

प्रवाहो नादिमानेष न विजात्येकशक्तिमान् ।
तत्त्वे यह्नवता भाव्यमन्वयव्यतिरेकयोः ॥ ६ ॥

एष कार्यकारणप्रवाहः नादिमान् अनादिः, विजातीयेषु
हणादिषु एकशक्तिमान् न प्रवाहः, अन्वयव्यतिरेकयोस्तत्त्वे
नियतत्वे निर्वाच्ये यह्नवता भाव्यं यह्नः करणीयः, वैजात्यं
कल्पनीयमिति भावः । वह्निसामान्यं प्रति तु विजातीयोष्ण-
स्पर्शवत् तेज एव कारणम् ॥ ६ ॥

'ननु यथा एक एव दीपः आलोककारी वर्तिविकारकारी
घटादिप्रकाशकारी च, तथा एकमेव ब्रह्म किं वा कार्य-
कारणयोरभेदात् प्रतिपुरुषं भिन्नभिन्नबुद्धेरभिन्ना प्रकृतिरेव
हेतुरस्तु, तथा च नादृष्टाधिष्ठातृत्वेश्वरसिद्धिः' इत्यत आह

एकस्य न क्रमः कापि वैचित्र्यं च समस्य न ।
शक्तिभेदो न चाभिन्नः स्वभावो दुरतिक्रमः ॥ ७ ॥

एकस्य कारणस्य नियम्यो न कार्याणां क्रमः, समस्य एक-

जातीयकारणस्य प्रयोज्यञ्च न कार्याणां वैचित्र्यं वैजात्यं, तथा च क्रमिककार्यनिर्वाहकतया क्रमिककारणसिद्धिः विजातीयकार्यजनकतया च विचित्रहेतुसिद्धिरित्यर्थः । 'शक्तिभेदादेव सजातीयादेकस्मात् कार्यवैजात्यं' इति शङ्कां निराकुरुते शक्तिभेदो न चाभिन्न इति । चो हेतौ, न शक्तिभेदः अभिन्नो यतः शक्तिशक्तिमतोरभेदात्, भेदे च तस्यैव कारणत्वस्वीकारे एकमात्रकारणलभङ्गप्रसङ्गे द्वैतापत्तिस्स्यैत्यर्थः । 'ननु स्वभावादेव एककारणस्य विचित्रकार्यनिर्वाहकत्वं' इत्यत्राह स्वभावो दुरतिक्रम इति । एकस्मिन् कार्ये जनयितव्ये यः स्वभावः, कार्यान्तरजननकाले तस्यानुवृत्तौ दहनस्यापि जलादित्वं स्यात्, स्वभावस्य दुरपह्नवत्वादित्यर्थः । प्रदीपस्थले तत्तत्कार्यसामग्रीभेदकल्पनादिति भावः ॥ ७ ॥

'ननु दण्डादिर्घटादौ हेतुरस्तु, न तु यागादिः स्वर्गादिहेतुः' इत्यत्राह

विफला विश्ववृत्तिर्नो न दुःखैकफलापि वा ।
दृष्टलाभफला नापि विप्रलम्भोऽपि नेदृशः ॥ ८ ॥

विश्वेषां परलोकार्थिनां स्वर्गाद्यर्थं यागादौ प्रवृत्तिर्विफला न, न वा दुःखमात्रफलिका प्रवृत्तेरिष्टसाधनताधीसाध्यत्वात्, न च दृष्टलाभफला पूजाख्यातिधनादिफला, तन्निर्पेक्षैरपि तदाचरणात् । 'केनचित् प्रतारकेन स्वर्गादिफलकतया यागादिकं प्रकल्प्य स्वयमनुष्ठाय धन्विता लोकः प्रवर्तते' इत्यत्राह विप्रलम्भोऽपि नेदृश इति । क एवं लोकोत्तरो यः

परप्रतारणार्थं नानाविधक्लेशहेतुकर्मभिरात्मानमवसादयेत्, तथा च यागादिप्रवृत्तिरेव खर्गादिफलकले यागादेर्मानमिति ॥ ८ ॥

'ननु यागादिकं खर्गादिहेतुरस्तु न तु तज्जन्याद्दृष्टं तथा' इत्याह

चिरध्वस्तं फलायालं न कर्मातिशयं विना ।
सम्भोगो निर्विशेषाणां न भूतैः संस्कृतैरपि ॥ ९ ॥

चिरध्वस्तं यागादिकर्म अतिशयं तत्फलानुकूलव्यापारं विना फलाय नालं न समर्थं, चिरध्वस्तकारणस्य व्यापारद्वारैव हेतुत्वं, यथा अनुभवस्य संस्कारद्वारकस्य स्मृतौ । 'ननु भोग्यनिष्ठमदृष्टं कारणमस्तु' इति जिज्ञासायामाह सम्भोग इति । निर्विशेषाणामदृष्टरूपविशेषगुणशून्यानाम् आत्मनां सम्भोगः प्रत्यात्मनियतो भोगः संस्कृतैरपि अदृष्टवत्तया स्वीकृतैरपि भूतैर्न स्यात्, भूतानां शरीरादीनां सर्वात्मसाधारण्यात्, तद्दृष्टादृष्टेरेव शरीरेन्द्रियादिभिस्सम्भोगजननादित्यर्थः ॥ ९ ॥

'ननु भोग्यादिनिष्ठ एव धर्मविशेषोऽतीन्द्रियः प्रतिनियतभोगादिनियामकोऽस्तु, यथा दाहादिनियामको वह्न्यादिनिष्ठः शक्तिभेदः, अन्यथा तादृशादेव करतलानलसंयोगात् सति प्रतिबन्धके दाहापत्तेः । न च मण्यादिभाव एव कारणमस्तु इति वाच्यं, कारणस्य भावत्वव्याघातात्, किन्तु शक्तिनाशं करोतीति मण्यादिः प्रतिबन्धक उच्यते, तथा च शक्तिः स्वीकार्या' इत्याह

भावो यथा तथाऽभावः कारणं कार्यवन्मतः ।
प्रतिबन्धो विषामयी तद्धेतुः प्रतिबन्धकः ॥ १० ॥

यथाऽन्वयव्यतिरेकादिना अभावो ध्वंसः कार्यः तथाऽभावः कारणमपि, 'कारणलं भावलव्याप्तं' द्रव्यत्वाप्रयोजकलात् । 'अकिञ्चित्करस्य प्रतिबन्धकलानुपपत्तिः' इत्यत्राच प्रतिबन्ध इति । विषामयी कारणाभावः, स च प्रकृते मण्याद्यभावस्याभावो मण्यादिः, तत्समवधानहेतुः पुरुष एव प्रतिबन्धकः, खार्थे कप्रत्ययेन च मण्यादौ प्रतिबन्धकपदप्रयोग इति भावः । मीमांसकनयास्तु "उत्तेजकाभावकूटविशिष्टमण्यभावलेन हेतुले गौरवात् लाघवाच्चक्किर्निला वह्न्यादौ कल्प्यते, प्रतिबन्धके सति शक्तिकुण्ठनम् । यन्तु 'शक्तिः प्रथमतो वह्निकारणज्ञया वह्निनिष्ठा, प्रतिबन्धकेन च तस्या विनाशे उत्तेजकेन पुनर्जननं । न च शक्तेरनियतहेतुकलमिति वाच्यं, शक्त्यनुकूलशक्तिमत्त्वेन कारणलात्' इति । तन्न, वह्निनिष्ठानांशक्तिकल्पनापेक्षया उत्तेजकाभावविशिष्टमण्यभावस्यैकस्यैव वरं हेतुलौचित्यात्, तथाचाकुण्ठितशक्तिरेव तत्र कारणतावच्छेदिका कल्प्यते" इत्याङ्गः । तन्न, शक्तिकुण्ठने प्रतिबन्धकस्य हेतुलमुत्तेजकस्य कुण्ठितलविनाशकलमित्याद्यनन्तशक्तिकल्पनापत्तेरिति दिक् ॥ १० ॥

"ननु 'व्रीहीन् प्रोक्षति, व्रीहीनवहन्ति' इत्यादौ प्रोक्षणजन्यः कालान्तरभाव्यवघातजनको व्यापारो व्रीहिनिष्ठः कल्प्यते, 'प्रोक्षिता एव व्रीह्योऽवघाताय कल्प्यन्ते' इति वाक्यशेषात् । किञ्च यो यदनुफलार्थितया क्रियते स तन्निष्ठफलजनकव्या-

पारजनकः यावत्। किञ्च व्रीह्यादीनामपरमाणुत्वभङ्गे व्रीह्यादिनियमानुपपत्तिः। एवं माषकर्षणादिना भूमिनिष्ठा ऋषिजन्या शक्तिर्निर्वाच्या"। अत्रोत्तरम्

संस्कारः पुंस एवेष्टः प्रोक्षणाभ्युक्षणादिभिः।
खगुणाः परमाणूनां विशेषाः पाकजादयः॥ २१॥

प्रोक्षणादिभिः संस्कारोऽदृष्टं पुंसः पुंसि दृष्टः खोक्तः, प्रतिव्रीहि नानाशक्तिकल्पनापेक्षया एकस्यैवादृष्टस्यात्मनिष्ठस्य प्रोक्षणादिजन्यावघातजनकस्य लाघवेन कल्पनात्, दृष्टद्वाराभावे सति विहितस्य कालान्तरभाविफलानुकूलस्य धर्मजनकत्वकल्पनाच्च। संस्कृतो व्रीहिरितिप्रत्ययबलाच्च तस्य खरूपसम्बन्धेनैव व्रीहिनिष्ठत्वं कल्प्यते, एतेनाभिमन्त्रितपयःपक्कवादावपि तत्तत्फलानुकूलमदृष्टं पुरुषनिष्ठं। व्रीहीनिति च शकून् प्रोक्षति दध्यादाविव प्रोक्षणादिजन्यजलसंयोगादिरूपपरसमवेतक्रियाजन्यफलशालितया कर्मता। 'यो यद्गतफलार्थितया क्रियते स तन्निष्ठफलजनकव्यापारजनकः' इति च यजुनिष्ठबधाचार्यक्रियमाणस्येनादौ खनिष्ठफलजनके व्यभिचारि। यवाद्युत्पत्तिनियमार्थमाद्य खगुणाः परमाणूनां पाकजाद्यो विशेषा विशेषकाः, तेन पाकजरूपपरषादिविशिष्टाः परमाणवस्तत्तत्कार्यमारभन्ते। चिकित्साखले तु धातुसाम्यमेव भेषजपानस्य रोगादिनाशे फले जनयितव्ये द्वारमिति भावः*॥ २१॥

'ननु यच्च पाकजो न विशेषस्तच्च वाय्वादौ कथमुद्भूतस्पर्शादि,

---

* माषकर्षणादिनापि न शक्तिर्जन्यते किन्तु कर्षणेन पूर्वभूमिनाशे सद्यैव जलानन्तरं विशद्रव्या भूमिर्जन्यते। एवमेव पद्मधरमिश्राः।

करकादौ च प्रतिरुद्धं द्रवत्वमिति, कथञ्च प्रतिमादौ प्रतिष्ठा-
देरुपयोग:, तथा च प्रतिष्ठाजन्या शक्तिश्चाण्डालादिसर्गेनाशा
पूज्यताप्रयोजिका स्वीकार्या' इत्याचष्ट

निमित्तभेदसंसर्गादुद्भवानुद्भवादच: ।
देवता: सन्निधानेन प्रत्यभिज्ञानतोऽपि वा ॥ १२ ॥

निमित्तभेद: अदृष्टभेद:, देवता: प्रतिष्ठाविधिना सन्निधा-
नेनाहङ्कारममकारादिना आराधनीयतामासादयन्ति, प्रति-
ष्ठाविधिना देवतानां प्रतिमादौ अहङ्कारममकारौ, चाण्डा-
लादिस्पर्शेन तादृशाभिमानाभाव:। देवताचैतन्यविवादेऽपि
यथार्थपूजितत्वधी: प्रतिष्ठितत्वधीश्च चाण्डालादिस्पर्शादभाव-
विशिष्टा पूज्यतानियामिका, तच्च चोपयोगिनी प्रतिष्ठा। वस्तु-
तस्तु प्रतिष्ठाकालीनयावत्स्पृश्यस्पर्शनादिसंसर्गाभाव: प्रतिष्ठा-
ध्वंसकालीन: पूज्यताप्रयोजक: 'प्रतिष्ठितं प्रपूजयेत्' इति क्षेन
प्रतिष्ठाध्वंसस्यैव प्राप्तेरिति दिक्॥ १२॥

'ननु तुलापरीचादौ परीचाविधिना शक्तिस्तुलादौ जन्यते,
तथा नमनोन्नमनादिकं फलं जन्यते' इत्याचष्ट

जयेतरनिमित्तस्य वृत्तिलाभाय केवलम् ।
परीच्यसमवेतस्य परीचाविधयो मता: ॥ १३ ॥

जयत्तरदितर: पराजय:, तन्निमित्तस्यादृष्टस्य परीचणीयपुरुष-
समवेतस्य वृत्तिलाभाय फलानुकूलसहकारिलाभाय परीचा-
विधयो मता: स्वीकृता:। योऽहमनेन परीचाविधिना तुला-
मारूढ: सोऽहं पापवान् निष्पापो वेति ज्ञानं सहकारि। यदा

वृत्तिलाभाय जननाय, तथा च प्रतिज्ञानुरूपां बुद्धिमपेच्य धर्मोऽबुद्धिमपेच्याधर्मो जन्यते । एतेन 'ब्रह्मवधाकरणादिना पुण्यजाजननात् कथं तस्य सहकारि तादृग्ज्ञानं स्यात्' इत्यपि पराख्तम् ॥ १३ ॥

साङ्ख्यास्तु "पुरुषश्चैतन्याश्रयः अकारणं, अत एव कूटस्थो नित्यः । प्रकृतिश्चाचेतना परिणामिनी नित्या एका, प्रकृतेश्च प्रथमपरिणामो बुद्धिर्महत्तत्त्वं, तचाष्टौ धर्माः ज्ञानाज्ञानैश्वर्यानैश्वर्यवैराग्यावैराग्यधर्माधर्मरूपाः, बुद्धिसुखदुःखेच्छादेषप्रयत्नधर्माधर्माश्चेत्यष्टौ वा, भावनाख्येरनङ्गीकारात् अनुभवस्यैव स्मृतिकाले सूक्ष्मतयाऽवस्थानात् । अचेतनायाः प्रकृतिकार्याया बुद्धेश्चैतन्याभिमानान्यथानुपपत्त्या स्वाभाविकचैतन्यस्वरूपः पुरुषः भिद्यः धर्माधर्मयोरभेदात् । तत्र प्रकृतेर्महान् महतोऽहङ्कारस्तस्माद्रूपरसगन्धस्पर्शशब्दतन्मात्राणीति सप्त, चक्षुःश्रोत्राणरसनात्वगाचमनानि वाक्पाणिपादपायूपस्थानि इन्द्रियाणि, तन्मात्रैः पञ्च महाभूतानि पृथिव्यप्तेजोवाय्वाकाशानि जायन्ते । तदुक्तम् 'मूलप्रकृतिरविकृतिर्महदाद्याः प्रकृतिविकृतयः सप्त । षोडशकस्तु विकारो न प्रकृतिर्न विकृतिः पुरुषः' (सां० का० ३) । पञ्च महाभूतान्येकादशेन्द्रियाणि चेति षोडश । चैतन्यस्य नित्यस्य स्वाभाविकेष्टानिष्टविषयावच्छिन्नस्वाभाव्येऽनिर्मोचः स्यात्, प्रकृत्यधीनत्वेऽपि विषयावच्छेद्यत्वस्य प्रकृतेर्नित्यतया तथैवानिर्मोचप्रसङ्गः, घटादेरनित्यस्यापि स्वाभाविकचैतन्यावच्छिन्नत्वे दृष्टादृष्टविभागानुपपत्तिश्च, इन्द्रियमात्रापेच्चो

यदि विषयचैतन्यावच्छेदस्तथापि व्यासङ्गानुपपत्तिः, अतो मनः स्वीकार्य्यं यदवलम्बनेन इन्द्रियस्य विषयीयचैतन्यावच्छेदनियामकत्वं । स्वप्नदशायां व्याघ्रलाभिमानिनो न नरोऽहमित्यभिमानः, अतस्तन्नियामय निचतविषयाभिमानव्यापारकोऽहङ्कारोऽपि स्वीकार्य्यः । जाग्रत्स्वप्नसुषुप्तिषु स्वाप्नप्रश्वासदर्शनात् सव्यापारं यदनुवर्तते तदुद्बुद्धितत्त्वं प्रागुक्तभावाष्टकयोगि स्वीकार्य्यं । तस्य ज्ञानरूपपरिणामेन सम्बद्धो विषयः पुरुषस्य स्वरूपतिरोधायकः, एवञ्च बुद्धितत्त्वनाशादेव विषयावच्छेदाभावात् पुंसो मोचः । भेदाग्रहाच्च चेतनोऽहं करोमीत्यभिमानः । तदुक्तं 'प्रकृतेः क्रियमाणानि गुणैः कर्म्माणि सर्व्वशः । अहङ्कारविमूढात्मा कर्त्ताहमिति मन्यते' (गी०) इति । सा च बुद्धिरंशत्रयवती, पुरुषोपरागः विषयोपरागः व्यापारावेश इति, ममेदं कर्त्तव्यमित्यच ममेति चेतनोपरागः बुद्धिचेतनयोर्भेदाग्रहात् अतात्त्विकः, इदमिति विषयोपरागः, तदुभयायत्तो व्यापारावेशः । बुद्ध्यावारोपितचैतन्यस्य विषयेण सम्बन्धः ज्ञानं, ज्ञानेन सम्बन्धेनोऽहं करोमीत्युपलब्धिः" इत्याद्यः । अत्राह

कर्त्तृधर्म्मा नियन्तारस्वेतिता च स एव नः ।

अन्यथाऽनपवर्गः स्यादसंसारोऽथ वा भुवः ॥ १४ ॥

कृतिसमानाधिकरणत्वाद्धर्म्माधर्म्मेच्छाः भोगस्य कृतिसामानाधिकरणात्, एवं चेतिता चेतनः स एव कृतिमानेव नोऽस्माकं मतः चेतनोऽहं करोमीति प्रत्यचबलात् । दूषणान्तरमाह अन्यथेति । यदि बुद्धिर्नित्या तदा बुद्ध्युपहिता-

त्मनः सर्वदावस्थानात् अनिर्मोच्यः स्यात्, यद्यनित्या तदोत्पन्ना वाच्या अनित्यभावस्थानुत्पत्त्यभावात्, तथा च तदुत्पत्तेः प्राक् तदाश्रितधर्मादेरप्यभावेन बुद्धितत्त्वस्थानुत्पत्तौ नियतशरीरेन्द्रियादिकार्यस्थानुत्पत्तौ असंसारः स्यादित्यर्थः ॥ १४ ॥

चार्वाकस्तु 'भवतु चेतनधर्मोऽदृष्टं चेतनस्य न नित्यविभुः किन्तु कायाकारपरिणतभूतविशेषः गौरोऽहं जानामीति प्रतीत्या रूपवत्त्वसिद्धेः' इत्याह

नान्यदृष्टं स्मरत्यन्यो नैकं भूतमपक्रमात् ।
वासनासङ्क्रमो नास्ति न च गत्यन्तरं स्थिरे ॥ १५ ॥

शरीरस्य चैतन्ये बाल्यदशायामनुभूतस्य यौवने स्मरणं न स्यात् चैत्रदृष्टस्य मैत्रेणास्मरणमिव । न च बाल्ययौवनयोरेकं भूतं शरीरम्, अपक्रमात् पूर्वशरीरविनाशात् परिमाणभेदेन द्रव्यभेदात् पूर्वपरिमाणनाशस्याऽऽश्रयनाशहेतुकत्वात् । न च कारणेनानुभूतस्य कार्येण स्मरणं स्यादिति वाच्यं वासनासङ्क्रमाभावात्, अन्यथा मात्राऽनुभूतस्य गर्भस्थेन स्मरणापत्तेः । 'ननूपादानवासनाया उपादेये सङ्क्रमः स्यात्' इत्याचेत् न च गत्यन्तरं स्थिर इति । स्थिरे स्थिरपक्षे पुञ्जात् पुञ्जान्तरोत्पत्तेरभावात् करादिशरीरस्योपादानं वाच्यं, तथा च विच्छिन्ने करादौ तदनुभूतस्य स्मरणं न स्यात्, खण्डशरीरे विच्छिन्नकरादेरनुपादानत्वात् । न च परमाणूनां चैतन्यं तेषाञ्च स्थिरत्वात् स्मरणं स्यादिति वाच्यं, तथा सति स्मरणस्यातीन्द्रियत्वप्रसङ्गात् तन्निष्ठरूपादिवत्, करपरमाण्वनुभूतस्य विच्छिन्नकरपरमाणुसन्निधावस्मरणप्रसङ्गाच्च ॥ १५ ॥

'ननु स्तु क्षणभङ्गः तथा च पूर्वपूर्वपरमाणुपुञ्जेनोपादेयो-
त्तरोत्तरपरमाणुपुञ्ज इति न स्मरणानुपपत्तिः' इत्याह

न वैजात्यं विना तत् स्यात् न तस्मिन्ननुमा भवेत् ।
विना तेन न तत्सिद्धिर्नाध्यं निश्चयं विना ॥ १६ ॥

वैजात्यं कुर्वद्रूपं विना न तत् क्षणिकत्वं स्यात् सिध्यतीत्यर्थः । स्थिर एव बीजादौ सहकारिलाभालाभाभ्यामेव कार्यजन्माजन्म-नोरुपपत्तेः बीजत्वादिनैवाङ्कुरादिजनकतोपपत्तेः, बीजव्यक्तिभे-दाभावे कुतः क्षणिकत्वं स्यात् । तस्मिन् जातिविशेषे च ऐन्द्रिय-कवृत्तावतीन्द्रियत्वेनाभ्युपगम्यमाने सत्यनुमानं न स्यात्, धूम-कुर्वद्रूपवह्निक्षिलादिनैव वह्न्यादेर्हेतुतया विजक्षणखकार्यजनकत्वेन सम्भावितस्य विजातीयधूमस्यैव वह्निजन्यत्वसम्भावनायां धूमसा-मान्ये हेतुत्वानिर्णयात्, तथा च कार्यकारणभावरूपविपक्षबाधक-तर्काधीनव्याप्तिनिर्णयस्यासम्भवेनानुमानमात्रोच्छेदप्रसङ्ग इति । तेनानुमानेन विना च क्षणिकत्वस्यासिद्धिः, तस्यानुमानैकगम्यत्वात्। न च तत्र प्रत्यक्षमेव मानमिति वाच्यं, निर्विकल्पकस्यैव तन्मते वि-षयजन्यतया प्रामाण्यं, तस्य च सविकल्पकोन्नेयतया 'क्षणिकः' इति सविकल्पकस्यासिद्धावसिद्धेः । किञ्चाङ्कुरकुर्वद्रूपं न जातिः शालित्वादिना सङ्करात्, शालित्वमपहाय यवे तस्य सत्त्वात्, शा-लित्वस्यापि कुमूलस्थे शालौ तदपहाय सत्त्वात्, कुर्वद्रूपे शालौ उभयोः समावेशादिति । अत एव रजतत्वादिभ्यां नानैव घटत्वं, *विजातीयसंस्थानवदवयवकलरूपमुपाधिमादाय घट इत्यनुगत-धीरिति ॥ १६ ॥

---

* विजातीयसंस्थानं कम्बुग्रीवादि ।

'ननु स्व चणिकले सन्देहः, न च प्रत्यभिज्ञाबलेन स्थैर्यसिद्धौ कथं स इति वाच्यं स एवायं घट इत्यच सन्देहसत्त्वात्' अत्राह स्थैर्यदृष्ट्यार्थं सन्देहो न प्रामाण्ये विरोधतः ।
एकतानिर्णयो येन चणे तेन स्थिरे मतः ॥ १७ ॥

स्थैर्ये न सन्देहस्य प्रत्यभिज्ञया विषयीकरणात्, न च प्रत्यभिज्ञानरूपे, तस्यापि तदनुव्यवसायेन निर्णयात्, प्रामाण्यमात्रेऽपि न सन्देहः विरोधात् सन्देहज्ञानस्य प्रामाण्यसन्देहे सन्देहस्याप्यसिद्धेः, प्रामाण्यस्यासिद्धौ प्रामाण्यसंशयस्याप्यभावः कोऽप्यनिर्णयात् । 'ननु प्रत्यभिज्ञायाः प्रामाण्ये संशयः लून-पुनर्जातकेशादौ त एवामी केशा इत्यादेर्भ्रमलदर्शनात्' तत्राह एकतेति । येन प्रमाणेन विरुद्धधर्मसंसर्गविरहेण, चणिके घटे यदि तस्मिन्नेव चणे न नानात्वं किन्त्वभेदः, तदा स्थिरे स्थिरपक्षेऽपि नानाचणवर्तित्वेऽपि घटस्य न नानात्वं किन्त्वेकत्वम्, एकस्य ज्ञानस्य नानाविषयसम्बन्धवत् एकस्य नाना-कालसम्बन्धेऽपि अविरोधात्, तत्तत्कारणक्रमाधीनलात् तत्तत्कालसम्बन्धस्य ॥ १७ ॥

तदेवं परलोकसाधनमागतं । तच्चेदं शङ्कते 'कारणं स्वाभाविकमौपाधिकं वा, आद्ये नीलस्य सर्वान् प्रति नीलत्ववत् कार्यस्य सर्वान् प्रत्यविशेषात् कारणमपि स्यात्,* द्वितीये उपाधेरपि स्वाभाविकत्वे तद्दोषतादवस्थ्यात्, औपाधिकत्वेऽनवस्था । किञ्च कारणस्य स्वाभाविकत्वे उत्पत्तेरारभ्य कार्यं स्यात्' । तत्राह

---
*तथा च सर्वं कार्यं सर्वस्य स्यादिति क्वचिदधिकं ।

D

हेतुशक्तिमनादृत्य नीलादपि न वस्तुसत्।
तद्युक्तं तच्च तच्छक्तमिति साधारणं न किम्॥ १८॥

हेतुशक्तिं कारणलं, अनादृत्य अनिश्चित्य, नीलाद्यपि न वस्तुसत् न प्रामाणिकं, तथा च 'यत् पारमार्थिकं तत् साधारणं यथा नीलादि, कारणलञ्च यदि न साधारणम् अतो न परमार्थसत्' इत्यपि न स्यात् दृष्टान्तस्यानित्यस्य नीलस्य कारणलस्वीकारेण सर्वचाभावात् नित्यस्य नीलादे: प्रमाणा-गोचरलात्। किञ्चेत्याद्युक्तं दूषयति तद्युक्तमिति। तद्युक्तं सह-कारियुक्तं, तत् कारणं, नच कार्य्यं, शक्तिमिति नोत्पत्तेरारभ्य कारणलम्। कारणलस्य साधारणे च दृष्टापत्तिमाह इति साधारणं न किमिति। नीलादेरपि सर्वसाधारणं यत् सर्वै-र्नीललादिना व्यवह्रियमाणलं, तादृशञ्च साधारणं सह-कारियुक्तस्य, जनकलमित्यस्यापि तथाव्यवहारस्य सर्वसिद्ध-लात्॥ १८॥

'नन्वात्मनिष्ठमदृष्टं नात्मजन्यं, नित्यविभोस्तस्य कालतो देशतश्च व्यतिरेकाभावात् व्यतिरेकसहकृतान्वयस्यैव कारण-ताग्राहकलात्, तद्व्यतिरेकप्रयोजकव्यतिरेकप्रतियोगिलस्यैव का-रणात्मकलाच्च, तथा च समवायिकारणाभावे असमवायि-कारणनिमित्ताभ्यामपि न कार्य्यं जननीयं तत्प्रत्यासन्नाभ्यामेव ताभ्यां जननादित्यदृष्टस्य नित्यलापत्ति:, तथा च न प्रति-नियतात्मदेशकालीनभोगजनकलं कल्प्येत' इत्यवाह

पूर्वभावो हि हेतुलं मीयते येन केनचित्।

व्यापकस्यापि नित्यस्य धर्मिधीरन्यथा न हि ॥ १८ ॥

व्यतिरेकगर्भं न कारणत्वं किन्त्वनन्यथासिद्धनियतपूर्वभावः । हि हेतौ, यतो ग्राहको न व्यतिरेकः धर्मिग्राहकमानेनापि तस्य प्रमापणात् द्व्यतो मीयते येन केनचित् व्यापकस्य नित्यस्यात्मनः येन केनचित् प्रमीयते, अन्यथा धर्मिधीरेव न स्यात्, तथा च धर्मिग्राहकप्रमाणसिद्धं तस्य हेतुत्वं, घटादिकं प्रति कपालादेरन्वयव्यतिरेकदर्शनात् समवेतकार्यं प्रति द्रव्यस्य द्रव्यत्वेन कारणत्वस्य कल्पनात् पृथिव्यादिबाधे परिग्रहेण ज्ञानेच्छादौ पृथिव्यादिभिन्नसमवायिनः सिद्धिः । वस्तुतस्तु समवायिकारणताघटकोऽन्योन्याभावः, 'यत्र कपालं तत्र घटवदितिवत् यो न आत्मा न तत्र ज्ञानादि' इति धीसम्भवात् । एवं यो न कालस्तत्र सम्बन्धविशेषेण न घट इति निमित्तकारणत्वाधिकरणीभूतस्य कारणताऽप्यन्योन्याभावरूपव्यतिरेकेण ग्राह्या ॥ एवञ्च मायाप्रकृत्यविद्यादिपदमप्येतत्परमिति न 'मायिकं जगत्' इत्यादिश्रुतिविरोधः, तथा चादृष्टाधिष्ठातृतया ईश्वरसिद्धिः ॥ १८ ॥

स्तवकार्थसंग्राहकश्लोकमाह

इत्येषा सहकारिशक्तिरसमा माया दुरुन्नीतितो
मूलत्वात् प्रकृतिः प्रबोधभयतोऽविद्येति यस्योदिता ।
देवोऽसौ विरतप्रपञ्चरचनाकल्लोलकोलाहलः
साचात् साचितया मनःस्थिमरतिं बध्नातु शान्तो मम ॥२०॥

इति प्रथमः स्तवकः ।

इति स्ववक्षसमाप्तौ, यस्येश्वरस्य सहकारिशक्तिः सहकारि-
रूपा शक्तिः कारणम्, एषा सहकारिरूपा माया, असमवं
सर्वकार्यापेच्चणीयत्वात्, दुरन्वेयत्वात् सादृश्यान्मायापदेऽदृष्टे
लचणा, मूलत्वात् प्रकृतिः सैव, तत्त्वज्ञानप्रतिबध्वत्वात् सैवा-
विद्या, उदिता उक्ता, असौ देवो मम मनसि स्वविषयां
साचादभिरतिं साचात्कारि ज्ञानं, बभ्रातु जनयतु, साचिनया
साचीभूय, निर्णायकतया साचित्वं, ज्ञान्तः रागादिगुणशून्यः,
प्रपञ्चस्य मिथ्याज्ञानादेः कल्लोलः मिथ्याज्ञानपरम्परा, तस्याः
कोलाहलः किंवदन्ती सा विरता यस्मादिति ॥ २० ॥

इति श्रीहरिदासभट्टाचार्यविरचितकुसुमाञ्जलिकारिका-
प्रथमस्तवकव्याख्यानम् ॥

कुसुमाञ्जलिः ।

द्वितीयः स्तवकः ।

अन्यथाऽपि परलोकसाधनानुष्ठानसम्भवादिति द्वितीयविप्रतिपत्तिः । 'अन्यथा ईश्वरं विनाऽपि परलोकसाधनयागाद्यनुष्ठानं सम्भवति यागादेः स्वर्गसाधनत्वस्य वेदगम्यत्वात्, नित्यनिर्दोषतया च वेदस्य प्रामाण्यं, महाजनपरिग्रहाच्च प्रामाण्यग्रह इति वेदकारणतया नेश्वरसिद्धिः, योगर्द्धिसमादितसार्वज्ञ्यकपिलादिपूर्वक एव वा वेदोऽस्तु' इत्यत्राह

प्रमायाः परतन्त्रत्वात् सर्गप्रलयसम्भवात् ।
तदन्यस्मिन्नविश्वासान्न विधान्तरसम्भवः ॥ ९ ॥

शाब्दी प्रमा वक्तृयथार्थवाक्यार्थधीरूपगुणजन्या इति गुणाधारतया ईश्वरसिद्धिः । 'ननु सकर्तृकेऽस्तु यथार्थवाक्यार्थधीर्गुणः, अकर्तृके च वेदे निर्दोषत्वमेव प्रामाण्यप्रयोजकमस्तु, महाजनपरिग्रहेण च प्रामाण्यग्रहः' इत्यत्र आह सर्गप्रलयसम्भवादिति । प्रलयोत्तरं पूर्ववेदनाशादुत्तरवेदस्य कथं प्रामाण्यं महाजनपरिग्रहस्याऽपि तदा अभावात् । शब्दस्यानित्यत्वं उत्पन्नो गकार इति प्रतीतिसिद्धं, प्रवाहाविच्छेदरूपनित्यत्वमपि प्रलयसम्भवात् नास्तीति भावः । 'कपिलादय एव

सर्गादौ पूर्वसर्गाभ्यस्तयोगजन्यधर्मानुभावात् साचात्कृतसकला-
र्थाः कर्तारः सन्तु' इत्यत आह तदन्यस्मिन्निति । विश्व-
निर्माणसमर्था अणिमादिशक्तिसम्पन्ना यदि सर्वज्ञास्तदा ला-
घवादेक एव तादृशः खीक्रियतां स एव भगवानीश्वरः, अनि-
त्यासर्वविषयकज्ञानवति च विश्वास एव नास्तीति वैदिक-
व्यवहारविलोप इति न विधान्तरसम्भवः ईश्वरानङ्गीकर्तनये
इति शेषः ॥ १ ॥

'ननु सर्गप्रलयसम्भवादिति न युक्तं प्रलये मानाभावात्
इति । अहोरात्र्याव्यवहिताहोरात्रपूर्वकलनियमात्, कर्मणां
विषमविपाकतया कालोपाधिकस्य भोगव्याप्यत्वात् युगप-
दृष्टस्य च वृत्तिनिरोधानुपपत्तेः, ब्राह्मणस्य ब्राह्मणजन्यत्वनि-
यमात् सर्गाद्युत्पन्नस्य ब्राह्मणलाभाभावात् उत्तरकालेऽपि ब्राह्म-
णव्यवहारानुपपत्तेः, प्रयोज्यप्रयोजकयोरभावात् सङ्केतग्रहा-
भावे शब्दव्यवहारानुपपत्तेः, घटादिनिर्माणे नैपुण्यस्य पूर्व-
दर्शनसापेक्षस्य सर्गादावभावात् घटादिसम्प्रदायोच्छेदा-
द्यादेर्बाधकाच्च' तत्राह

वर्षादिवद्ध्वोपाधिवृत्तिरोधः सुषुप्तिवत् ।
उद्भिद्दृष्टिकवद्वर्षा मायावत् समयादयः ॥ २ ॥

यथा वर्षादिनस्याव्यवहितवर्षादिनपूर्वकले साध्ये रात्रि-
विशेषावच्छिन्नरविकालपूर्वकलमुपाधिस्तथाऽहोरात्र्याव्यवहि-
ताहोरात्रपूर्वकलेऽव्यवहितसंसारपूर्वकलमुपाधिः, भवोपाधिः
संसारावच्छेदककालोपाधिः स एव उपाधिरित्यर्थः । सुषुप्ति-

द्वितीयः स्तवकः ।

काले कतिपयव्यक्तिनिष्ठभोगजनकादृष्टनिरोधवत् कालविशेषात् समस्तात्मनां समस्तादृष्टनिरोधादिदमुक्तं वृत्तिरोधः सुषुप्तिवदिति । तद्वित् द्राक्विशेषः, तस्य यथा तण्डुलकणात् द्राक्विशेषबीजाच्च उद्भवः, यथा वा वृश्चिकस्य गोमयादृश्चिकाच्च उद्भवस्तथा कालविशेषेऽदृष्टविशेषात् केवलात् इदानीञ्च ब्राह्मणात् ब्राह्मणोत्पत्तिः, बीजात्वस्य कार्यतावच्छेदकत्वात् न व्यभिचारः । यथा मायावी स्वमन्त्राराधिष्ठितदारुपुत्रकं कृत्वा दारुपुत्रकं घटमानयेत्यादि नियोज्य घटानयनं सम्पाद्य बालकस्य व्युत्पत्तौ प्रयोजकस्त्वयेश्वरोऽपि प्रयोज्यप्रयोजकभावापन्नं शरीरद्वयं परिगृह्य व्यवहारं कृत्वा तदानीन्तनानां शक्तिं ग्राहयति । एवं घटादिसम्प्रदायमपि स्वयं कृत्वा शिच्यति, तदिदमुक्तं मायावत् समयादय इति । समयः शक्तिग्रहः ॥ २ ॥

बाधके निरस्ते बाधकमप्याह

जन्मसंस्कारविद्यादेः शक्तेः स्वाध्यायकर्मणोः ।
ह्रासदर्शनतो ह्रासः सम्प्रदायस्य मीयताम् ॥ ३ ॥

सम्प्रदायस्य वेदादिसम्प्रदायस्य ह्रासोऽनुमीयतां, कुतः जन्मादेर्ह्रासदर्शनात् । प्रयोगश्च, वेदादिसम्प्रदायोऽयमत्यन्तमुच्छिद्यते ह्रसमानत्वात् प्रदीपवत् । स्वरूपासिद्ध्युद्धाराय आह जन्मेति । पूर्वं मानस्यः प्रजास्ततः पुत्रमात्रार्थितापूर्वकमैथुनजाः सम्प्रति सम्भोगकामिप्रवृत्त्यावर्जितजन्मान इति जन्मह्रासः । पूर्वं चर्भप्रभृतिषु संस्कारः ततो गर्भे ततो जननानन्तरम्

इदानीं कथञ्चिदिति संस्काराद्ह्रासः । पूर्वं सहस्रशाखस्य चतुर्वेदस्याध्ययनं तत एकस्याः शाखाया इत्यादिक्रमेण विद्याह्रासः । विद्यादेरित्यादिना वृत्तिधर्मादिसंग्रहः, पूर्वमुञ्छशिलवृत्तयस्ततोऽयाचितवृत्तयस्तत ऋत्यादिवृत्तयस्ततः सेवावृत्तय इति वृत्तिह्रासः । पूर्वं तपोज्ञानयज्ञदानात्मकश्चतुष्पाद्धर्मस्तत्तेतादौ एकैकह्रासः कलौ च विसंष्टुलः खलद्वानेकपादिति धर्मह्रासः । पूर्वं यज्ञशेषभुजस्ततोऽतिथिशेषभुजस्तत् स्वार्थसाधितभुजस्ततो ह्यादिसहभुज इत्यपि धर्मह्रासः । ख्याख्यायस्याध्ययनस्य कर्मणो यागादेः शक्तेः सामर्थ्यस्य ह्रासात्, अध्ययनशक्तेः कारणस्य ह्रासात् विद्याशक्तेः कार्यस्य ह्रास इति पृथङ्निर्देशः । एवञ्च ब्रह्माण्डनाशे तदन्तर्गतप्राणिनां नाश इति प्रलयसिद्धिः । यच्चप्येयाद्वैतरागजीविकाकुतर्काभ्यासव्यताभिसन्धिपाषण्डसंसर्गप्रतारणादिनिबन्धनान्या या प्रवृत्तिर्यागादौ तद्वान् महाजनः, तत्प्रियत्वात् वेदप्रामाण्यमिति ॥ ३ ॥

स्वकार्यसंग्रहश्लोकमाह

कारं कारमलौकिकाद्भुतमयं मायावशात् संचरन्
द्वारं द्वारमपीन्द्रजालमिव यः कुर्वन् जगत् क्रीडति ।
तं देवं निरवग्रहस्फुरदभिख्यानानुभावं भवम्
विश्वस्यैकभुवं शिवं प्रति नमन् भूयासमन्तेष्वपि ॥ ४ ॥

इति द्वितीयः स्तवकः ।

कुसुमाञ्जलिः।

द्वितीयः स्तवकः।

तदभावावेदकप्रमाणसम्भवादिति द्वितीयविप्रतिपत्तिः। 'भूतले घटाभाववदीश्वरस्याप्यनुपलब्धेरभावस्य ग्रहात्, परमात्मनोऽयोग्यतया योग्यानुपलब्धेरभावात् नाभावग्रहो यदि तदा शशशृङ्गस्याप्ययोग्यस्य नाभावः सिध्येत्' इत्याशङ्कते

योग्यादृष्टिः कुतोऽयोग्ये प्रतिबन्धिः कुतस्तराम्।
क्वायोग्यं बाध्यते घट्टङ्कं क्वानुमानमनाश्रयम्॥ १॥

अयोग्ये परमात्मनि योग्यानुपलब्धिः कुतः, सैव बाधिका, या चास्ति सा न बाधिका, अन्यथाऽऽकाशधर्माधर्मादिविलयापत्तेः। घट्टङ्कन्तु योग्यमेव तथा च कुतः प्रतिबन्धिः। अयोग्यन्तु शशशृङ्गं न बाध्यते किन्तु साधकाभाव एव तत्र। प्रकृते पञ्चमस्तवके साधकस्य वक्तव्यत्वात्। 'ननु कर्त्त्वव्यापकशरीर-प्रयोजनाभिसन्धानयोरभावात् ईश्वरस्याभावोऽनुमेयः' इत्याशङ्क्यानुमानमनाश्रयमिति। ईश्वरस्याश्रयस्य प्रत्यक्षासिद्धेः, सिद्धौ च धर्मिग्राहकमानेन अनुमानबाध एव॥ १॥

'ननु असत्ख्यात्युपनीत ईश्वरस्तत्र कुत्त्वाभावः तस्यैव वाऽभावः साध्यः' इत्याशङ्क्य

व्यावर्त्याभाववत्त्वैव भाविकी हि विशेष्यता।
अभावविरहात्मत्वं वस्तुनः प्रतियोगिता॥ २॥

व्यावर्त्यः प्रतिचेष्यः, तदभाववक्ता भाविकी पारमार्थिकी
चि यतः विश्येष्यता अभावस्याश्रयता, तथा चालोकं न विश्ये-
ष्यमित्यर्थः। अभावविरहात्मकं प्रतियोगिलमवस्तुनो नेति ना-
लोकस्य प्रतिषेधाधिकरणलवत् प्रतिषेध्यलमपीति भावः॥ २॥

'ननु अयोग्यस्याप्यनुपलब्ध्या कथं नाभावग्रहः' इत्यत आह
दुष्टोपलम्भसामग्री घ्रघ्रष्टङ्गादियोग्यता।

न तस्यां नोपलम्भोऽस्ति नास्ति साऽनुपलम्भने॥ ३॥

योग्यानुपलब्धिरेवाभावग्राहिका, अन्यथाऽतोन्द्रियमाचो-
च्छेदापत्तेः। योग्यता च प्रतियोगितव्याप्येतरयावदुपलम्भसाम-
ग्रीसमवधानम्*, एवञ्च घ्रघ्रष्टङ्गे योग्यता दुष्टा दोषघटिता
उपलम्भसामग्री वाच्या, तस्यां सत्यामनुपलम्भिर्न किन्तूपलब्धि-
रेव स्यात्, अदृष्टे च सा योग्यता नास्तीति॥ ३॥

'नन्वात्मा किञ्चिदनभिज्ञः खनिष्ठकर्हेलानिरूपकचितिको
वा आत्मलात्' इत्यत्राह

---

* प्रतियोगितव्याप्याभ्यां इतरा यावती उपलम्भस्य प्रतियोगिप्रध्व-
स्तस्य सामग्री कारणसमूहस्त्याः समवधानं मिलनमित्यर्थः। एतां-
दृश्योग्यतासहिता अनुपलब्धिः असद्विषयस्थले कदापि न सम्भवति।
तथा हि प्रत्यक्ष्यस्य द्विविधा सामग्री प्रमास्थले विषयसहितः चच्-
रादिकारणकलापः, भ्रमस्थले च विषयरहितः पित्तादिदोषसहितः
चच्रादिकारणसमुदायः। तत्र प्रथमा विषयसहिता द्वितीया च
सर्वदैव विषयरहिता इति फलितं, एतयोरन्यतरसत्त्व एव प्रत्यक्षं जा-
यते। घ्रघ्रष्टङ्गस्य असद्रूपलेन तत्प्रत्यक्षसामग्री द्वितीया वाच्या, तत्-
सत्त्वे च घ्रघ्रष्टङ्गस्य प्रत्यक्षमेवेति न प्रत्यक्षाभावरूपानुपलब्धिः, तद्-
सत्त्वे च तत्स्वरूपा उक्तयोग्यतैव नास्तीति विसंवादेन घ्रघ्रष्टङ्गादि-
स्थले योग्यतासहिता अनुपलब्धिः न कदापि सम्भवतीति भावः॥

दृष्टसिद्धिः प्रसिद्धेऽग्रे हेतुसिद्धिरगोचरे ।
नान्या सामान्यतः सिद्धिर्जातावपि तथैव सा ॥ ४ ॥

प्रसिद्धे संसार्यात्मनि पक्षे दृष्टसिद्धिः सिद्धसाधनम्, अगोचरे अज्ञाते ईश्वरे हेतुसिद्धिः हेतोरज्ञानं, आत्मत्वेन सामान्यतः सिद्धः पक्षश्चेत् तच्चाद्यप्रदर्शितेतर आत्मा वा पक्ष इति विकल्पे सिद्धसाधनं हेतुसिद्धिर्वा । 'नन्वात्मत्वं जातिः पक्षः' तत्राह जातावपि तथैव सेति । आत्मत्वं जातिर्न चितिकर्त्री इत्यचेष्टसिद्धिः सिद्धसाधनं, हेतोश्च तच्चत्वमिति हेतुसिद्धिरित्यर्थः ॥ ४ ॥

'नन्वागमादिसिद्धात्मनि अकर्तृत्वं साध्यं' तत्राह

आगमादेः प्रमाणत्वे बाधनादनिषेधनम् ।
आभासत्वे तु सैव स्यादाश्रयासिद्धिरुद्धता ॥ ५ ॥

आगमादेः प्रमाणत्वे तत एव ईश्वरस्य कर्तृत्वादिसिद्धौ कर्तृत्वाद्यभावसाधने बाधः । आगमादेरप्रमाणत्वे सैवाश्रयासिद्धिः उद्धता उत्कटा ॥ ५ ॥

अत्र चार्वाकाः "योग्यताविशेषणेन किं, 'यन्न प्रत्यक्षं तन्नास्ति' इत्यनुपलब्धिमात्रमेव बाधकं स्यात्, अनुमानविक्षेपष्टष्ट एव धूमदर्शनान्न्लरं वह्न्यर्थप्रवृत्तिश्च सम्भावनामात्रात्" इति तत्राह

दृष्टदृष्योर्न सन्देहो भावाभावविनिश्चयात् ।
अदृष्टिबाधिते हेतौ प्रत्यक्षमपि दुर्लभम् ॥ ६ ॥

सम्भावना हि सन्देहः, स च दृष्टे नास्ति तस्य निश्चयात्, अदृष्टे च नास्ति अनुपलब्धौ तदभावस्यैव निर्णयात् । एवम्

दृष्ट्या अनुपलब्ध्या, चेतौ प्रत्यचकारणे चचुरादौ बाधिते सति प्रत्यचमपि प्रमाणं न स्यात्, अनुपलब्धिकालेऽपि तस्य सत्त्वे तु व्यभिचारात् नानुपलब्धिरभावावधारणे हेतुः । एवञ्च घटद्द्व्यधिगतस्यार्वाक्: पुत्रदाराद्यभावमवधार्य विक्रोश्येत्, पराट्टतो ऽपि कुटुम्बं नासादयेत्, तदा तेषां सत्त्वे चानुपलब्धिर्व्यभिचारिणी न हेतुः स्यादिति ॥ ६ ॥

'ननु यदनुपलब्धमात्रं नाभावसाधकं तदा अयोग्योपाधि-शङ्कया धूमादावपि व्यभिचारशङ्कया न व्याप्तिनिश्चयः स्या-दिति गतमनुमानेन' इत्यत्राह

शङ्का चेदनुमाऽस्त्येव न चेच्छङ्का ततस्तराम् ।
व्याघातावधिराशङ्का तर्कः शङ्कावधिर्मतः ॥ ७ ॥

तद्धेशत्तत्कालयोर्व्यभिचाराभावनिश्चयात् कालान्तरदेशा-न्तरस्थयोर्व्यभिचारशङ्का स्यात् कालान्तरदेशान्तरस्थज्ञान-ज्ञानुमानादेवेति सिद्धमनुमानं । शङ्का न चेत्, ततः शङ्का-विरहे तरां सुतरामनुमानम् । 'ननु किं शङ्कानिवर्तकं' तत्राह तर्कः शङ्कावधिर्मत इति । विपक्षबाधकतर्काच्छङ्काविरहे मतः सम्मतः इत्यर्थः । 'ननु तर्कस्यापि व्याप्तिमूलकत्वेऽनवस्था' इत्यत्राह व्याघातेत्यादि । तर्कमूलव्याप्तौ न शङ्का व्याघातात्, कृषकारणं विना कार्योत्पत्तिशङ्कायां हव्ययं भोजनादौ पर-प्रतिपत्त्यर्थञ्च शब्दप्रयोगादौ न प्रवर्तेतेति । एवञ्च तर्कानवतारे शङ्कितोपाधिरेवाप्रयोजक इत्युच्यते । तदुक्तं 'यावच्चाव्यति-रेकिलं ज्ञातांऽग्निनापि शङ्क्यते । विपक्षस्य कुतस्तावद्धेतोर्गमनि-

काबलम्'। विपचस्य विपचे हेतोर्व्यतिरेकिंत्वं सत्त्वं यावच्छङ्क्यते तावद्धेतोर्न गमकत्वमिति भावः। व्यभिचारशङ्का च उपाधिशङ्काधीना। तदुक्तम् 'अन्ये परप्रयुक्तानां व्याप्तीनामुपजीवकाः। तैदृष्टैरपि नैवेष्टा व्यापकांशावधारणा' इति। अन्ये केचन हेतवः परप्रयुक्तानां व्याप्तीनामुपजीवकाः, तथा हि उपाध्यवच्छिन्नहेतुनिष्ठा व्याप्तिः हेतुतावच्छेदकावच्छिन्नहेतु- वृत्तितया ज्ञायते, अत एव उप समीपवर्तिनि खसमानाधि- करणे स्वधर्मे व्याप्तिं आदधाति बोधयतीति उपाधिशब्दो जवाकुसमादिसाधारणः, तैः सोपाधिभिर्दृष्टैरपि पचे व्याप- कांशस्यावधारणा निश्चयो नेष्यते साधारणधर्मेण साध्यसंशय- जननादित्यर्थः ॥ ७ ॥

'ननूपमानमीश्वरे बाधकं स्यात्' अचोपमानव्यतिरिक्तप्रमा- णत्वानभ्युपगमात् न बाधकत्वमिति वैशेषिकाद्यः। तच सादृ- श्यस्य पदार्थान्तरस्य ग्राहकमुपमानमिति केचित्, सादृश्यं न द्रव्यं गुणः कर्म वा गुणसमवेतत्वात्, न सामान्यं सप्रतियोगिकत्वात्* सामान्यादिवृत्तित्वाच्च, नाभावः सप्रतियोगिकत्वेनाप्रत्ययात्। तच न प्रत्यक्षगम्यमिन्द्रियपातमात्रेणाप्रतीतेः, नापि प्रतियो- गिज्ञानसहकृतमिन्द्रियं ग्राहकमिति वाच्यं गोसदृशो गवय इति ज्ञानानन्तरं सा गोगवयसदृश्यप्रतीत्यसन्निकृष्टगोविशेष्यकस्य तस्या- प्रत्यक्षत्वात्, नाप्यनुमानगम्यं लिङ्गाप्रतिसन्धानेऽपि ज्ञायमा- नत्वात्, न शब्दगम्यं तस्याशाब्दत्वादिति तच्च

---
* उपमानसापेक्षत्वात्।

परस्परविरोधे हि न प्रकारान्तरस्थितिः ।
नैकतापि विरुद्धानामुक्तिमात्रविरोधतः ॥ ८ ॥

न प्रकारान्तरस्थितिः न नोभयात्मकत्वं*, हि यतः, परस्पर-विरोधात्, नैकतापि न भावाभावात्मकत्वमपि, विरुद्धानामिति हेतुगर्भविशेषणं परस्परविरोधिरूपत्वात् । विरोधमेव प्रतिपादयति उक्तिमात्रविरोधतः । नाभाव इत्युक्ते च भाव-त्वप्रतीतेः कथमभावता, न भाव इत्युक्ते चाभावत्वप्रतीतेर्न भाव-त्वम् । अयमभिप्रायः सादृश्यं भावोऽभावो वा उभयकोट्य-तिरिक्तत्वाप्रसिद्धेः, अभावत्वे सप्तमपदार्थत्वं भावत्वे च गुणवत्त्वे द्रव्यत्वं निर्गुणत्वे सामान्यवत्त्वे च गुणत्वं तदन्यत्वे गुणत्वं निर्गुणनिःसामान्यभावत्वे, समवेतत्वे च समवायत्वं सम-वेतत्वे च अनेकाश्रितत्वे सामान्यत्वं एकाश्रितत्वे विशेषत्वम् । एवं शक्तिसंज्ञाद्योऽपि पदार्था निराकार्याः ॥ ८ ॥

'ननु भवतु सादृश्यं समानधर्म एव, तद्ग्राहकमेवोपमानं मानान्तरं स्यात्' इत्यचाह

साधर्म्यमिव वैधर्म्यं मानमेवं प्रसज्यते ।
अर्थापत्तिरसौ व्यक्तमिति चेत् प्रकृतं न किम् ॥ ८ ॥

अयं गोविसदृग् इति ज्ञानानन्तरं सा गौरेतद्विसदृग्गीति धीः प्रमाणान्तरादेवास्तु । अथ 'एतत्त्व तद्वैधर्म्यं तस्मिन्नेतद्वैधर्म्यं विनाऽनुपपन्नमित्यर्थापत्तिरेव' इति, गोसादृश्यं गवयस्य गो-

---

* नोभयात्मकत्वं उभाभ्यामन्यत्वमित्यर्थः ।

गवयसादृश्यं विनाऽनुपपन्नमित्यर्थापत्तिरेवेति न मानान्तरं सादृश्यग्राहकं मन्तव्यमिति ॥ ९ ॥

वैशेषिकादिभिरुपमाने दूषिते नैयायिकः प्राह

सम्बन्धस्य परिच्छेदः संज्ञायाः संज्ञिना सह ।
प्रत्यचादेरसाध्यत्वादुपमानफलं विदुः ॥ १० ॥

फलमित्यनन्तरं इतीर्द्यध्याहार्यं, संज्ञायाः गवयादिसंज्ञायाः, संज्ञिना गवयत्वादिविशिष्टेन सह, सम्बन्धस्य शक्तेः, परिच्छेदः निश्चयः, उपमानस्य मानान्तरस्य फलमुपमितिः, प्रत्यचादेर-साध्यत्वात् इन्द्रियलिङ्गशब्दानामसामर्थ्यात् ॥ १० ॥

"ननु गोसदृशो गवयपदवाच्य इत्यतिदेशवाक्यादेव शक्ति-धीरस्तु, 'गवयत्वविशिष्टो धर्मी गवयपदवाच्यो गोसदृशत्वात्' इत्यनुमानादास्तु" तत्राह

सादृश्यस्यानिमित्तत्वान्निमित्तस्याप्रतीतितः ।
समयो दुर्ग्रहः पूर्वं शब्देनानुमयापि वा ॥ ११ ॥

समयः गवयत्वादिजातिपुरस्कारेण शक्तिरूपसम्बन्धः, स च दुर्ग्रहः शब्दादनुमानाद्वा न सम्भवति, गवयत्वस्य तेन पुरा-ऽगृहीतत्वात्। न च सादृश्यमेव प्रवृत्तिनिमित्ततया शङ्कयतां *तस्य गुरुत्वेनाप्रवृत्तिनिमित्तत्वात् ॥ ११ ॥

'ननु प्रथमतो गवयत्वस्याप्रतीतत्वेऽपि यदा गवयं प्रत्यचं

---

* तस्य तद्धिन्नत्वे सति तद्धर्मवत्त्वरूपसादृश्यस्य, अप्रवृत्तिनिमि-त्तत्वात् शक्यतावच्छेदकत्वात्, सम्भवति लघौ धर्मे गुरुर्धर्मो नाव-च्छेदक इति नियमात्।

तदा गोसदृशे गवयपदवाच्यत्यतिदेशवाक्याल्लक्षणया गवय-
त्वपरात् तेन रूपेण शक्तिधीरस्तु' तच्चाह

श्रुतान्वयाद्नाकाङ्क्षं न वाक्यं ह्यन्यदिच्छति ।
पदार्थान्वयवैधुर्यात् तदाचिह्नेन सङ्गतिः ॥ १२ ॥

गोसादृश्यसामानाधिकरण्येन गवयपदवाच्यत्वविषयकज्ञा-
नजनकतया शब्दस्य गवयत्वादिना शक्तिबोधे नाकाङ्क्षा
अन्वयस्य पर्यवसानात्, यत्र पदार्था एवान्वयविधुराः केनापि
रूपेणान्वयायोग्याः तत्र तदाचिह्नेन तेन लक्षणीयेनार्थेन
सङ्गतिरन्वयः यथा गङ्गायां घोष इत्यादौ ॥ 'ननु गवय-
पदं सप्रवृत्तिनिमित्तकं साधुपदत्वादिति सामान्यतो दृष्ट-
मनुमानमितरप्रवृत्तिनिमित्तकत्वबाधे गवयत्वस्य प्रवृत्तिनि-
मित्तत्वमवगाहतां' इति चेन्न व्यापकतावच्छेदकरूपेणैवानु-
मितेर्व्यापकविषयकत्वात् । 'गवयपदं गवयत्वप्रवृत्तिनिमित्त-
कम् इतराप्रवृत्तिनिमित्तकत्वे सति सप्रवृत्तिनिमित्तकत्वात्'
इति व्यतिरेकि च साध्याप्रसिद्ध्या न सम्भवति, व्यतिरेकव्या-
प्तिप्रतिसन्धानेऽपि गवयत्वाश्रयो गवयपदवाच्य इति धियोऽनु-
भवसिद्धत्वाच्च उपमानं प्रमाणान्तरम् । एवं धिक्करभमितिदो-
र्घग्रीवमतिकठोरकण्टकाग्निनमपसदं पशूनामित्यादिवाक्यार्थ-
ज्ञानानन्तरं तादृशपिण्डदर्शने करभपदवाच्यतायद्वेऽप्युप-
मानादेवेति । उपमानं तु शक्तिमात्रपरिच्छेदकतया नेश्वरे
बाधकमिति भावः ॥ १२ ॥

'शब्दस्तु नेश्वरे बाधकत्वेन शङ्कनीयः अनुमानानतिरेकात्

इति वैशेषिकाः, "पदश्रवणानन्तरं पदार्थस्मरणे 'एते पदार्थाः परस्परं संसर्गवन्तः आकाङ्क्षायोग्यताषत्तिमत्पदस्मारितत्वात् दण्डेन गामभ्याजेतिपदस्मारितपदार्थवत्' (१) इत्यनुमानात् संसर्गसिद्धेः, किं वा 'एतानि पदानि स्मारितपदार्थसंसर्गप्रमा-पूर्वकाणि आकाङ्क्षादिमत्पदत्वात्' (२) इत्यनुमानात् तत्सिद्धेः, ज्ञानज्ञानस्य तद्विषयविषयकत्वनियमात्*" इति, अत्राह—

अनैकान्तः परिच्छेदे† सम्भवे च न निर्णयः ।
आकाङ्क्षा सत्तया‡ हेतुर्योग्यासत्तिरवम्भना ॥ २३ ॥

अत्र पदार्थपञ्चकानुमाने (१) संसृष्टा एवेति यदि संसर्गवत्त्वं साध्यते, सम्भावितसंसर्गका इति संसर्गखरूपयोग्यत्वं वा, आद्ये पक्षया सिच्चतीत्यादावनैकान्तः§, द्वितीये न संसर्गनिर्णयः, अन्वयप्रयोजकरूपवत्त्वरूपयोग्यताया हेतुविशेषणीकृतत्वेन सि-द्धसाधनञ्च‖। द्वितीये प्रयोगे (२) आकाङ्क्षा सत्तया इति। आकाङ्क्षा हि समभिव्याहृतपदस्मारितपदार्थजिज्ञासा, घटमि-त्युक्ते आनय पश्येति, आनयेत्युक्ते घटं पटं वेति जिज्ञासादयः।

---

* ज्ञानस्य प्रकृते पदार्थसंसर्गप्रमाया यत् ज्ञानं उक्तानुमितिरूपं तस्य, तस्य उक्तसंसर्गप्रमारूपज्ञानस्य यो विषयः संसर्गरूपः स एव विषयो यस्य तत्त्वनियमादित्यर्थः, अयं भावः संसर्गप्रमापूर्वकत्वज्ञानं संसर्गरूपविशेषणगोचरमेवेति न पुनःसंसर्गज्ञानाय प्रमाण्यान्तरा-पेक्षा इति।

† परिच्छेदे नियमे।
‡ सत्तया विद्यमानया, न तु ज्ञातया।
§ करकादिस्थिरजलेन सेकासम्भवात्।
‖ अन्वयप्रयोजकरूपं प्रकृते पक्ष्त्वादि, अयंभावः हेतुविशेष-तयैव साध्यस्य सिद्धौ पुनः साधनापेक्षैव नास्तीति।

'ननु योग्यताविदिता आसक्तिरेव हेतुरस्तु', तत्राह योग्या-
क्तिरिनबन्धना इति व्याप्तिशून्या, अयमिति पुत्रो राज्ञः पुरुषोऽप-
सार्यतामित्यत्र   निराकाङ्क्षयोराजपदपुरुषपदयोर्व्यभिचारात्
॥ १३ ॥

प्राभाकरास्तु "वेदस्यापौरुषेयतया तत्र वक्तृज्ञानानुमाना-
सम्भवात् शब्दः प्रमाणं, लोके तु आप्तोक्तलब्धज्ञानमपेक्षितं,
तथाच 'अयं वक्ता स्वप्रयुक्तवाक्यार्थयथार्थज्ञानवान् भ्रमाद्य-
जन्यवाक्यार्थज्ञानजन्यवाक्यप्रयोक्तृत्वात्' इत्यनुमानाद्वक्तृज्ञानाव-
च्छेदकतया,* उत्तरकालं वा 'एते पदार्थाः परस्परं संसृष्टाः
वक्तृयथार्थज्ञानविषयत्वात्'इत्यनुमानात् साक्षात् वाक्यार्थसिद्धेः,
क्लृप्तसामर्थ्यात् शब्दात् पुनरन्वयधीरित्यनुवादको लौकिकः
शब्दो न प्रमाणं" इति† प्राञ्चः, तत्राह

निर्णीतशक्तेर्वाक्याद्धि प्रागेवार्थस्य निर्णये ।
व्याप्तिस्मृतिविलम्बेन लिङ्गस्येवानुवादिता ॥ १४ ॥

वेदेऽवधारितसामर्थ्याच्छब्दाल्लोकस्थलेऽपि   प्रागर्थनिर्णये
लिङ्गस्येवानुवादकत्वं, व्याप्तिस्मृतिविलम्बेनानुमानस्य शब्दापेक्ष-
या विलम्बितधीजनकत्वात्॥ १४ ॥

'ननु आप्तोक्तलस्य संशये व्यतिरेके च शाब्दज्ञानानुत्पत्त्या नि-
र्णयो हेतुर्वाच्यः, आप्तोक्तलञ्च प्रकृतवाक्यार्थगोचरयथार्थधीजन्य-
त्वमिति, वाक्यार्थधीः प्रथमतोऽनुमानादेव वाच्या' इति, अत्राह

---

* अवच्छेदकतया विशेष्यविधया, यस्य 'सिद्धेः' इत्यनेनान्वयः ।
† अष्टचोत्याद्यचितं प्रमाणत्वमिति प्राभाकरसिद्धान्तः ।

तृतीयः स्तवकः ।

व्यस्तपुंदूषणाशङ्कैः स्मारितत्वात् पदैरमी ।
अन्विता इति निर्णीते वेदस्यापि न तत् कुतः ॥ १५ ॥

आम्नातत्वनिश्चयस्य हेतुत्वे मानाभावः, बाधकप्रमाविरह-रूपयोग्यताज्ञानविलम्बादेवायोग्येऽन्वयधीविलम्बसंभवात्, अन्यथा वेदेऽपि अपौरुषेयत्वधीर्हेतुरस्तु, तथाच तत्रापि 'अमी वैदिका अर्थाः 'अन्विताः' परस्परं संसृष्टाः व्यस्तपुंदूषणाशङ्कैः पदैः स्मारितत्वात्' इत्यनुमानात् संसर्गे निर्णीते तत् अनुवादकत्वं वेदस्यापि न कुतः ।

यत्तु "पदं न कारणं किन्तु पदार्थ एव, अत एव पदार्थकरणकवाक्यार्थज्ञानात् कविकाव्यादिकं,* द्वारमित्यञ्च द्वारोपस्थितावपि पदार्थनिष्ठाकाङ्क्षाविरहेणान्वयाबोधः,† 'शाब्दी ह्याकाङ्क्षा शब्देनैव प्रपूर्यते' इति न्यायात् । अतएव 'पदार्थानामवच्छेदकत्वं पदजन्योपस्थितिं विना पदार्थान्वयाबोधात्,‡ तदुक्तम् 'प्राथम्यादभिधात्वात् तात्पर्योपगमादपि । पदानामेव सा शक्तिर्वरमभ्युपगम्यताम्' । अभिधात्वात् पदा-

---

* तत्र हि पदं विनापि लिपिमात्रदर्शनेन वाक्यार्थबोधोत्तरमभिप्रेतार्थबोधो जायते ।

† अत्र विधेहीतिपदाभावात् नान्वयबोध इति न, किन्तु समभिव्याहृतपदार्थजिज्ञासाभावादेव, श्रुतपदस्यार्थेन समं श्रुतपदार्थान्वय एवाकाङ्क्षोदयनियमादिति भावः ।

‡ अयं भावः पदस्य व्यवहितस्यापि अन्वयव्यतिरेकाभ्यां कारणत्वं सिद्धं, पदार्थस्य पदार्थोपस्थितिविशेषणविधया कारणतावच्छेदकत्वमात्रम् ।

र्य्यापस्थापकत्वात्' इति गुरुमतमपास्तं, पदानामित्यच्च आम्रा-नामिति प्रच्छेपेणापि आम्रोत्कलखावच्छेदकत्वापातात्,* त-थाचावस्थितोकार्य्यपदार्थोपस्थितौ पदमन्यथासिद्धं न कर-णम्" इति, तन्न पदार्थानामतीतादिरूपतया अकारण-त्वात्, पदार्थस्मरणस्यापि निर्व्यापारतया अकरणत्वात्, पद-ज्ञानस्यैव करणत्वात्, पदार्थस्मृतेर्व्यापारत्वात्, कविकाव्यादि-स्थले च मानसज्ञानं† हेतुरिति ॥ १५ ॥

'ननु शब्दोऽतिरिच्यतां प्रमाणं, स एव बाधकोऽस्तु, त-थाहि 'प्रकृते: क्रियमाणानि गुणै: कर्माणि सर्वश: । अह-ङ्कारविमूढात्मा कर्ताहमिति मन्यते' इति गीतां पठन्ति, प्रकृतेर्बुद्धितत्त्वस्य, गुणै: सत्वादिभि:, क्रियमाणानि कर्माणि मोहादहं कर्तेति चेतनो मन्यते, तेनाभिमानिकं कर्तृत्वं न पारमार्थिकं, न च सर्वत्रत्यभिमान: विशेषदर्शनात्, कर्तेति हन्निति न षष्ठी' इति, अत्राह

न प्रमाणमनाप्तोक्तिनादृष्टे क्वचिदाप्तता ।
अदृष्टदृष्टौ सर्वज्ञो न च नित्यागम: क्षम: ॥ १६ ॥

अर्थ हि सर्वकर्तृलाभावादेदक: शब्द: अनाप्तोक्तत्वेन प्रमा-णं, आप्तोक्तत्वे एतदर्थगोचरज्ञानवतो नित्यसर्वविषयकज्ञानवत्त्वम्

---

* अयं भाव: यथा प्राथम्यादित्वेऽपि नाम्न: कारणं किन्तु आम्रोक्त-त्वज्ञानमेव, तथा पदस्य प्राथम्यादित्वेऽपि न कारणत्वमिति ।
† पदस्येति शेष:, हेतु: शाब्दबोधस्य हेतु:, यदा तत्र न काव्यार्थस्य शाब्दबोध: किन्तु मानसज्ञानमेव, तदेव चमत्कारहेतुरिति ।

इन्द्रियाद्यभावात्, आगमस्य च नित्यत्वं दूषितमेव प्रागिति वेदकारो नित्यः सर्वज्ञः सिद्ध्यति ॥ १६ ॥

'ननु सत्त्वबोधकागमानां का गतिः', तत्राह

नचासौ क्वचिदेकान्तः सत्त्वस्यापि प्रवेदनात् ।
निरञ्जनावबोधार्थो न च सन्नपि तत्परः* ॥ १७ ॥

अषावागमो नासत्त्वमात्रपर एव, सत्त्वस्यापि बङ्गभ:'मत्तः सर्वं प्रवर्तते' इत्यादिभिः प्रतिपादनात्, तयोश्च न मुख्यार्थत्वं विरोधात्, विनिगमकचिन्तायां विशेषगुणशून्यात्मस्वरूपस्य ध्येयत्वतात्पर्यकत्वं बाधकश्रुतीनां, साधकश्रुतीनाञ्च कार्यकारणभावादितर्कमूलकानुमानसाचिव्येन मुख्यार्थकत्वात् ॥ १७ ॥

'ननु यद्यसौ सर्वज्ञः स्यात् अनुपदिष्याऽपि प्रवर्तयेदित्युपदेशानुपपत्तिरेवास्तु ईश्वरे बाधिका, नह्ययमनुपदिश्य स्वयं प्रवर्तयितुं न जानाति सर्वज्ञत्वानुपपत्तेः, अर्थापत्तिश्च मानान्तरं', तत्राह

हेत्वभावे फलाभावात् प्रमाणेऽसति न प्रमा ।
तदभावात् प्रवृत्तिर्न कर्मवादेऽप्ययं विधिः ॥ १८ ॥

प्रमाणेऽसति न प्रमा, प्रमाणरूपहेत्वभावे फलाभावात् प्रमाविरहात्, प्रमाविरहे च न प्रवृत्तिः कारणाभावात्, प्रमाकारणत्वाग्निष्ठोऽमेनेत्यादिविधिरेव इति नोपदेशवैयर्थ्यता,

---

* निरञ्जनस्य निर्धर्मकस्य आत्मनः । सन्नपि सत्त्वबोधकोऽपि तत्परः असत्त्वतात्पर्यकः ॥

अन्यथा कर्मवादेऽप्ययं विधिः अदृष्टादेव प्रवृत्तेरुपपत्तेः
वेदस्यानर्थक्यापत्तिः । न वार्थापत्तिर्मानान्तरम् ॥ १८ ॥

तदेवाह

अनियम्यस्य नायुक्तिर्नानियन्तोपपादकः ।
न मानयोर्विरोधोऽस्ति प्रसिद्धे वाप्यसौ समः ॥ १९ ॥

जीवी देवदत्तो गेहे नास्तीति ज्ञानानन्तरं वहिरस्तीति
धीरुदाहरणं, तच्चानियम्यस्याव्याप्यस्य नायुक्तिर्नानुपपत्तिः,
अनियन्ता अव्यापको नोपपादकः, व्यापकव्यतिरेकेण व्याप्य-
स्यैव व्यतिरेकात्, तादृग्ज्ञानुपपत्तिज्ञाने व्यतिरेकव्याप्तिधीरेव ।
यदपि 'क्वचिदस्ति गेहे नास्तीतिज्ञानानन्तरं विरोधज्ञा-
नेऽविरोधाय गेहान्यविषयता क्वचिदस्तीत्यर्थापत्तिः' इति,
तदपि न, न हि वास्तवो मानयोर्विरोधः, तथा सति एकं
मानं भज्येत, विरोधज्ञानस्य तु विषयभेदव्यवस्थापकम-
नुमानविधच्चैव, तथाहि विरोधो भिन्नविषयकः एकविषय-
तायां विरुद्धले सति प्रमाणसिद्धत्वादिति, अन्यथा धूमोऽप्यनु-
पपद्यमानो वह्निं गमयेदित्यर्थापत्तिरिति प्रसिद्धमप्यनुमानं
न स्यात्, अर्वाग्भागावच्छेदेन वह्न्यनुपलम्भः धूमस्य वह्निसा-
धनमिति विरोधेऽपरभागावच्छेदेन वह्निव्यवस्थापनमप्यर्थाप-
त्तेरेव स्यात्, अनुमानाभावेऽपि च व्याप्तिग्राहकमानस्य वह्नि-
साधकत्वमर्थापत्तेरित्यनुमानविलोपः स्यादिति ॥ १९ ॥

अनुपलब्धिस्तु नेश्वरे बाधिकेति योग्यादृष्टिरित्यादिनोक्तम्,
वस्तुतोऽनुपलब्धिर्मानान्तरमेव नेत्याह

द्वितीयः स्तबकः ।

प्रतिपत्तेरपरोक्त्यादिन्द्रियस्यानुपचयात् ।
अज्ञातकरणत्वाच्च भावावेशाच्च चेतसः* ॥ २० ॥

यच्चाज्ञातानुपलब्धिः कारणं तत् प्रत्यक्षं, ज्ञातानुपल-
ब्धिजन्याभावज्ञानस्यानुमानत्वात्, जन्यापरोक्षज्ञानस्य इन्द्रिय-
जन्यत्वात्, अपरोक्षत्वञ्च ज्ञानकरणकान्यत्वं, घटादिप्रत्यक्ष इव
घटाभावप्रत्येतेऽपीन्द्रियस्यान्यानुपचीणत्वात् करणं, अधिक-
रणप्रत्यक्षाभावेऽपि शब्दादिध्वंसस्य, वायौ रूपाभावस्य च ग्रहात्
अधिकरणग्रहेऽप्यनुपचयात्, अज्ञातकरणजन्यज्ञानत्वेन इन्द्रि-
यजन्यत्वानुमानाच, भावावेशाच्च 'चेतसः' मनसः, अस्मदा-
दिवाह्यानुभवस्य भावभूतकरणश्चिवमनोजन्यत्वनियमात् ना-
नुपलब्धिः करणं किन्त्विन्द्रियमेवेति ॥ २० ॥

साधकान्तरमाह

प्रतियोगिनि सामर्थ्याद्व्यापाराव्यवधानतः ।
अन्यग्यत्वादोषाणामिन्द्रियाणि विकल्पनात् ॥ २१ ॥

इन्द्रियाणि करणमिति साध्यं, प्रतियोगिग्राहकत्वात्, य-
च्चानुमानं घटस्येव तदभावस्यापि ग्राहकं तदिन्द्रियमपि ।
'ननु प्रतियोगिग्राहकत्वमतन्त्रं, अनन्यथासिद्धतुल्योपाधित्वात्,
आश्रयग्रहेण इन्द्रियस्यान्यथासिद्धे:' इत्यत आह व्यापाराव्य-
वधानत इति । व्यापारेणाधिकरणप्रत्यक्षेण इन्द्रियस्यान्यथा-

---

* अयं भावः अभावज्ञानस्य प्रत्यक्षत्वं तत्र च अनुपलब्धेर्हेतुत्वं
उभयवादिसिद्धं, विशेषस्त्वयं पूर्वपक्षवादिनयेऽनुपलब्धिरेव करणं
नत्विन्द्रियं, सिद्धान्ते तु प्रत्यक्षसामान्यस्यैव इन्द्रियं करणमतो भाव-
प्रत्यक्षेऽपि तदेव करणमिति ॥

मिद्याभावात्, अन्यथा संयोगेन चचुरादिकमन्यथासिद्धं भाव-
ग्रहेऽपि स्यात्। किञ्चाभावभ्रमस्य दुष्टकरणजन्यत्वमवश्यं वाच्यं,
दोषस्येन्द्रियादिनिष्ठ एव, अनुपलब्धेर्दोषवत्ताभावात्, पित्तादि-
ना इन्द्रियस्यैव दुष्टत्वात्, तदिदमुक्तम् अन्याश्रयत्वाद्दोषाणा-
मिति। अधिकरणाभावग्राहिविशिष्टधीर्नेन्द्रियजा अभावधीत्वात्,
नानुपलब्धिकरणजा भावधीत्वात् अतो विशिष्टग्राहीन्द्रियं खी-
कार्यं तदिदमुक्तं विकल्पनात् विशिष्टविषयकज्ञानात्* ॥ २९ ॥

'नन्वनुपलब्ध्या घटाभावस्य ज्ञानं ततश्च घटाभाववद्भू-
तलमिति ज्ञानं, घ्राणजधैरभोपनयानन्तरं सुरभि चन्द-
नमितिचाक्षुषवत् द्रव्याभावग्राहिकाऽनुपलब्धिः करणतया
वाच्या, निर्विकल्पकविषयीकृत एव इन्द्रियेण सविकल्पकविष-
यतया गृह्यते तथादर्शनात्। अभावेनेन्द्रियप्रत्यासत्तेरभावात्
कथं वा प्रत्यक्षं, विशेषणतायाः सम्बन्धान्तरगर्भत्वात्† अव-

---

* अयं भावः घटाभाववत् भूतलं इति विशिष्टबुद्धिर्न केवलं इन्द्रिय-
मात्रजन्या अभावविषयकत्वात् अपि तु अनुपलब्धिरपि तत्र का-
रणमस्तु, तथापि तस्याः तत्र करणत्वं न सम्भवति भूतलरूपविशेष्यांशे
भावग्राहितया तदंशे इन्द्रियस्य करणतायाः उभयवादिसिद्धत्वात्
इतरांशेऽपि तस्यैव करणत्वमुचितमिति॥

† उक्तविशिष्टज्ञाने इन्द्रियं करणमस्तु निर्विकल्परूपघटाभा-
वज्ञाने तु अनुपलब्धिः करणमिति को दोषः। किञ्च अभावस्य संयोगस-
मवायादिसम्बन्धाभावेन कथं वा इन्द्रियसम्बद्धत्वं, याऽपि च विशेषण-
ता साऽपि सम्बन्धान्तरसापेक्षतया न सम्बन्धत्वमुपैति, तथाहि विशेष-
णत्वं नाम केनापि सम्बन्धेन कस्मिंश्चिद्वृत्तित्वं, यथा संयोगसम्बन्धेन
भूतले घटस्य वृत्तित्वमिति घटस्य भूतलविशेषणता, नायमभावः
केनापि सम्बन्धान्तरेण कुत्रापि वर्त्तते येन तस्य विशेषणता स्यादिति
पूर्वपक्षतात्पर्यम्॥

द्वितीयः स्तवकः ।

यन्नृप्रकारणताकानुपश्रम्भे रेव करणलं नेन्द्रियस्य' इत्यत्राह

अवच्छेदग्रहग्रोव्याद ग्रौव्ये सिद्धसाधनात् ।
प्राप्त्यन्तरेऽनवस्थानान्न चेदन्योऽपि दुर्घटः* ॥ २२ ॥

अवच्छेदग्रहस्य प्रतियोगिग्रहस्य, अभावप्रत्यच्चे हेतुत्वात् नियमतः सविकल्पकज्ञानसामग्रीसत्त्वान्निर्विकल्पकलं, घटादिग्रहे तु निर्विकल्पकमेव प्रथमतः, विशिष्टज्ञानहेतुविशेषणज्ञानाभावात्, प्रतियोग्यनुपर्चितस्याभावस्य भानाभ्युपगमे तु अभावस्यापि निर्विकल्पकविषयतेति सिद्धसाधनम् । सम्बन्धान्तरेऽनवस्थानात् स्वरूपमेवाभावस्याधिकरणेन सम्बन्धः, वैशिष्ट्यस्याभावसम्बन्धस्याङ्गीकृतस्यापि सम्बन्धधारायामनवस्थानात् स्वरूपसम्बन्धस्वीकारस्यावश्यम्भावात्, इन्द्रियसम्बद्धविशेषणताया घटाभावादिप्रत्यच्चे सन्निकर्षतया कल्पनात् । न चेदेवं, तदाऽनुपलब्धिकरणतापत्तेरपि अन्यप्रकारो दुर्घटः,

---

* सिद्धान्तस्वर्यं, यन्मतेऽभावप्रत्यच्चं प्रति प्रतियोगिज्ञानं कारणं, तन्मते अभावस्य निर्विकल्पकमेव नास्ति, प्रतियोगिज्ञानादेव नियमतो प्रतियोगिविशिष्टाभावज्ञानस्योदयात्, यन्मते प्रतियोगिज्ञानं न तत्र कारणं, तन्मतेऽभावस्य निर्विकल्पकसत्त्वेऽपि इन्द्रियादेव तदुत्पत्तिः सम्भवति । नापि विशेषणतायाः उक्तरूपेण सम्बन्धान्तरगर्भता, तस्याः स्वरूपसम्बन्धरूपत्वात्, स्वरूपसम्बन्धस्य नातिरिक्तः किन्तु अभावस्य अधिकरणस्य वा स्वरूपमेव, अतिरिक्तत्वे यथा संयोगस्य समवायः सम्बन्धान्तरं तथा स्वरूपसम्बन्धस्यापि सम्बन्धान्तरं एवं तस्य तस्यापीति अनवस्था स्यात्, इन्द्रियसम्बद्धेऽभावस्य तादृश्स्वरूपसम्बन्धरूपविशेषणतैव सन्निकर्षः, उक्तसम्बन्धाभावे भूतले घटाभावसम्बन्धावगाहिन्याः घटाभाववद्भूतलमितिप्रतीतेः वायुरूपवान् इत्यादिवत् भ्रमत्वमापद्येतेति ।

तथा हि सर्वैरेव प्रमाणैः परम्परया निर्विकल्पकविषय एव गृह्यते, अनुमानादावपि वह्न्यादेः पूर्वं कदाचिन्निर्विकल्पकस्वीकारात्, घटाभाववदभूतलमित्यादिविशिष्टप्रत्ययबलात् अभावेनाधिकरणस्य प्राप्तेर्भवतापि स्वीकारात् ॥ २२ ॥

स्ववकार्यसंग्राहकश्लोकमाह

प्रत्यक्षादिभिरेभिरेवमधरो दूरे विरोधोदयः
प्रायो यन्मुखवीचणैकविधुरैरात्मापि नासाद्यते ।
तं सर्वानुविधेयमेकमसमस्वच्छन्दलीलोत्सवम्
देवानामपि देवमुद्भवदतिश्रद्धाः प्रपद्यामहे ॥ २३ ॥

इति तृतीयः स्तवकः ।

यस्येश्वरस्य मुखनिरीक्षणैकविधुरैर्धर्मिग्राहकमानबाधितैः* प्रत्यक्षादिभिरात्मैव नासाद्यते, विरोधोदयो यतोऽधरोऽधः, अत एव दूरे, सर्वमनुविधेयं वश्यं यस्येति, असमा स्वच्छन्दा चेतनान्तराप्रयोज्या या लीला सैवोत्सवो यस्य स तथा, दुःखाभावैकनिदानत्वात्, अतएव उद्भवदतिश्रद्धाः, देवानामपि देवं स्तुत्यं, प्रपद्यामहे ॥ २३ ॥

॥ इति तृतीयस्तवकव्याख्यानम् ॥

---

* ईश्वरो नास्तीत्यादिरीत्या ईश्वरधर्मिकासत्त्वसाधकतया उपन्यस्तानि प्रत्यक्षादीनि प्रमाणानि स्वधर्मिभूतेश्वरसाधकप्रमाणेन बाध्यमानानि प्रमाणतामेव नासादयन्तीति भावः ।

कुसुमाञ्जलिः ।

चतुर्थः स्तवकः ।

सत्त्वेऽपि तस्याप्रमाण्वादिति तुरीयविप्रतिपत्तिः । 'ईश्वरो न प्रमाणं तज्ज्ञानस्याग्रहीतग्राहिलाभावेन प्रमात्वाभावात्, ईश्वरस्य प्रमाकर्त्तृत्वं प्रमाकरणत्वञ्च नास्तीति अप्रमाणपुरुषस्य वचः कः श्रद्ध्यात्' इत्याशङ्कते

अप्राप्तेरधिकप्राप्तेरलक्षणमपूर्ववृक् ।
यथार्थोऽनुभवो मानमनपेक्षतयेष्यते ॥ १ ॥

अपूर्ववृक्त्वं अगृहीतग्राहित्वं न प्रमालक्षणं धारावहनबुद्ध्याप्राप्तेः इदं रजतमितिभ्रमातिव्याप्तेः । क्षमते लक्षणमाह यथार्थ इति । अनपेक्षतयेति स्मृतेः जनकानुभवसमानविषयकतया तत्प्रामाण्याधीनप्रामाण्यकतया सापेक्षत्वात् तत्र न प्रमाव्यवहारस्तान्त्रिकाणामिति ॥ १ ॥

'ननु धारावाहिके नाव्याप्तिः, ज्ञानेन हि विषयनिष्ठो धर्मः कश्चिज्जननीयः, अन्यथा ज्ञानस्य विषयं प्रति नियमो न स्यात्*,

---

* अयं भावः घटज्ञानस्य घट एव विषयः न तु पटः इति नियमो हि तदैव उपपद्यते यदि घटज्ञानेन घटे कश्चित् विशेषः स्यात्, अन्यथा घटपटोभयं प्रत्येव ज्ञानस्य औदासीन्येन घट एव विषय इति नियमानुपपत्तिः, स च विशेषः ज्ञाततानाम्नकः, ताद‍ृशो विशेषस्तु येन ज्ञानेन यस्मिन् जायते तस्य स एव विषयो नान्य इति मीमांसकसिद्धान्त इति ।

तथा च तमादायागृहीतग्राह्यिलमेव* । किञ्च स धर्मस्तदुपा-
दानज्ञानजन्यो न वा, आद्ये उपादानज्ञानस्य उपादान-
विषयतानियमार्थं धर्मान्तरस्वीकारे तत्राप्येवमित्यनवस्था,
द्वितीये कार्यं किं हेतुः तच्चैव उपादानज्ञानजन्यत्वव्यभिचारीति
नेश्वरस्य चित्यादिकर्तृतया सिद्धिः' इत्याचष्ट

स्वभावनियमाभावादुपकारो हि दुर्घटः ।
सुघटत्वेऽपि सद्यर्थेऽसति का गतिरन्यथा ॥ २ ॥

स्वभावविशेष एव विषयतानियामकः, अन्यथा ज्ञाततायाधा-
नेऽपि नियमानुपपत्तिः इति स्वभाव एव नियामकस्त्वेति ।
किञ्च वर्तमानविषये तदुत्पत्तावपि अविद्यमाने विषये
ज्ञातताया उपादानविरहात् अनुत्पत्तौ विषयतानियमानु-
पपत्तिरिति स्वभाव एव तत्र नियामक इति ॥ २ ॥

'ननु क्रियया कर्मणि किञ्चिज्जननीयमितिव्याप्तेर्ज्ञानक्रि-
ययाऽपि विषयनिष्ठो धर्मो जननीयः' इत्याचष्ट

अनैकान्तादसिद्धेर्वा न च लिङ्गमियं क्रिया ।
तदैव विषयप्रकाशत्वाद्ध्यध्यक्षानुभवोऽधिके ‡ ॥ ३ ॥

---

* पूर्वगृहीतां प्रथमज्ञानजन्यज्ञाततामादाय द्वितीयज्ञानस्य, द्वि-
तीयज्ञानादिजन्यज्ञाततादिकमादाय तृतीयादेरगृहीतग्राहित्वमिति
भावः ।

† तच्चैव ज्ञाततानामकधर्म एव, तस्य जन्यत्वेन कार्यत्वात् ।

‡ तस्य ज्ञानस्य वैशिष्ट्यं सम्बन्धः, तत्प्रकाशत्वात् तद्विषयकत्वात्
अधिके ज्ञातत्वरूपधर्मे न अध्यक्षानुभवः न प्रबन्धं प्रमाणमित्यर्थः ।

क्रिया यदि धात्वर्थस्तदा 'शरेण गगनं युनक्ति' इत्यत्र संयोगेन गगननिष्ठकिञ्चिदजननात् अनैकान्त:, यदि करण-व्यापार: क्रिया तदापीन्द्रियसंयोगादिना घटादिनिष्ठकिञ्चि-दजननात् व्यभिचार:, अथ क्रिया सन्दृतदा ज्ञानस्य सन्दृ-नात्मकत्वादसिद्धि: । 'ननु ज्ञातो घट: साचात्कृतो घट इत्यादि प्रत्यचमेव ज्ञाततायां मानं' इत्याचष्टे तद्दैत्रिच्छेति । सर्वञ्च विशिष्टज्ञाने विशेषणविशेष्ये तदुभयसम्बन्धो विषय:, स च सम्बन्ध: क्वचित् संयोगादि: क्वचित्तु खरूपं, तदिह 'घट-ज्ञानं' इत्यत्रेव घटज्ञानयो: खरूप एव सम्बन्ध: 'ज्ञातो घट:' इत्यत्रापि भासते, अन्यथा 'दृष्टो घट:' 'कृतो घट:' इत्यत्र दृष्टताकृततयोरप्यापत्ते: ॥ ३ ॥

स्वभावसम्बन्धादुपपत्तिसुख्या तदुच्यते

अर्थेनैव विशेषो हि निराकारतया धियाम् ।
क्रिययैव विशेषो हि व्यवहारेषु कर्मणाम् ॥ ४ ॥

यथा घटादिना ज्ञाने विशिष्टधी: यथा च क्रिययैव कर्मणां घटादीनां व्यवहारेषु विशिष्टबुद्ध्यादिषु विशेषस्तथा ज्ञातो घट इत्यादौ ज्ञानेनैव घटादौ विशिष्टधीर्न धर्मान्त-रादिति* ॥ ४ ॥

---

* घटादिना विशेषणेन, ज्ञाने विशिष्टधीर्घटज्ञानमिति बुद्धि, क्रिययैव विशेषणीभूतत्वख्या एव, अस्याञ्च विशेष इत्यनेनान्वय: । विशिष्टबुद्ध्यादिषु 'कृतो घट:' इति प्रतीत्यादिषु, ज्ञानेनैवेति विशे-षणेनेति शेष:, धर्मान्तरात् ज्ञाततारूपादित्यर्थ: ।

'ननु तथापि नेश्वरज्ञानं प्रमा प्रमाणजन्यत्वाभावात्, एव-मीश्वरो न प्रमाता न वा प्रमाणं प्रमाकर्त्तृकरणत्वयोरभावात्' अत्राह

मितिः सम्यक्परिच्छित्तिस्तदवत्ता च प्रमात्वता ।
तद्योगव्यवच्छेदः प्रामाण्यं गौतमे मते ॥ ५ ॥

यथार्थानुभवत्वमेव प्रमात्वमजन्यत्वेऽपीश्वरज्ञानस्याविरुद्धं, प्रमात्वं प्रमासमवायित्वं तच्च अकारणत्वेऽपि प्रमाया ईश्व-रस्याविरुद्धम्। एवं प्रमया सद्योगव्यवच्छेदेन सम्बन्धित्वये-श्वरस्य प्रमाणत्वमपि न तु करणत्वमपि तच्च नियामकमिति, 'मन्त्रायुर्वेदवत् तत्प्रामाण्यमात्रप्रामाण्यात्' इति सूत्रे (न्यायसू० २।१।६८) ईश्वरस्य प्रामाण्यमुक्तं। न चेश्वरस्य पञ्चमप्रमाणत्वा-पत्त्या विभागव्याघातः प्रमाकरणाभिप्रायेण विभागसम्भवात्। न चेश्वरज्ञानस्य भ्रमविषयकत्वे भ्रमविषयावगाहित्वेन भ्रम-त्वापत्तिरिति वाच्यं व्यधिकरणप्रकारकत्वाभावेनाप्रमात्वाभा-वात्, भ्रमनिष्ठं युक्तिविषेय्यकत्वं रजतत्वप्रकारकत्वञ्च सदेव तदवगाहितया ईश्वरज्ञानस्य प्रमात्वाच्यते ॥ ५ ॥

स्वकार्यसंग्राहकश्लोकमाह

साचात्कारिणि नित्ययोगिनि परद्वारानपेक्षस्थितौ
भूतार्थानुभवे निविष्टनिखिलप्रस्ताविवस्तुक्रमः ।
लेशाद्दृष्टिनिमित्तदुष्टिविगमप्रभ्रष्टशङ्कातुषः
शङ्कोन्मेषकलङ्किभिः किमपरैस्त्वन्ये प्रमाणं शिवः ॥ ६ ॥

इति चतुर्थः स्तवकः ।

चतुर्थः स्तवकः ।

भूतार्थानुभवे यथार्थानुभवे, साक्षात्कारिणि प्रत्यक्षे, नि-
विष्टो विषयीभूतो निखिलप्रस्तावविवक्षितानां नानापदार्थानां
क्रमो यस्य स तथा अनुभवविषयसकलविश्वक इत्यर्थः, नित्य-
योगिनि सदातनयुक्ते, अतएवेन्द्रियाणां द्वाराणामनपेक्षा
स्थितिर्यस्य, क्षेत्रतोऽप्यक्षतोऽपि अदृष्टिर्विशेषादर्शनं तन्निमि-
त्तिका या दुष्टिः रागद्वेषमोहात्मिका तद्गमेन प्रभ्रष्टः
शङ्कातुषः वेदाप्रामाण्यशङ्कालेशो यस्मादित्यर्थः, प्रमाणं
शिवः, एवम्भूते त्वयि प्रामाण्यशङ्कारूपकलङ्कवह्नि पाषण्डैः किं
कर्त्तव्यमिति भावः* ॥ ६ ॥

इति चतुर्थस्तवकव्याख्यानम् ।

---

*'एवम्भूते' इत्यादिपाठः प्राचीनपुस्तकद्वये नास्ति ।

कुसुमाञ्जलिः ।

पञ्चमः स्तवकः ।

'तत्साधकप्रमाणाभावात्' इति पञ्चमविप्रतिपत्तिः 'नन्वी-
श्वरे साधकप्रमाणमेव नास्ति' इत्याह

कार्यायोजनधृत्यादेः पदात् प्रत्ययतः श्रुतेः ।
वाक्यात् सङ्ख्याविशेषाच्च साध्यो विश्वविदव्ययः ॥ १ ॥

इत्यादि सकर्त्तृकं कार्यत्वात् घटवत् सकर्त्तृकञ्च उपादान-
गोचरापरोक्षज्ञानचिकीर्षाकृतिमज्जन्यत्वम् । आयोजनं कर्म
एवञ्च सर्गाद्यकालीनद्वयणुकारम्भकपरमाणुद्वयसंयोगजनकं कर्म
चेतनप्रयत्नपूर्वकं कर्मत्वात् अस्मदादिशरीरक्रियावत् । धृतीति
ब्रह्माण्डादि पतनप्रतिबन्धकीभूतप्रयत्नवदधिष्ठितं धृतिमत्त्वात्
वियति विद्यङ्गमघ्राहकाष्ठवत् धृतिश्च गुरुत्ववतां पतनाभावः ।
धृत्यादेरित्यादिपदात् नाशपरिग्रहः, ब्रह्माण्डादि प्रयत्नवद्वि-
नाशं विनाश्यत्वात् पाच्यमानपटवत् । पदात् पद्यतेऽनेनेति
व्युत्पत्त्या पदं व्यवहारः, पटादिसम्प्रदायव्यवहारः स्वतन्त्र-
पुरुषप्रयोज्यः व्यवहारत्वात् आधुनिकलिप्यादिव्यवहारवत् ।
प्रत्ययतः प्रामाण्यात्, वेदजन्यज्ञानं कारणगुणजन्यं प्रमात्वात्
प्रत्यक्षादिप्रमावत् । श्रुतेर्वेदात्, वेदः पौरुषेयो वेदत्वात् आ-
युर्वेदवत् । किञ्च वेदः पौरुषेयो वाक्यत्वात् भारतवत्, वेद-

वाक्यानि पौरुषेयाणि वाक्यत्वात् अस्मदादिवाक्यवत् । 'सङ्ख्या-विशेषात्', ह्यणुकपरिमाणं सङ्ख्याजन्यं परिमाणप्रचयाजन्यत्वे सति जन्यपरिमाणत्वात् तुल्यपरिमाणककपालद्वयारब्धघट-परिमाणात् प्रकृष्टतादृशकपालत्र्यारब्धघटपरिमाणवत्*, अणु-परिमाणञ्च न परिमाणजनकं, नित्यपरिमाणत्वात् अणुपरि-माणत्वाद्वा, एवञ्च सर्गादौ ह्यणुकपरिमाणहेतुपरमाणुनिष्ठ-द्विसङ्ख्या च नास्मदाद्यपेक्षाबुद्धिजा, अतस्तदानीन्तनापेक्षा-बुद्धिरीश्वरस्यैवेति । विश्वविद्यश्च इति विशिष्टस्याव्ययत्वं, तेन नित्यसर्वविषयकज्ञानसिद्धिः† ॥ ९ ॥

'ननु शरीरविशिष्टस्य कर्तृतया विशेषणबाधात्मको विशिष्ट-बाध इति (१), कर्तृजन्यत्वव्यापकशरीरजन्यत्वाभावात् कर्तृज-न्यत्वाभाव इति सत्प्रतिपक्षता च (२), यद्वा 'कर्ता शरीर्येव' इति व्याप्तिविरोधिनो (३), यद्वा व्याख्या यथादर्शनप्रवृत्तया शरीरी कर्ता उपनेयः, पञ्चधर्मतया च चित्यादावप्रशरीरीति विशिष्टसाध्याप्रसिद्धिः विशेषणविशेष्यविरोधश्च (४), यद्वा शरी-

---

* यादृशपरिमाणयुक्तेन कपालद्वयेन एको घटो जन्यते, तादृश-परिमाणयुक्तेनैव कपालत्रयेण द्वितीयोऽपि घटो जातः, परन्तु पूर्वघटपरिमाणापेक्षया द्वितीयस्य उत्कृष्टपरिमाणवत्त्वं प्रत्यक्षसिद्ध-मिति, तच्च कारणचिन्तायां प्रथमस्य कपालद्वयजन्यत्वात् द्वितीयस्य तत्त्रयजन्यत्वाच्च परिमाणवैलक्षण्यमङ्गीकार्यं, तथा च द्वितीय-घटपरिमाणं कपालगतत्रित्वसङ्ख्याजन्यमिति प्रकृतदृष्टान्तता ।

† विशिष्टस्य विश्वज्ञानवतः, अव्ययत्वं नित्यत्वं, साध्यते इति शेषः, तेनेति विशिष्टान्वयस्थले विधेयस्य विशेषणविशेष्योभयान्वितत्वनिय-मादिति हृदयम् ।

रजन्यत्वाद्युपाधिना व्याप्यत्वासिद्धिः (५), इति कार्यत्वहेतौ पञ्च दोषाः*, तचाह

न बाधोऽख्योपजीव्यत्वात्, प्रतिबन्धो न दुर्बलैः ।
सिद्धासिद्ध्योर्विरोधो न, नासिद्धिर्रनिबन्धना ॥ २ ॥

ईश्वरे धर्मिणि शरीरबाधात् कर्तृत्वबाधो (१) न, अधिकरणज्ञानं विना अभावज्ञानासम्भवात् अस्य कार्यत्वस्य धर्मिसाधकस्य† अधिकरणज्ञानजनकतया अवश्यापेच्चणीयत्वेन बलवत्त्वात्, एवञ्च न विशेषणबाधात्मको विशिष्टबाधः प्रत्यत्त्वात्मक इति, ईश्वरो न कर्ता अशरीरत्वात् इत्यनुमानबाधोऽपि नेत्यर्थः । चित्यादि न सकर्तृकं शरीराजन्यत्वात् इति (२) न प्रतिबन्धकं, सत्प्रतिपच्चहेतोः शरीरांशवैयर्थ्यात् व्याप्यत्वासिद्धा‡ दुर्बलत्वात् । द्वितीयेऽपि कार्यत्वव्याप्तेः पच्चधर्मत्वसहकारात् विपच्चबाधकतर्कावताराच्च§ बलवत्त्वम्, उपन्यस्ताया: 'कर्ता शरीर्येव' इति व्याप्तेर्दुर्बलतया न प्रतिबन्धः । चतुर्थे च यदि पच्चधर्मतया अशरीरी उपस्थितस्तदा न विरोधः, कर्तृ-

---

* नैते पच्चविधहेत्वाभासरूपाः पच्च दोषा इति तदुपपादनाय यत्नोनाशम् ।

† धर्मी ईश्वरः ।

‡ अयमभिसन्धिः, व्याप्तिलच्चणे व्याप्तावच्छेदकधर्मान्तराघटितत्वरूपविशेषणसत्त्वात् शरीराजन्यत्वहेतोरजन्यतात्वरूपव्याप्तावच्छेदकधर्मान्तरघटिततया व्याप्यत्वासिद्धिरिति ।

§ पच्चेति चित्यादिरूपपच्चेऽशरीरिकर्तृकत्वस्यैव सम्भवादित्यर्थः । विपच्चबाधकतर्कञ्च उत्तरकारिकायामुक्तः ।

स्वाशरीरिसमानाधिकरणखोपलब्धात्, तदनुपस्थापने तु न विरोधः, विरोधाश्रयस्यासिद्धेः। पञ्चमे च विपक्षबाधकतर्क-सत्त्वात् तदभावनिबन्धना अज्ञानरूपासिद्धिर्व्याप्यत्वासिद्धिर्वा न, शरीरजन्यत्वोपाधेरपि विपक्षबाधकाभावेनापास्तत्वात्*॥

॥ २ ॥

'ननु यदीश्वरः कर्ता स्यात्, शरीरी स्यादिति प्रतिकूल-तर्कावतारोऽनुकूलतर्काभावश्च', तत्राह

तर्काभासतयान्येषां, तर्काभ्युद्धिरदूषणम्।
अनुकूलस्तु तर्कोऽत्र कार्यलोपो विभूषणम्॥ ३ ॥

प्रतिकूलतर्कास्तावदीश्वरासिद्धा आश्रयासिद्धा इत्याभा-साः। कर्तारं विना कार्यं न स्यादिति तर्कस्तु 'विभूषणं' उप-कारकः। 'अहं सर्वस्य प्रभवो मत्तः सर्वं प्रवर्तते' (गीता०) इत्यागमश्च†। 'आर्षं धर्मोपदेशञ्च वेदशास्त्राविरोधिना। यस्तर्केणानुसन्धत्ते स धर्मं वेद नेतरः' (मनु० अ० १२) इति तर्कानुगृहीतस्यागमस्य बलवत्त्वम्॥ ३ ॥

'ननु कार्यत्वं प्रयत्नजन्यत्वेऽप्रयोजकम्', अत्राह

स्वातव्ये जडताहानिः, नादृष्टं दृष्टघातकम्।
हेतुभावे फलाभावः, विश्लेषस्तु विश्लेषवान्‡ ॥ ४ ॥

---

* विपक्षबाधकावतारेणापास्तत्वादिति पाठान्तरम्।

† आगमश्चेत्यस्य उपकारक इत्यग्रिमेणान्वयः।

‡ विश्लेषः क्रियाविशेषचेष्टारूपः, विश्लेषवान् प्रयत्नविश्लेषरूपहेतु-मान्, तथा च 'यद्विश्लेषयोः कार्यकारणभावस्तत्सामान्ययोरपि' इति न्यायात् क्रियासामान्ये प्रयत्नसामान्यस्य हेतुत्वं सिध्यति।

न हि कर्तारं हेतुं विना कार्यं* । परमाणोरेव यद्वत्त्वे-ऽचैतन्यानुपपत्तिः, अचेतनस्य चेतनप्रेरितस्यैव जनकत्वात्। अदृष्टमपि दृष्टकारणसहकारेणैव फलजनकम्। न च 'चेष्टायामेव भोक्तृप्रयत्नो हेतुः, न तु क्रियासामान्ये' इति, चेष्टायां विशेषप्रयत्नस्य हेतुत्वेऽपि क्रियासामान्ये प्रयत्नसामान्यस्य कारणत्वानपायात्, अन्यथा बीजविशेषस्याङ्कुरविशेषे जनकत्वेनाङ्कुरसामान्यं प्रति बीजत्वेन हेतुताया अपि विलोपापत्तेः ॥ ४ ॥

'ननु धृत्यादीनां प्रयत्नजन्यत्वे किं मानम्' इति, अत्राह
कार्यत्वान्निरुपाधिकमेवं धृतिविनाशयोः ।
विच्छेदेन पदस्यापि†, प्रत्यघादेश्च पूर्ववत् ॥ ५ ॥

धृतिविनाशयोः प्रयत्नजन्यत्वान्निरुपाधिकम्। विच्छेदेनान्तराप्रयत्नेन आद्यान्द्यभावात् अर्वाग्दर्शि नाद्यव्यवहारमूलं, व्यवहारानभिज्ञत्वादिति सर्गाद्यकालीनघटादिव्यवहारप्रवर्तकः पुरुषः सिध्यति। एवं प्रत्यघादेर्वेदजन्यधीप्रामाण्यादेरपि निरुपाधिकम्‡।

अथवा कार्यत्यादिकं (१ का०) अन्यथा व्याख्यायते, कार्यं तात्पर्यं, तात्पर्यविषय एव शब्दप्रामाण्यमिति तात्पर्यं हि यस्य

---

* इदञ्च हेत्वभाव इत्यंशस्य विवरणम्।
† ननु घटादिव्यवहारः पूर्वपूर्वकुलालपरम्पराप्रयोज्य एवास्तु, तदर्थमीश्वरेणालमित्यत आह विच्छेदेनेति पदस्य व्यवहारस्य, अस्यापि निरुपाधिकत्वमित्यनेनान्वयः।
‡ अन्तराप्रयत्नेन तत्प्रामाण्यस्य अर्वाक्दर्शिप्रयोज्यत्वासम्भवादिति भावः।

वेदे स एवेश्वरः । आयोजनं व्याख्यानं, वेदास्तदर्थविद्याख्या-
ताः महाजनपरिगृहीतवाक्यत्वात्, अव्याख्यातत्वे पदार्थानव-
गमेऽननुष्ठानापत्तेः, एकदेशदर्शिनश्च व्याख्यायां नाश्वासः । एवं
धृतिर्धारणं, धृत्यादेरित्यादियत्नात् अनुष्ठानसङ्ग्रहः* । ए-
वमीश्वरादिपदार्थतया ईश्वरसिद्धिः, तदुक्तम् 'उद्देश्य एव
तात्पर्यं, व्याख्या विश्वदृश्यः सती । ईश्वरादिपदं साधुं लोक-
वृत्तानुसारतः', उद्देश्य इच्छाविशेषः, एवं 'अहं सर्वस्य प्रभवः'
इत्यादावेवंपदं स्वतन्त्रोच्चारचिह्नपरं, लोकस्थले सतात्पर्यक-
शब्दस्यैव प्रमाणत्वात् 'य एव लौकिकास्त एव वैदिकाः' इति
लौकिकाहमादिपदवल्लौकिकेऽपीयमेव व्यवस्था । प्रत्ययतः
विधिप्रत्ययात्, आप्ताभिप्रायो विध्यर्थः, यस्याभिप्रायः†, स
एवेश्वरः ॥ ५ ॥

प्रवृत्तिः कृतिरेवाच, सा चेच्छातः, यतश्च सा ।
तज्ज्ञानं, विषयस्तस्य विधिः, तज्ज्ञापकोऽथवा ॥ ६ ॥

विधिजन्यज्ञानात् प्रवृत्तिर्दृश्यते, सा च इच्छातत्सिद्ध्यर्षात्,
चिकीर्षा च कृतिसाध्यत्वेष्टसाधनताज्ञानात्, तज्ज्ञानस्य विषयः
कार्यत्वं दृष्टसाधनत्वञ्च विधिरिति प्राचां मतं, स्वमतमाह
तज्ज्ञापकोऽथवेति दृष्टसाधनत्वानुमापक आप्ताभिप्रायो विधि-
प्रत्ययार्थः ॥ ६ ॥

---

* धारणं धारणाख्यसंस्कारः, वेदास्तदर्थविद्वता अनुष्ठिता वेद्यादि-
रीत्या प्रयोगः ।

† अभिप्राय इति वेदे इति शेषः ।

प्रवृत्तिप्रयोजकेच्छाहेतुज्ञानविषयं परिग्रहयति*
दृष्टहानेरनिष्टाप्तेरप्रवृत्तेर्विरोधतः ।

असत्त्वात् प्रत्ययत्यागात् कर्तृधर्मो न सङ्करात् ॥ ७ ॥

स्कन्दस्य‡ कर्तृधर्मस्य प्रवृत्तिप्रयोजकत्वे 'आत्मानं विजानी-
यात्' इत्यत्राप्रवृत्तिप्रसङ्गात्, ग्रामं गच्छतीत्यत: प्रवृत्त्यापत्तेश्च ।
यद्बलस्य विधित्वे दोषमाह अप्रवृत्ते:, आख्यातान्तरेण यत्न बोधि-
तेऽपीष्टसाधनत्वाप्रतिसन्धाने अनिष्टसाधनत्वज्ञाने वाऽप्रवृत्ते: ।
इच्छाया विधित्वे दोषमाह विरोधत इति । इच्छाया विधित्वे
इच्छ्यैव तज्ज्ञानं जननीयं, इच्छाया ज्ञानेन चेच्छा जननीया
इत्यन्योन्याश्रय:§, तदिदमुक्तं विरोधत इति । ननु 'इच्छाज्ञानं
लिङ्गं जननीयं∥' इति, अत्राह असत्त्वादिति । इच्छाज्ञाने जाते
प्रवृत्तिहेतुस्वरूपसदिच्छाभावात् प्रवृत्तिर्न स्यात्, इच्छाया:
स्वरूपसत्त्या एव प्रवृत्तिहेतुत्वात्, न च लिङ्गश्रवणकाले इच्छा

---

* परिग्रहयति इतरस्मिन् बाधप्रदर्शनेन परिग्रहात् 'आस्माभि-
प्राय एव विध्यर्थ:' इति व्यवस्थापयति ।

† विध्यर्थं इति शेष: ।

‡ स्कन्दस्य चेष्टादिरूपक्रियाया: । अयं भाव:, स्वज्ञानद्वारा प्रवृत्तौ
प्रयोजको य:, स एव विध्यर्थं इत्यविवादं, तच क्रियाया तद्गतत्वे ज्ञानस्य
क्रियालाभावेन विजानीयादिबोधौ प्रवृत्त्यनुपपत्ति:, गच्छतीत्यादौ तु
गमनक्रियाया अवगमात् प्रवृत्त्यापत्तिस्रेति ।

§ अयं भाव:, विध्यर्थज्ञानेनैव जायमाना इच्छा प्रवर्तयतीति
नियमात् प्रवृत्त्यनुकूला इच्छा विध्यर्थज्ञानमपेक्षते, इच्छारूपविध्यर्थ-
ज्ञानञ्च मानसप्रत्यक्षरूपं स्वविषयमिच्छामपेक्षते इत्यन्योन्याश्रय: ।

∥ तथा च इच्छाया शाब्दबोध:, स च न स्वविषयमिच्छामपे-
क्षते इति न दोष: ।

पञ्चमः स्तवकः ।

स्वरूपसतीत्यर्थः । 'ननु लिङेव इच्छाजनिका' इति, अत्राह प्रत्ययत्यागादिति । इच्छाकारणत्वेन गृहीतस्य प्रत्ययस्य ज्ञानस्य कारणस्य त्यागापत्तेः व्यभिचारादित्यर्थः* । 'लिङ्श्रुतिकाले सुखत्वादिप्रकारकधीजन्येच्छा लिङर्थः†' इति, अत्राह सङ्करादिति । इष्टसाधनताज्ञानस्य उपायेच्छाहेतोरवश्यस्वीकारात्, तत्र‡ च कारणान्तराभावात् लिङ्पदमेव कारणम्, अतः फलेच्छाज्ञानं न प्रवृत्तिहेतुः, तद्विनापि प्रवृत्तिसम्भवात्, तथाच सङ्करात् इष्टसाधनत्वज्ञानरूपसाधनसद्भावात्, इच्छाज्ञानस्येच्छाजनकत्वे मानाभावेन तस्य लिङ्पदजन्यत्वे मानाभावाच्चेति ॥ ७ ॥

'ननु यत्रज्ञानमेव प्रवर्तकमस्तु, आख्यातान्तरञ्च न यत्नवाचकम्, अनुकूलव्यापारमात्र एव आख्यातशक्तेः, रथो गच्छतीत्यादौ तथाकल्पनात्', तत्राह

कृताकृतविभागेन कर्तृरूपव्यवस्थया ।
यत्न एव कृतिः, पूर्वा परस्मिन् नैव भावना ॥ ८ ॥

---

* अत्रायमाशयः, नियतपूर्ववर्तिन एव कारणत्वात् इष्टसाधनताज्ञानरूपप्रसिद्धकारणाभावेऽपि केवलं लिङ्ग इच्छोत्पत्तौ तस्य नियतपूर्ववर्तित्वाभावप्रसङ्गेन कारणत्वैव न स्यादिति ।

† 'फलेच्छाज्ञानं उपायेच्छां प्रति कारणं' इति मतमाश्रित्येदं, तथा च सुखरूपमुख्यफलेच्छा विषयधर्मत्वज्ञानञ्च उपायेच्छायां हेतुः, सा च प्रवृत्ताविति नोक्तदोषावसर इति पूर्वपक्षः । सिद्धान्तस्तु, फलेच्छाज्ञानस्य उपायेच्छां प्रति कारणतायां प्रमाणाभावेन नोक्तप्रक्रियासम्भव इति ।

‡ तत्र इष्टसाधनताज्ञाने ।

घटः कृतोऽङ्कुरो न कृत इति व्यवहारात्* कुलालादिः कर्ता न कारकान्तरमिति कृञ्धात्वर्थः कृतिः।† 'ननु यत्न-पर्यायता‡ स्यात्', अत आह पूर्वेति। परस्मिन्नुत्तरकाल-वर्तिनि फले विद्यमाने, सैव कृतिरेव, पूर्वा साधनीभूता, भावना, फलानुकूलतापन्नयत्न एवाख्यातार्थः। यद्वा फलानु-कूलव्यापारधात्वर्थप्रचयजनिका पूर्वापरस्मिन् पूर्वापरीभूतले सति, कृतिराख्यातार्थः, तथा च प्रयत्नवत्त्वमनुकूलं पूर्वा-परीभूतमिति चयमर्थः§ ॥ ८ ॥

'ननु धातुना यत्नः प्रतीयते, आख्यातस्य च अनुकूलव्या-पारमात्रार्थकत्वम्, आक्षेपादेव च यत्नलाभः॥' इति, अत आह

---

* अयं भावः, करोतेरनुकूलव्यापारार्थकत्वेऽङ्कुरादावपि अस्मदा-दीनां साक्षात् परम्परया वाऽनुकूलव्यापारसत्त्वादयं व्यवहारो नोप-पद्यते, प्रयत्नार्थकत्वे च घटाङ्कुरयोर्यथाक्रमं अस्मदादीनां कर्तृताप्रयो-जकप्रयत्नसत्त्वासत्त्वाभ्यामुपपन्नोऽयं व्यवहारः, अत एव च घटानु-कूलव्यापारवतामपि दण्डादीनां प्रयत्नाभावात् न कर्तृत्वं किन्तु कुला-लस्यैवेति।

† तथा च य एव करोतेरर्थः स एवाख्यातस्यापीति कृतिरेवाख्या-तार्थ इति भ्रमः।

‡ आख्यातस्येति भ्रमः।

§ एतादृग्विशिष्टार्थकल्पनायां प्रकृतावच्छेदकगौरवादिदोषप्रस-ङ्गादिति भ्रमः। विशिष्टार्थलाभस्तु परस्परमन्वयबलादिति भावः।

॥ कृञ्धातोर्यत्नार्थकत्वेऽपि नाख्यातार्थो यत्नः, आख्यातस्थले यत्न-बोधस्तु 'तस्य तदनुकूलव्यापारस्य तस्मिन् यत्नं विनाऽनुपपन्नः' इत्या-क्षेपादेवेति पूर्वपक्षः।

भावनैव हि यद्धात्मा सर्वाख्यातस्य गोचरः ।
तथा विवरणान्नोव्यादाक्षेपानुपपत्तिः ॥ ९ ॥

तथा ह्याख्या तदाचकपदेन, पचति पाकं करोतीति विवर-णात् तत्र शक्तिः, अनुकूलव्यापारस्य यत्नानाक्षेपकत्वात्, वर्त-मानपाकानुकूलव्यापारस्याचेतनेऽपि भावात् । आदनमिति-कर्मपदोत्तरं पचति भुङ्क्ते वेति जिज्ञासा च कर्मणः क्रियाव्याप्य-त्वप्रतिसन्धानेन* यथा पचतीत्यनन्तरं कर्मादौ जिज्ञासा ॥ ९ ॥

'ननु कर्तुरपि विवरणात् तत्रापि शक्तिराख्यातस्य स्यात्', तत्राह

आक्षेपलभ्ये संख्येये नाभिधानस्य कल्पना ।
संख्येयमाक्षलाभे तु शाकाङ्क्षेण व्यवस्थितिः ॥ १० ॥

आख्यातवाच्यया संख्यया आश्रयस्य आक्षेपादेव लाभान्न कर्तरि शक्तिकल्पना†, प्रथमान्तपदोपस्थाप्यत्वे सति आख्याता-र्थविशेष्यत्वमाक्षेपलभ्यं, भुक्त्वा इत्यादौ क्रान्तार्थानन्तर्यवार-णाय विशेष्यत्वम्, सुयते इत्यादौ वर्तमानत्वविशेष्यत्वं स्था-स्यापोति सत्यन्तदलम् । चैत्रस्तण्डुलं पचतीत्यत्र द्वितीयार्थ-कर्मतावरूद्धत्वात् तण्डुलस्य, न तत्र भावनाऽऽकाङ्क्षेति भावना

---

* न त्वनुकूलव्यापारस्य यत्नाक्षेपकतया, कर्मादाविति क्ष्त्तेः कर्मा-दिव्याप्यकत्वप्रतिसन्धानेनेति प्रेयः । अयं भावः, कर्मणः क्रियाव्याप्यतया कर्मणैव सामान्यतः क्रियुपस्थितौ सत्यां 'पचति भुङ्क्ते वा' इति भवति क्रियाविशेषजिज्ञासा, सामान्यप्रकारकज्ञानस्य विशेषजिज्ञासाहेतु-त्वादिति ।

† 'अनन्यलभ्यः शब्दार्थः' इति नियमात् ।

ध्रुद्धप्रातिपदिकार्थान्वयिनी, अतएव 'यं यं भावनाऽन्वेति, तं
तं सङ्ख्याऽपि' इति, एकपदोपात्तभावनान्वयबलात्, कर्त्रादि-
सङ्ख्याभिधान एव च प्रथमेति। एवं कर्मापि नाख्यातपदवा-
च्यम्* ॥ १० ॥

'ननस्तु कर्मधर्मो विधिः', तच्चाह

अतिप्रसङ्गान्न फलं, नापूर्वं तच्चदानितः ।
तदलाभान्न कार्यञ्च, न क्रियाऽप्यप्रवृत्तितः ॥ ११ ॥

कर्म खर्गादि, तद्धर्मः कार्यत्वं यदि विध्यर्थः, तच्चाह अति-
प्रसङ्गान्न फलं। खर्गे कार्यत्वज्ञाने सति खर्गासाधनेऽपि प्रवृत्त्या-
पत्तेः। यदि कर्म अपूर्वं, तद्धर्मः कार्यत्वं विध्यर्थः, तच्चाह नापूर्वं
तच्चदानितः। शाब्दबोधात् पूर्वं नोपस्थितमित्यत एवापूर्वं, पूर्व-
मुपस्थितौ च न तत्त्वम्, अनुपस्थितौ च कथं तत्र शक्तिधीः।
'ननु कार्यत्वरूपेण शक्तिधीः, शाब्दबोधे तु योग्यतया अपूर्वस्य
कार्यविशेषस्य भानं', तच्चाह तदलाभान्न कार्यञ्चेति। नित्यनि-
षेधापूर्वयोरलाभप्रसङ्गात्, तत्र फलकामस्य नियोज्यत्वाभा-
वात्† । यदा 'ननु कार्यत्वेनोपलक्षितायामपूर्वव्यक्तौ शक्तिग्रहः,
गन्धवत्त्वेनोपलक्षितायां पृथिवीत्वविशिष्टायां व्यक्तौ पृथिवी-

---

* अस्य 'ग्रामो गम्यते इत्यादिकर्माख्यातस्थले' इति आदि।
† अयं भावः, काम्यस्थले काम्यरूपभविष्यत्खर्गादिफलसाधनत्वेन
उपस्थितानां यागादीनामाशुविनाशिनां तत्साधनत्वासम्बन्धेन तदन्य-
त्वानुपपत्त्याऽपूर्वं कल्प्यतं, नित्यस्य निषेधस्य च फलाभावेन तच्चापूर्व-
कल्पनायां प्रमाणाभावात् 'सन्ध्यामुपासीत' 'अष्टम्यां मांसं नाश्रीयात्'
इति नित्यनिषेधस्थलीयविधिप्रत्ययस्य निरर्थकत्वापत्तिरिति।

पञ्चमः स्तवकः ।

पदस्येव*', इत्याह तदलाभात्। अपूर्ववैशिष्ट्यापूर्व्यञ्जनुप-
स्थितेः, गन्धवत्त्वेनापि हि पृथिवीत्वविशिष्टस्य स्मरणमनुमानं वा
सम्भवति, प्रागनुभवात्, प्रकृते तथात्वेऽपूर्वत्वव्याघातादित्यर्थः ।
'ननु कर्म यागादि, तद्धर्मः कार्यत्वं विधिः', तत्राह न
क्रियापीति । अनिष्टसाधनताधीकाले प्रवृत्त्यदर्शनात् । अत्र
अपिना नापूर्वमपि, उक्तदोषादित्यर्थः ॥ ११ ॥

'ननु करणं शब्दः, तद्धर्मोऽभिधा, तज्ज्ञानं प्रवर्तकम्', अत्र
एवाङ्गः "अभिधां भावनामाङ्गरन्यामेव लिङादयः । अर्था-
त्मभावना लभ्या सर्वाख्यातस्य गोचरः", अभिधा यागप्रव-
र्तिका इतिधीः शब्दात्, आख्यातार्थश्च उत्पादना उत्पत्त्यनु-
कूलक्रियारूपा' इति, अत्राह

अशक्यादप्रवृत्तेश्च नाभिधाऽपि गरीयसी ।
बाधकस्य समानत्वात् परिश्लेषोऽपि दुर्लभः ॥ १२ ॥

अभिधायां मानाभावात्, अभिधाशब्दतोऽभिधाज्ञानेऽपि
अप्रवृत्तेः, गरीयसी उचिता, लिङर्थतयेति शेषः । 'ननु अन्यस्य

---

* यथा हि 'गन्धवती पृथिवीपदशक्या' इत्युपलक्षणविधया शक्ति-
ग्रहः, न तु 'गन्धवत्त्वेन गन्धवती पृथिवीपदशक्या' इति गन्धवत्त्वं
शक्यतावच्छेदकोक्त्या शक्तिग्रहः, तथा कार्यत्वेन कार्यं विधिशक्यमिति
न शक्तिधीः, किन्तु कार्यं विधिशक्यमिति उपलक्षणविधयेति भावः ।
सिद्धान्तस्तु पृथिवीत्वजातेः प्रागुपस्थितिसत्त्वेन तस्य शक्यतावच्छे-
दकत्वे लाघवप्रतिसन्धानात् गन्धवत्त्वस्य उपलक्षणविधयैव भानं, प्रकृते
ऽपूर्वत्वस्य प्रागनुपस्थित्या नैवं सम्भवतीति ।

लिङर्थत्वे बाधात् परिशेषेणाभिधा लिङर्थः' इति, अचाच
बाधकस्तेति । प्रकृतेऽपि बाधकसम्भवात्* ॥ १२ ॥

'ननु करणस्य चागादेर्धर्मो दृष्टसाधनत्वं विध्यर्थोऽस्तु' तचाच
हेतुत्वादनुमानाच मध्यमादौ वियोगतः ।

अन्यत्र कृत्स्नासामर्थ्यान्निषेधानुपपत्तिः ॥ १३ ॥

विध्यर्थस्य दृष्टसाधनतायां 'हेतुत्वात्' लिङ्गतयोपन्यासात्,
न च खस्य खलिङ्गत्वमिति, अग्निकामो दारुणी मन्थीयादित्युक्ते
कुत इत्याकाङ्क्षायां वक्तारो वदन्ति यतो दारुद्वयमथनसन्निसा-
धनमिति । 'अनुमानात्' अर्थवादादिष्टसाधनताबोधान्तरमपि
विधेरनुमानात्, यदि चानुमितेनापि विधिना दृष्टसाधनत्वमेव
बोध्यम्, तदा तदनुमानवैयर्थ्यम्, 'तरति मृत्युं, तरति ब्रह्म-
हत्याम्†' इत्यादौ मृत्युब्रह्महत्यासन्तरणकामोऽश्वमेधेन यजे-

---

* मीमांसकमतेनेदम्, तन्मतं यथा, धात्वर्थोत्पादानुकूलो व्यापारो
भावना, सा च अर्थभावना शब्दभावना चेति द्विधा, तचाद्या फल-
भावनापदाभिधेया कृत्निष्ठा प्रयत्नादिरूपा आख्यातप्रत्ययसामान्य-
स्यार्थः, अस्याञ्चयमस्ति, तथा हि 'स्वर्गकामो यजेत' इत्यादावा-
ख्यातेन भावनायामुपस्थितायां किं भावयेत्, केन भावयेत्, कथं
भावयेदित्याकाङ्क्षायां स्वर्गकामपदादिभिः, 'स्वर्गं भावयेत्, यागेन
भावयेत्, आग्न्याधानादिभिरूपकारं सम्पाद्य भावयेत्' इतिरीत्या
भाव्यकरणेतिकर्तव्यतासमन्वय इति भाव्यार्थप्रत्ययवतीयम् । शब्दभा-
वना च स्वविधापदाभिधेया वैदिकशब्दनिष्ठा लिङादिरूपविधिप्रत्य-
यागम्या, अस्याश्च अर्थभावना भाव्या, विधिलिङ्गादि करणं, अर्थ-
वादिकी स्तुतिरितिकर्तव्यतेत्येषामपि भाव्यार्थप्रत्ययत्वमधिकेन ।

† अस्य 'योऽश्वमेधेन यजते' इति शेषः । इत्यादाविति अत्र 'इष्ट-
साधनताबोधान्तरमपि' इति पूरणीयम् ।

पञ्चमः स्तवकः।

नेति विध्यनुमानस्य सर्वतन्त्रसिद्धत्वात्*। 'मध्यमादौ वियोगतः' मध्यमोत्तमपुरुषे लिङ् दृष्टसाधनताविषयोगात्, कुर्याः कुर्यामित्याद्याद्यादिकं प्रतीयते, आज्ञा तु अभिप्राय एव इति प्रथमपुरुषेऽपि दृष्टा अर्थः । 'अन्यच्च लक्षणासामर्थ्यात्' अद्वेषणादिलिङ्गम् दृष्टावाचकत्वकल्पनात्‡ । 'निषेधानुपपत्तितः' 'न कलञ्जं भक्षयेत्' इत्यत्रेष्टसाधनत्वनिषेधस्य बाधितत्वात्§ । बलवदनिष्टाननुबन्धित्वञ्च न विषयार्थः, 'श्येनेनाभिचरन् यजेत्' इत्यादौ असम्भवात्‖, अप्रवर्तमानपुरुषस्य च बलवद्द्वेषविषयत्वात् बलवद्द्वेषविषयदुःखजनकत्वसामान्याभावस्य बाधितत्वादिति ॥ १३ ॥

मतमाह

---

* सर्वतन्त्रसिद्धत्वात् सर्वतन्त्रसिद्धान्तसिद्धत्वात्, स च 'सर्वतन्त्राविरुद्धस्तन्त्रेऽधिकृतः सर्वतन्त्रसिद्धान्तः' इति न्यायसूत्रे (१अ०।१आ०। ५प०) दर्शितः।

† आदिना सङ्कल्पपरिग्रहः, अनुपदमनुष्ठीयमानकर्मणः स्वान्यकर्तृत्वेनेच्छा आज्ञा, स्वकर्तृत्वयाऽभिप्रायस्तु सङ्कल्पः। केचित्तु 'आज्ञा त्वभिप्राय एव' इत्युत्तरग्रन्थदृष्ट्या आदिपदमत्र नास्तीत्यनुमिमते।

‡ सत्कारपुरःसरनियोगेच्छा अद्वेषणा, यथा गुरो नामध्यापय इत्यादौ।

§ अयं भावः, एतन्मते नञर्थविशेष्यकान्वयस्याचासम्भवेन 'नञ्रार्थत्वे यस्य विधेयत्वं, नञा तदभाव एवावगम्यते' इति नियमानुसारेण प्रकृते कलञ्जभक्ष्यां नेष्टसाधनं इत्येवार्थो वर्णनीयः, स च न सम्भवति, कलञ्जभक्ष्यस्य दृष्टिप्रेष्टसाधनतया तत्र तदभावविरुद्धादिति।

‖ अयमाशयः, श्येनेन हि उच्चार्यन्तया हिंसारूपेण उच्चय इव नरकोऽपि भवति, स च बलवान् अनिष्ट इति तदनुबन्धिनि श्येने कुतस्तदभाव इति।

विधिर्वक्तुरभिप्रायः प्रवृत्त्यादौ लिङ्गादिभिः।
अभिधेयोऽनुमेया तु कर्तुरिष्टाभ्युपायता ॥ १४ ॥

प्रवृत्तिनिवृत्तिविषये आज्ञाभिप्रायः लिङ्गादिभिः प्रत्य-
यैरभिधेयः, इष्टसाधनता अनुमेया। वस्तुतस्तु ईश्वरेच्छायाः
सर्वविषयकत्वात् निषेधे बाधः, बलवदनिष्टाननुबन्धित्वेनेच्छा-
याः शक्यत्वे गौरवमिति प्राचीनमतमेव साधीयः:* ॥ १४ ॥

---

* वक्त्रभिप्रायस्य विध्यर्थत्वे वैदिकविधिप्रत्ययस्य वक्तुरीश्वरस्या-
भिप्राय एवार्थः, अभिप्रायस्त्विच्छैव इति 'न कलञ्जं भक्षयेत्' इत्यादौ
कलञ्जभक्षणं नेश्वरेच्छाविषय इत्येवार्थो वक्तव्यः, स च बाधितः, कार्य-
सामान्यं प्रत्येव ईश्वरेच्छाया हेतुतया कलञ्जभक्षणेऽपि तदनपायात्
निषेधस्थले बाध इति तात्पर्यम्।

अथेदं बोध्यं, वृत्तिवैचित्र्येण विधिसमभिव्याहृतनञर्थः विषेध्य-
तयैवान्वेतीति कलञ्जभक्षणाभाव ईश्वराभिप्रेत इत्येवाचान्वयः, 'यदी-
च्छेद्बहूना वासं पुत्रसम्पदमात्मनः। एकादश्यां न भुञ्जीत पक्षयो-
रुभयोरपि' इत्यादिकाम्यनिषेधविधिस्थले नित्यनिषेधस्य फलवत्त्वे च
नञर्थविषेध्याकान्वयस्य सिद्धत्वात्। यदा विध्यर्थस्येच्छाया विषयता-
सम्बन्धेन धात्वर्थे नान्वयः, किन्तु धात्वर्थतावच्छेदकरूपेण धात्वर्थे
उद्देश्यतासंसर्गेणेवेति, तथा च कलञ्जभक्षणस्य कार्यत्वेन ईश्वरेच्छा-
विषयत्वेऽपि विप्रेषतत्तदिच्छोद्देश्यत्वाभावान्निषेधोपपत्तिः। यदि च,
'इच्छा सामान्यं नाभिप्रायः, किन्तु तत्त्वावत् इच्छाविशेष एवाभिप्रायः,
स च अन्येच्छानधीनः कर्तव्यत्वेनेच्छारूपः, इच्छात्वव्याप्याभिप्रायत्व-
जातिमान् वा, अतएव 'अज्ञात्वा मयेदं कृतं न तु ममाभिप्रेतमिदम्'
इत्यादिप्रयोगः' इत्यादिकं विभाव्यते, तदा प्रतिषिद्धक्रियायामीश्वरा-
भिप्रायाभावात् निषेधस्थले बाधाशङ्कैव नोदेति। 'श्येनेनाभिचरन्
यजेत' इत्यादावभिचारस्य सामान्यतः कर्तव्यत्वेनेश्वरेच्छाभावेऽपि
जिघांसोः कर्तव्यत्वेन तदभिप्रायोऽस्त्येवेति न दोषः, अतएव मीमांसा-
भाष्ये (१अ०।१पा०।२सू०) 'कथं पुनरनर्थः कर्तव्यतयोपदिश्यते?' इति
पूर्वपक्षयित्वा 'उच्यते, नैव श्येनादयः कर्तव्या विज्ञायन्ते, यो हि

पञ्चमः स्तवकः ।

श्रुतेरित्यस्य व्याख्यान्तरमाह

कृत्स्न एव च वेदोऽयं परमेश्वरगोचरः ।
स्वार्थद्वारैव तात्पर्यं तस्य स्वर्गादिवद्विधौ ॥ १५ ॥

सर्वत्र वेदभागे ईश्वरः प्रतिपादितः, 'यज्ञो वै विष्णुः' (तै॰सं॰) 'पश्यत्यचक्षुः' (श्वे॰उ॰) इत्यादिश्रुतिषु 'एतस्य वा अक्षरस्य प्रशासने गार्गि द्यावापृथिव्यौ विधृते तिष्ठतः' (बृहदा॰) इत्यादिषु च, न तु सिद्धार्थतया अमोघमन्यत्र तात्पर्यं, यथा स्वर्गनरकादिबोधकानां, तथा 'ईश्वरमुपासीत' इति विधेककवाक्यतया तेषां लब्धमपि प्रामाण्यमेव, अन्यथा स्वर्गादिपदानामपि स्वार्थे प्रामाण्यं न स्यात्, तदेतदुक्तं स्वार्थद्वारैवेति । स्वार्थप्रतिपादनद्वारा एव विधौ सिद्धार्थतात्पर्यात्* । 'वाक्यात्', वैदिकप्रशंसानिन्दा-

---

हिंसितुमिच्छेत्, तस्यायमभ्युपाय इति हि तेषामुपदेशः, "श्येनेनाभिचरन् यजेत" इति हि समामनन्ति, न त्वभिचरितव्यमिति' इति भगवत्स्वामिनः समादधिरे । यच्च बलवदनिष्टेत्यादिकं नव्यैरनुक्तमपि उक्तमिति कृत्वा गौरवमभिहितं, तदपि प्राचीनमतापेक्षया लाघवमेव, बलवदनिष्टेत्यादिकमप्यपेक्षमाणस्य तन्मतस्य गुरुतरत्वादिति प्राचीनदोषदुष्टमपि प्राचीनमतं प्राचीनानामेव साधीयः, नव्यानां पुनर्नवीनसरणिरेवानुसरणीयेत्यलम् ।

* अयं निष्कर्षः, क्रियाबोधनायैव प्रवृत्तस्य वेदस्य यदंशे क्रिया नावगम्यते, भूतार्थादिबोधकस्य तस्य न स्वार्थे प्रामाण्यं परन्तु विध्यङ्ग एव तात्पर्यमिति 'यज्ञो वै विष्णुः' इत्यादिविध्यनात्मकश्रुतेर्भूतार्थतया न स्वार्थे प्रामाण्यमिति कथमनया ईश्वरसिद्धिरिति मीमांसकाशङ्का । अत्र च तन्मतमाश्रित्यैवायं सिद्धान्तः, 'यत्र दुःखेन सम्भिन्नम्' इत्यादीनां भूतार्थानामपि स्वर्गादिबोधकवाक्यानां 'स्वर्गकामो यजेत' इत्यादिविध्येकवाक्यतया यथा स्वार्थे प्रामाण्यं स्वीकृतम्, तथा 'ईश्वरमुपासीत' इत्यादिविध्येकवाक्यतयैव 'यज्ञो वै विष्णुः' इत्यादीश्वरप्रतिपादकवाक्यानां प्रामाण्यमकामेनाप्यङ्गीकार्यमिति ।

वाक्यानि प्रशंसानिन्दाज्ञानपूर्वकाणि प्रशंसानिन्दावादवाक्य-
लात् परिणतिसुरसमाघ्रफलमित्यादिवत्॥ १५ ॥

संख्याविशेषादित्यस्य व्याख्यान्तरमाह

स्यामभूवं भविष्यामीत्यादौ संख्या प्रवर्तृगा ।
समाख्याऽपि च शाखानां नाद्यप्रवचनाद्दते॥ १६ ॥

वैदिकोत्तमपुरुषेण स्वतन्त्रोच्चारयितुः सङ्ख्या वाच्या, 'तत्
ऐचत एकोऽहं बहु स्याम्' (छान्दो॰) इत्यादिबहूत्तमपुरुष-
श्रुतेः। सङ्ख्यापदार्थमन्यमाह* समाख्येत्यादि । सर्वासां शाखानां
हि काठककालापकाद्याः समाख्याः संज्ञाविशेषाः श्रूयन्ते, ते च
नाध्ययनमात्रनिबन्धनाः, अर्थैहतूनामानन्त्यात् †आदावन्धैरपि
तदध्ययनात्, तस्मादतीन्द्रियार्थदर्शी भगवानेव कारुणिकः
सर्गादावस्वदादृग्दृष्टाङ्गष्टकाठकादिशरीरविशेषमधिष्ठाय यां
शाखामुक्तवान् तस्याः शाखायास्तन्नाम्ना व्यवदेश इति सिद्धु-
मीश्वरमलनं मोच्चहेतुः ॥ १६ ॥

तस्येश्वरे न विश्वासस्तं प्रत्याह

इत्येवं श्रुतिनीतिसंभवजलैर्भूयोभिराचान्तिते
येषां नास्पदमाददासि हृदये ते शैलसाराशयाः।
किन्तु प्रस्तुतविप्रतीपविधयोऽप्युच्चैर्भवच्चिन्तकाः
काले कारुणिक त्वयैव कृपया ते तारणीया नराः॥१७॥

इतिशब्दः स्वरूपे, एवंशब्दः प्रकारार्थः, शैलसारः लोष्टं,

---

* त्वन्नं 'संख्यायते विग्रेषेण चाप्यतेऽनया' इति कृत्यत्तिबललभ्यं
समाख्यारूपमपरमर्थम्। † अनादाविति पाठे संसार इति मेघः।

अतिकठिनशिथिला वा । प्रस्तुते ईश्वरे विप्रतीपविधयः प्रतिकू-
लपराः, तादृशा अपि उच्चैरतिशयेन काले भवच्चिन्तकाः,
शङ्काकलङ्कशून्याः कार्याः ॥ १७ ॥

अस्माकन्तु निसर्गसुन्दर चिराच्चेतो निमग्नं यथि
त्वद्धयानन्दनिधौ तथापि तरलं नाद्यापि सन्तृप्यते ।
तन्नाथ त्वरितं विधेहि करुणां येन त्वदेकायतां
याते चेतसि नाप्नुवाम शतशो याम्याः पुनर्यातनाः ॥ १८ ॥

अद्धा तत्त्वं, सन्तृप्यत इति कर्मकर्त्तरि* ।

दृष्ट्येष नीतिकुसुमाञ्जलिरुज्ज्वलश्री-
र्यद्दास्यदपि च दक्षिणवामकौ† द्वौ ।
नो वा, ततः किममरेश्वगुरोर्गुरुस्तु
प्रीतोऽस्त्वनेन पदपीठसमर्पणेन ॥ १९ ॥

इति पञ्चमः स्तवकः ।

नो वास्यचेत् ततः किमस्माकम् ।

इति श्रीहरिदासभट्टाचार्यविरचितकुसुमाञ्जलिकारिका-
व्याख्यानं समाप्तम् ॥

---

* कर्मकर्त्तरीति लट्प्रत्ययनिष्पन्नमिति श्लेषः । तथा च यत् चेतो
संह्रष्णोमि तत् स्वयमेव संतृप्यते नेत्यर्थः ।
† अमरेश्वगुरोर्दक्षिणवामकौ तत्त्वस्वीकारेऽनुकूलप्रतिकूलपक्षौ,
अथ च दक्षिणवामकराविति श्लेषः । अमरेश्वगुरोर्बृहस्पतेरपि गुरु-
रिति वाऽन्वयः ।

शुद्धिपत्रम्।

पृ०	प०	अशुद्धम्।	शुद्धम्।
७	१०	अन्वय०	अन्वय०
१३	१२	धर्माधर्मिणोः	धर्मधर्मिणोः
३८	२२	भावप्रयच्छे	अभावप्रयच्छे
५८	१२	क्रिया०	क्षति०

KUSUMÁNJALI,

OR

THE HANDFUL OF FLOWERS.

FIRST CLUSTER.

I.—May this handful of flowers of faultless logic, devoted to the twofold proof* of God, delight my mind without hindrance while bee-like hovering over it,—this handful of flowers, opening under favourable auspices, and affording a banquet to the upright by the inhaling of its fragrance,—one which will not fade, however closely handled,—the home of a honey that distils the nectar of immortality.†

II.—" But is there not an absence of evidence to establish any connection between such a fruit as liberation and your argument devoted to the twofold proof of the existence of God,—since the word *soul* which signifies that soul which is the object of the so-called essential knowledge,‡ merely means that individual soul which is the object of

---

* *I. e.* the arguments which establish his existence, and the discussion as to the validity of the premises which becomes necessary if these are not accepted. The words may also mean 'laid at the feet of God.'

† The latter half of this s'loka (the former in the original) has a double meaning, as nearly every word has a technical or logical sense,—" this handful of flowers, which reveals the knowledge of true minor terms and affords a banquet to the intelligent by the perception of an undoubted universal connection [between the middle and major terms] &c."—I may add that the proverb alluded to in the commentary क्वद्चिस्ति भावो द्रव्यवत् प्रकाश्यते is quoted to shew that though *rasa* properly denotes an attribute, it here means the subject which possesses it.

‡ Alluding to such passages as that in the Brihadárany. Upanishad (ii. 4, 5,) 'behold the soul *(átmá)* is verily to be seen, heard, contemplated and profoundly meditated upon.'

the illusory knowledge that is the cause of the sensible world; and therefore the contemplating of *this* is the true means of liberation?"*
To meet this doubt he replies,

II.—That Being, whose worship the wise consider as the means of the two heaven-like liberations,—He, the Supreme Soul, is here ascertained (as the object of our contemplation).

The 'two heaven-like liberations' [as intensely desirable from the absence of all pain,] are the liberation while still remaining in this life, and the absolute emancipation. The contemplation of God is a means of liberation through the merit produced thereby or through the knowledge of one's own soul. This S'ruti† is the proof that it is such a cause, 'having known him only one goes beyond death; there is no other path to obtain it.' And that the knowledge of one's own soul is the cause of liberation is proved by the s'ruti,‡ 'When a man truly discriminates the soul and says " I am he," what can he wish for? or in desire of what object can he follow the continuous onflow of mundane events?'

III.—Now although with regard to that Being whom all men alike worship, whichever of the [four wellknown] ends of man they may desire,—(thus the followers of the Upanishads as the very Knower,—the disciples of Kapila as the perfect first Wise,—those of Patanjali as Him who, untouched by pain, action, fruit or desert, having assumed a body in order to create, revealed the tradition of the Veda and is gracious to all living beings,—the Mahápás'upatas as the Independent one, undefiled by vaidic or secular violations,—the S'aivas as S'iva,—the Vaishnavas as Purushottoma,—the followers of the Puránas as the great Father (Brahmá),—the Ceremonialists as the Soul of the sacrifice,—the Saugatas as the Omniscient,—the Jainas as the Unobstructed,—the Mímánsakas as Him who is pointed out as

---

* This being the seat of the great error, it is to this that our contemplations should be directed.
† S'wetás'watara Upanishad, iii. 8.
‡ Brihadár. Up. iv. 4, 12.—S'ankara read सञ्जरेत् for संसरेत्.

to be worshipped,—the Chárvákas as Him who is established by the convention of the world,—the followers of the Nyáya as Him who is all that is said worthy of Him,—why farther detail ? whom even the artizans themselves worship as the great artizan, Vis'wakarman,)—although, I say, with regard to that Being, the adorable S'iva, whom all recognise throughout the world as universally acknowledged like castes, families, family invocations of Agni, schools, social customs, &c. how can there arise any doubt? and what then is there to be ascertained?—Still this logical investigation may be well called the contemplation of God, and this is really worship when it follows the hearing the S'ruti. Therefore that adorable one who hath been often heard mentioned in the S'ruti, Smṛiti, narrative poems, Puráṇas, &c., must now be contemplated, according to such a S'ruti as 'He is to be heard and to be contemplated,' and such a Smṛiti as 'by the Veda, inference and the delight of continued meditation,—in this threefold manner producing knowledge, a man obtains the highest concentration.' Now there is, in short, a fivefold opposition to our theory,—as based, first, on the non-existence of any supernatural cause of another world (as *adṛishṭa*, the merit and demerit of our actions) ;—or secondly, on the possibility of our putting in action certain causes of another world (as sacrifices,) even if God be allowed to be non-existent ;—or thirdly, on the existence of proofs which show the non-existence of God ;—or fourthly, on the opinion that, even if God does exist, he cannot be a cause of true knowledge to us ;—or fifthly, on the absence of any argument to prove his existence.

"Very"—without any second ; "knower"—existing in the form of pure knowledge ; "first wise"—existing in the form of intelligence at the first beginning of creation ; "perfect"—as possessed of the eight divine faculties ; ignorance, egoism, desire, aversion, and tenacity of mundane existence, are the five "pains;" sacrifice, injuring others, &c.

as causing merit and demerit, are the " actions ;" rank, length of life and enjoyment are the " fruits ;" merit and demerit the " deserts" left as a residue in the mind. " Revealed"—*i. e.* manifested [as a previously existing object], since the Veda is eternal. He is " gracious" as being the original instructor in arts, as of making jars, &c. " S'iva," void of the three qualities ; the " great Father" as the father even of the father ; " omniscient" with a momentary omniscience.* The " obstructions" are ignorance, desire, aversion, delusion, and tenacity of mundane existence,—" pointed out as to be worshipped" as the Vaidic mantras, &c.—possessed of " all that is said worthy of him" in the various descriptions of God. " School" *(charaṇa)* means here recension *(s'ákhá).*† Although the existence of God is indeed established by the S'ruti's evidence, yet, if we wish to employ inference, the absence of doubt need not be a fault in our argument.‡ He therefore proceeds towards the close of the passage to propose a doubt, according to the principle of satisfying an opponent.

IV.—We have to meet the opponent's first objection by establishing the existence of a supernatural cause of another world in the form of merit and demerit, and, if this be established, then it follows that a God is established as the superintendent thereof, since a non-intelligent cause can only produce its effect by the superintendence of something intelligent. He therefore proceeds to establish this.

IV.—From dependence,—from eternity,—from diversity, —from universal practice,—and from the apportionment to each individual soul,—mundane enjoyment implies a supernatural cause [*i. e.* ' desert.']

Our proposition is that there exists a supernatural cause of another world, *i. e.* a cause beyond the reach of the senses. *a.* First of all, then, to establish the class of causes in general, he says " from dependence." Dependence means here that the effect is occasional. All effects must have a cause since they are occasional, like the gratification produc-

---

* The Mádhyamika Bauddhas hold that everything is momentary, πάντα ῥεῖ.

† For the original difference between charaṇa and s'ákhá cf. Müller's Ancient Sanskrit literature, p. 125. On *pravara*, see ibid., p. 386.

‡ In ordinary cases people do not take the trouble of arguing if there is no doubt to be solved.

ed by food; [otherwise, if they did not depend on a cause, they could be found everywhere and always]. *b.* " But if the cause of a jar, &c. were eternal, would it not follow that the jar, &c. would also be eternal, and therefore we must assume the jar's cause to be itself only occasional, and therefore the perpetual series of causes must be all occasional, each dependent on its previous cause ?" To meet this objection of a regressus in infinitum he says "from the eternity [of the succession of cause and effect]," like the continued series of seed and shoot,*—the meaning being that a regressus in infinitum ceases to be a fault, if, like this one alleged in our illustration, it can be proved by the evidence of our senses. *c.* " But [if you require a cause,] why not say [with the Vedántin] that Brahma alone is the cause, or [with the Sánkhya] Nature in the form of various individual intellects ?" To meet this, he says " from the diversity [of effects, as heaven, hell, &c.]"—as the effects imply a diversity of causes, from their being diverse as effects. *d.* " But why not accept a visible cause as sacrifices, &c.—why have recourse to an invisible desert *(adrishṭa)* ?" To meet this, he adds " from the universal practice," *i. e.* from the fact that all men, desiring fruit in another world, do engage in sacrifices, &c. It is only the conviction that they do produce heaven, &c. as their fruit, which makes men engage in sacrifices, &c.; and these [passing away when the action is over] cannot produce this fruit unless by means of some influence which continues to act after the rite is over,—and hence is this invisible influence, called merit or demerit, established. *e.* " But why not say that this desert does not reside in the same subject as the enjoyment [*i. e.* the individual soul,] but produces the enjoyment by abiding in the thing enjoyed ?" He replies " from the apportionment to each soul." Since the enjoyment resides in each soul severally, we should be unwarranted to attribute its production to a desert residing elsewhere.

V.—" But why may we not suppose that the effect arises without a cause, according to the adversary's opinion given in the Nyáya Sútras (iv. 22), ' there is an origination of entities from no cause, for we see the sharpness of a thorn, &c. ?' " He replies,

---

* Cf. Cowper's remarks on his cucumber, " I raised the seed that produced the plant, that produced the fruit, that produced the seed, that produced the fruit I sent you."

V.—" Without a cause" cannot mean the denial of a cause or of production, nor can it imply that the effect itself or an unreal thing is the cause ; and if you suggest " spontaneously," it cannot mean *that*, from effects being definitely limited.

Does your " without a cause" mean that *a.* there is no cause at all ? or *b.* does it deny all production ? or *c.* does it imply the rejection of all foreign causes ? or *d.* of all *real* causes ?* Under either pair of alternatives the ultimate result is that you have no cause at all, and under the latter pair, the additional absurdity of a false cause.†—Or *e.* does it mean " spontaneously ?" But effects are definitely limited, since, if they were not, occasionalness would be at an end, [as they might then arise always and everywhere.]

VI.—" But if we are to assume an eternal succession of causes and effects (as otherwise we cannot account for the occasionalness of effects,)—still even then, as that which is distinguished by the nature of fire (*scil.* fire) will not always be found only where straw, &c., are, these latter will have to be excluded from being causes, and therefore we shall again have our old difficulty of occasionalness being precluded, as no other cause can be mentioned." Here the Mímánsakas come in and maintain that we must assume as a cause the fact of there being present a capacity favourable to fire, and thus "capacity" must be allowed to be a separate category‡ varying according to each individual, non-eternal in the non-eternal thing, *described as it is in the line*

'Eternal in the eternal, and in the non-eternal produced by the cause of that thing in which it resides.'

Or as another opinion holds [that of S'ríkaráchárya] " there is an eternal capacity favourable to fire, abiding in straw, the *araṇi* wood, and the burning gem."—The Naiyáyikas however maintain that there is an actual difference of class which accompanies the being produced from straw, araṇi or the burning gem,—since, if we assumed a capacity favourable to one and the same thing (*i. e.* to fire,) and yet itself existing in things of different classes (as straw, &c.,) then on seeing

---

* That is, there can be imagined false causes.

† Under any one of the four cases you have really no proper ' *cause*' at all (thus in the third, the thing must precede itself to fulfil the definition of a cause ;) and hence any supposed cause (as in *c.*, and *d.*,) can only be a false one.

‡ Cf. Siddhánta Muktávali, pp. 3, 4.

smoke, &c., you could not draw the inference of fire, &c.* And again, [if this assumption were correct], we should not have such respective colligations of concurrent causes of fire, as straw and blowing, *arani* wood and rubbing, or the burning gem and the reflected rays of the sun, since we see in other cases that that which possesses the property that determines causation (*i. e.* according to the present theory, capacity) will produce its effect in conjunction with anything which similarly possesses some other property that determines causation; and therefore, in the present case, we should be led to expect fire to result from such a conjunction as the gem and blowing. If you would meet this by assuming that there is one capacity favourable to fire, which resides not in any one thing alone (as straw,) but in the several combinations, as straw and blowing, and the rest,— this is not the true solution, but you must rather accept (from its greater simplicity) my theory that a difference of class resides in the various fires produced by straw, &c., as is seen by the evidence of the senses, like the fire of a lamp, &c.† Hence Capacity is not to be assumed as a separate category. These discussions are condensed in the following couplet.

VI.—This succession of causes and effects has no beginning, nor has it one capacity abiding in things of different classes [as straw, &c.]; we must diligently strive for ourselves to fix the several limitations, by determining the constant accompaniments and separations.‡

The meaning of this is that we must assume a difference of class (i. e. species,) in effects produced by different causes. [If you ask "Then, in reference to *what* cause, is the class of fire (as the genus,) the determining notion of all the various special fires as effects, I reply,] heat as possessing a peculiar hot quality to the touch§ is the cause in the case of all the various fires. [In the case of the different species of fire

---

* Fire would not be the cause of smoke, in its nature as fire, but simply as having a capacity for producing smoke; and therefore on seeing smoke, our true inference would be that the mountain has not "fire" but "a capacity for producing smoke."

† The fire in a lamp lights the house, while fire from wood or cow-dung produces little or no light.

‡ *E. g.* Fire may be found, and yet no straw, but a gem; and vice versâ.

§ This epithet is added to exclude 'gold.'

we have different causes, straw, &c., but in all alike we have the general cause 'heat,' *i. e.* heat is the necessary and universal antecedent].

VII.—" But may we not say that as one and the same lamp gives light, destroys the wick and illumines different objects as jars, &c., so we may have one common cause, either as the one Brahma (with the Vedántin,) or as Nature (with the Sánkhya) which is not to be distinguished from the various intellects apportioned to the different souls, as the cause and effect are identical;—and hence the existence of God will not be established as the superintendent of merit and demerit, [since our supposed causes will evolve their own effects, and we therefore need not assume *adṛishṭa* as the special cause of the world] ?"

To meet this he says,

VII.—Of *one* there can be no succession, of the *same* there can be no variety; it is not a special capacity since this cannot be severed,—nature is hard to be violated.

From one cause alone there can be no determinate *succession* of effects [as they would be all produced simultaneously;] and from the same cause, *i. e.* one general cause (as the Sánkhya's prakṛiti) there cannot be a variety of effects, *i. e.* effects of different kinds; and therefore since we find successive effects produced, we must conclude that there are successive causes, and, since we find effects of various kinds, we must conclude the causes to be likewise various in kind.

He now refutes the doubt that perhaps various effects might be produced from one general cause by special capacities, by the words "it is not a special capacity, since this cannot be severed" from the subject in which it resides, as the power and that which possesses the power are really identical; and if you sever them, then we shall have to accept the power as the true cause, and in this way your unity of cause is destroyed, and duality follows.—" May we not hold that one cause can produce various effects simply by its own nature?" He replies "nature is hard to be violated." If that same nature which existed when one effect had to be produced, continued to exist at the time of the production of another, then the nature of water, &c., might exist in fire,—that is, a thing's real nature cannot remain concealed. The instance of the lamp is not in point, as it can be explained by a difference in the concurrent causes necessary to produce the different effects.*

VIII. "But why may we not say that the potter's staff, &c. may be a cause in the case of jars, &c., but not sacrifices, &c. in the case of heaven, &c. ?" He replies,

> VIII. The universal practice is not fruitless, nor can it have trouble as its only fruit; nor can it have as its fruit some visible gain; nor can there be such a deception [as this would involve if all were false].

The activity in performing sacrifices to obtain heaven, which all display who desire another world, cannot be fruitless, nor can it have trouble as its sole result,—since activity arises only from a conviction that such a course will be a means to obtain the desired object. Nor can we say that its fruit is the attainment of some visible object, *i. e.*, reputation for sanctity, wealth, &c., since even those perform sacrifices who have no regard to such objects. Should you reply that some knave first devised the custom of offering sacrifices as means of obtaining heaven, and the rest of mankind were cajoled into following his example, this is met by the words "nor can there be such a deception." For who could be so utterly different from the rest of mankind as for the mere sake of deceiving others to impose upon himself a round of actions which necessarily cause all sorts of trouble? and hence we may safely infer that the universal practice of sacrifice is a proof that sacrifices do produce heaven as their result.

IX. "Well, then, why not say that sacrifices, &c., may be the direct causes of [our obtaining] heaven, &c., and not any merit which they are said to produce?" He replies,

> IX. A thing long passed cannot produce its result without some continuant influence over and above. The souls, having no distinction, could not have enjoyment even though the objects were affected by *adrishṭa*.

---

* Thus for the giving light we have the conjunction of the flame and wick, &c.; for the burning of the wick we have the destruction of the conjunction previously existing between the particles of the wick; for the illumining of objects we have the conjunction of the eye with the jar, and that of the jar with the light.

A " thing long passed," *i. e.* the sacrifice, &c., " without some continuant influence over and above," *i. e.* an operation favourable to producing the result, cannot produce that result; for a cause which has long ceased to be, can only act as a cause by means of some operation [or influence] that continues to exist after it, just as the transient perception of the senses only produces recollection by means of the impression which it leaves in the mind, [to produce the actual recollection we require some reminding association to arouse the dormant impression.]—" May we not say that *adṛishṭa* may be the cause, as residing in the thing to be enjoyed [and not as merit in the person enjoying ?]" He replies by the subsequent line. If the souls had no distinction, one from the other, in the form of different kinds of merit, they could not receive different degrees of enjoyment [as we see they do] from different bodies [higher or lower in the scale], even though these were affected by adṛishṭa,—since these bodies are properly common to all souls. In other words, the varying enjoyment can only be produced by the different bodies and their organs as attracted, in each case, by the respective merit of the individual souls.

X. " But" [the Mímánsaka will say,] " why not allow a certain imperceptible property [*i. e.* the before-mentioned capacity] residing in the objects to be enjoyed, which produces the enjoyment in each particular case, just as we accept a particular kind of capacity which abides in fire, &c., and produces their special effects, as burning, &c.? Otherwise [*i. e.*, if the fire burns of itself and not by its capacity,] we should have to expect the effect of burning to be produced wherever there was contact between the fire and the hand, even though the latter wore the fire-extinguishing gem. Nor may you say that the absence of this gem should be considered as also a cause of burning,—because causation must always imply presence and existence.* The true statement is that the gem produces the destruction of the burning capacity, and hence its common name 'the obstructor;' and hence we maintain that the category of Capacity must be accepted." He replies,

X. As existence, so too non-existence is held to be

---

* See Jaimini Sútras i., Mitákshará iii.

a cause as well as an effect; obstruction is the absence of means, and that which causes this is 'an obstructor.'

As we prove by constant accompaniment and separation that absence or non-existence (*abháva,*) *i. e.* emergent non-existence,* may be an effect, similarly we can prove that it may be a cause,—since there is no reason to establish such a maxim as yours, that 'causation must imply presence and existence.'—The second line replies to the objection that an inanimate thing cannot be said to be an obstructor. Obstruction (*pratibandha*) signifies "the absence of means," *i. e.* of causes to produce such and such an effect; and this in our present topic would be "the absence of the extinguishing gem's absence," *i. e.* the presence of the gem itself. Properly speaking the man who places the gem is the obstructor (*pratibandhaka*); but by the grammatical rule which allows the affix *ka* to be added pleonastically, we may accept *pratibandhaka* to be used for *pratibandha*, the 'obstructor' for the 'obstruction.'

The modern Mímánsakas, however, maintain that "there is a needless complication in assuming such a cause as the absence of such a fire-extinguishing gem as is attended by the absence of all [excitants as the fire-exciting gem, charms, &c.;]† it is more simple to assume an eternal capacity in fire, &c., and, when the gem is present, this capacity is deadened. (Nor may you say that 'a capacity is first produced from the straw, &c. the causes of the fire,—this capacity resides in the fire, and is destroyed by the extinguishing gem and resuscitated by the exciting gem; and any objection on the ground of the indeterminate nature of the cause of the capacity‡ might be met by the assumption that its cause is only such a cause by virtue of itself possessing a capacity favourable for producing the former capacity.' This, we repeat, is unwarranted, because

---

* Emergent non-existence is the destruction of a thing previously existing. We prove that it is an effect because the destruction of a jar is only seen when it is preceded by some cause as the blow of a hammer, &c. and wherever these are not found, there the jar is not destroyed. The Mímánsá holds that abháva, being really nothing, cannot be a cause. But he proves that absence can be similarly shewn to be a cause,—where absence of the fire-extinguisher is, there is burning, and where there is not this absence, there is no burning.

† If the fire-extinguishing gem were present *with* the fire-exciting gem, its effect would be neutralised. Cf. Siddhánta Muktávali, p. 4.

‡ Its cause being sometimes straw, &c. and sometimes the exciting gem.

rather than assume such a multitude of successive capacities residing in the fire, it would be more simple to assume [with our opponents, the followers of the Nyáya,] that the one cause is the absence of such an extinguishing gem as is attended by the absence of a fire-exciting gem.) Therefore we maintain that in the case of burning we must assume, as the determining notion of causation, the presence of an undeadened capacity." Thus hold the modern Mímánsakas; but we cannot agree with them, because we should then have to assume an endless number of different capacities, as that of the extinguishing gem to cause the deadening of the burning capacity, that of the exciting gem to destroy the deadening, &c. This is a brief summary of the discussion.

XI. But the Mímánsakas reply, "In the Vaidic injunction 'he sprinkles the rice, he shells the rice,' do we not assume an operation or capacity [*i. e. sanskára*,] produced by the sprinkling, which abides in the rice and produces the future shelling, since what we understand by the expression is that only that rice which is sprinkled is capable of being shelled ? and it may be taken as a general rule that whenever anything is done through desire of an effect which will reside in some other thing, the former produces an operation which produces the result residing in the latter, as is the case with sacrifices. [Sacrifices are done for the sake of happiness (as heaven, &c.) residing in the man; therefore the means thereto, the merit produced by the rite, must also reside in the man.] And again, unless we accept a continuant capacity, how can we account for rice, and rice only, being produced from sown rice, though the seed is dissolved in the ground into its component atoms? and similarly we must say that ploughing in the month Mágha (Jan.—Feb.) produces a capacity residing in the ground [which eventually produces a good harvest in Nov. and Dec.]" He answers,

XI. We accept an influence produced in man by such acts as sprinkling the rice, &c.;* the qualities of the atoms, as form affected by contact with fire, &c., cause the distinction.

---

* Some say that there are three ways of sprinkling—*prokshana* with the supine hand, *abhyukshana* with the inverted hand, and *avokshana* by a motion of the hand sideways. But other authorities give them differently.

By sprinkling, &c. there is produced in man an influence which we call 'desert,'—since it is simpler to assume one single influence residing in the soul directly producing the shelling which is indirectly produced by sprinkling, &c.,* than to assume a variety of capacities for each parcel of rice,—and since some power or attribute must be assumed to be produced by a veda-commanded act which tends to a future result, as there is no visible means for the result being brought about. From the phrase "purified rice" we assume that the influence resides in the rice by a connection† which is the same as the nature of the thing [while it resides in the man by the so-called intimate relation ;] and so too in the case of consecrated water, branches, &c. there is produced an influence or merit residing in the man favourable to producing such and such a result [as the consecration of the jar.] [Nor may you say that "if the merit produced do not reside in the rice but in the man, then why is *vrihín* in the objective case, as wherever there is this objective case we find the effect residing there, as in 'he cooks rice,'—here the effect produced by cooking, *i. e.*, softening, resides in the rice, &c."—as we reply that] your vaidic example stands on the same footing as such a common secular phrase as "he sprinkles the fried barley flour,"—here there is no Vaidic injunction, yet we find an objective case used, the real meaning of which is this, viz. the possessing a result produced by the action of another (*i. e.* the man), which result is the conjunction of the water produced by that action, *i. e.* the sprinkling. Besides your general maxim that 'whenever a thing is done through desire of an effect, &c.' fails in such cases as the hawk-sacrifice, which is performed for the sake of the slaughter of an enemy [which slaughter of course resides in him,] while it produces a result [hell] which resides in the performer.

---

* In other words *adrishṭa* is the *vyápára* of the sprinkling, according to the principle *taj-janyatwe sati taj-janya-janako hi vyápárah*.

† In Hindu philosophy there are three principal relations,—1. the *samaváya* or intimate relation, *i. e.* that which exists between the whole and its parts, a substance and its qualities, or both these and their genus ; 2. the *sanyoga* or conjunction, as between a pot and the soil on which it stands ; and 3. *swarúpa* or the nature of the thing. This last may be generally said to take up all those relations which are not included in the two former, such as the relation between an object and the knowledge of it *(vishayatá)*, that between abháva and the spot of ground from which the absent thing is absent, &c., and that between a distinguishing attribute (not a proper quality or action) and its subject, as ákás'atwa in ákás'a. Hence the swarúpa sambándha is sometimes called vishayatá-sambandha. The two former are something *other* than the things related ; the swarúpa sambandha is really one or the other of them.

He now explains by the second line the determined production of barley, &c., from the several seeds as sown. The qualities of the atoms, such as form affected by contact with fire, &c.* produce the distinction, *i. e.* the atoms as possessed of the qualities of form, moisture, &c. affected by contact with fire, tend to produce such and such effects [rice or barley, as it may be,—the desert of the individual acting as the concurrent cause.] In the case of healing [where the opponent might allege that the medicine produced an after effect by means of his supposed continuant capacity,] the drinking of the medicine produces an equilibrium between the three humours, and this is the means of the subsequently produced destruction of the disease.†

XII. " But how then [except by the assumption of our special category ' Capacity,'] will you account for sensible touch, &c. in the case of air, &c. [which seem cold, &c. to the body,] where there is no form produced by contact with fire, [as there is in earth ?] or again how is the natural liquidity of water stopped in ice, &c. ? or how in images, &c. do such ceremonies become effectual as those for inviting the deity to take up his residence therein, &c. ? We hold therefore that we must admit such a thing as a capacity produced by the rite *pratishṭhá*‡ which can be destroyed by the touch of impure persons as the Chándála, &c., which capacity renders the image a fit object of worship." He replies,

> XII. The perceptible form, &c. and their absence [in ice and air] arise from contact with special causes; the deities are worshipped through their coming [into the image] or through the worshipper's consciousness of having duly performed the rite.

The 'special causes' are the various kinds of merit in the person [gratified by the cold air or ice.] The deities become conciliated by

---

* It is a peculiarity of the element earth that its form, taste (or moisture,) smell and touch are changed by contact with fire.

† Our author does not notice the objection of the ploughing in Mágha. Another writer Pakshadharamitra in his Padártha Málá supplies the omission. According to him " Through the ploughing in Mágha the original soil is destroyed by the series of acts tending to the separation of the atoms which destroys their original conjunction, and subsequently by the disintegration a new soil is produced, and through this is the ploughing in Mágha a cause of the excellent harvest afterwards."

‡ The ceremony of consecrating an image of a deity.

the ceremony of consecration, and shew it by coming to take up their residence, *i. e.* by their appropriation of the image and transference of self-consciousness thereto ; but by the touch of an impure person such appropriation and self-consciousness are rendered void. Even on the Mímánsaka view which disputes the intelligence of the deities, we can say that it is the idea [in the worshipper's mind] that the worship has been performed in due manner, and that the image has been duly consecrated,—this idea being also necessarily accompanied by the absence of the touch of any impure person,— which constitutes the image's fitness as an object of worship, and the ceremony's importance lies in its contributing to produce this idea. But in reality it is the absence of any impure contact as with a Chándála, &c. at the time of the *pratishṭhá* ceremony and also after the ceremony is over, which constitutes the fitness of the image as an object of worship; since the rule "let him worship it when duly inaugurated by the ceremony *pratishṭhá*" implies that the ceremony must be already over. Such is a summary of the discussion.

XIII. " But ought we not to say that in the weighing ordeal, &c. a power or capacity is produced in the scales by the ceremony of the ordeal, and by that a result is produced such as the rising or sinking of the defendant in the scales ?"* He replies,

  XIII. Only for the discovering of the concurrent of the cause of victory or defeat,—which cause abides as an attribute in the person examined,—are the rules of the ordeal instituted.

Only to discover the concurrent, favourable to the desired result (*i. e.* the rising or sinking in the scale),—the concurrent of the desert which is the proper cause of the victory or defeat in the ordeal,—are the rules of the ordeal instituted. " I who according to the rule of the ordeal now mount the scales am innocent or guilty,"—this consciousness in the man's own mind is the concurrent.—Or another interpretation is " only to discover the residing of (*i. e.* to produce,) merit or demerit are the rules of the ordeal instituted," and thus in relation to innocence such as is conformable

---

* For this kind of ordeal see Professor Stenzler's essay on 'die Indischen Gottesurtheile' in the Zeitschrift d. D. M. G. vol. ix. p. 665.

to his protestation merit is produced, and demerit in relation to his guiltiness.* The second mode is preferable, as in this way an objection is obviated which would apply to the former, viz.,—"in the case of a man falsely accused of killing a Bráhman, &c., as his not having done it is not meritorious, how could his consciousness of innocence be a concurrent cause?"†

XIV. But here the Sánkhyas come in with their system,—"There is Soul, the abode of intelligence, but not a cause of anything, and consequently unchangeable and eternal; and Nature which is one, unintelligent, subject to development and eternal; the first development from Nature is Intellect, the so-called 'great' first principle,—in it are eight attributes, viz. knowledge, ignorance, might, weakness, freedom from passion, subjection to passion, merit and demerit, or the eight may be otherwise enumerated as knowledge, pleasure, pain, desire, aversion, effort, merit, and demerit,—as this school does not accept the Naiyáyik self-reproductive quality of imagination, *bhávaná*, since they hold that at the time of memory the perception itself does remain in a very subtil form. As without the assumption of soul we cannot account for the unintelligent product of Nature, Intellect, imagining itself to be intelligent, we conclude that the existence of soul is hence established,—identical with its essential attribute intelligence, since the subject and attribute are always undistinguishable. From Nature arises the Great one, from the Great one Egoism, from Egoism the five subtil elements, form, flavour, smell, touch and sound, and the organs [of perception and action], the eye, skin, nose, tongue, ear, and mind, and the voice, hand, foot, anus and generative organ; while from the subtil elements are produced the gross elements, earth, water, fire, air and ether. This has been thus described, [in the Sánkhya Káriká,] "Original Nature is not an evolute; the seven, intellect, &c. are evolvent and evolute; the set of sixteen are only evolute; while Soul is neither evolvent nor evolute." The set of sixteen is made up by the five gross elements and the eleven organs of perception and action. [Should you ask why we assume mind as our eleventh organ, we reply,] *a.* if the eternal Soul were

---

* By the former interpretation merit and knowledge act conjointly in producing the result, by the second merit alone.

† This negative knowledge could not be the *sahakári* of a previous *puṇya*, as there is no *puṇya* in the absence of an action.

itself associated with the objects of inherent joy and pain, it would follow that there could be no liberation; *b.* if the connection with objects took place in dependence on Nature, it would equally follow that, since Nature is eternal, there could be no liberation; *c.* if the non-eternal objects, jars, &c., were associated with the essential intelligence, it would follow that there could be no such distinction as 'seen' and 'not seen,' [as all the things now existing would necessarily be seen at one and the same moment;] and *d.* if the association of objects and intelligence depended on the external organs only, we could not account for the perceptions through different organs not being simultaneous; and hence we must assume the existence of a distinct organ, mind, in connection with which the external organs produce the association of the object and intelligence. In dreams when a person thinks himself a tiger, &c. there is not present to him the consciousness that he is a man; hence we must also assume the existence of a faculty, egoism, whose function is the assuming the consciousness of various objects. Since we see inspiration and expiration ceaselessly going on, in waking, dreams, and sound sleep, we must assume the existence of a faculty which continues acting throughout, viz. the principle of Intellect endued with the eight attributes before mentioned; the object being brought into connection with Intellect's development, viz. cognition, conceals the real nature of Soul, and hence it is that liberation arises when, from the destruction of the principle Intellect, there ceases to be any connection with objects; while the idea 'I, the intelligent, act' arises from the nonperception of the difference between the (witness) soul and the active intellect. This has been explained in the Bhagavad Gítá "actions are ever done by the qualities of nature, the soul blinded by egoism thinks 'I am the doer.'" And this Intellect consists of three portions, the reflection of the Soul, the reflection of the object, and the arising determination, as in the thought 'this must be done by me,'—here '*by me*' shews the reflection of the intelligent Soul, which is not an actual intercourse, but only illusory in consequence of the nonperception of the distinction between the Soul and Intellect; '*this*' shews the reflection of the object; and the arising resolve '*must be done*' is dependent upon both these. The connection of the Soul, as reflected in Intellect, with the object, is what we call knowledge, and the connection of the Soul with this knowledge is seen in the determination 'I, the intelligent, act,'" [whereas in reality the intelligent cannot act and the acting faculty cannot think.]

To meet this, he says,

> XIV. The attributes of the agent are the determiners [that knowledge and action reside in the same subject]; and the intelligent is our only agent; otherwise, we should necessarily have no liberation or else no mundane succession of events.

The attributes merit, demerit, desire and aversion must reside in the same subject with action, since experience of happiness and misery resides in the same subject with action [and these produce all such experience]; and in the same way we hold that the intelligent soul is alone the agent, as is proved by the impression 'I, the intelligent, act.' The second line adds another refutation of the Sánkhya doctrine. If Intellect were eternal, then there could be no liberation, as the Soul would always remain associated with Intellect; if it were noneternal, then it must be allowed to have been produced, as a noneternal thing cannot but have been produced; and in this case, previously to its production, as the attributes belonging to it would be also then non-existent, it would follow that their effects, the various bodies, organs, &c., assigned to individuals, would as yet be equally unproduced, and consequently there would be no mundane succession of events, [and therefore no bondage of soul, and consequently no need of liberation.]

XV. Here steps in the Chárváka, " well, let desert be an attribute of an intelligent being; but this intelligent being is not eternal and all-pervading, but a certain kind of element modified in the form of the body, since such phrases as 'I, the pale one, know' prove that it has form [and form is a corporeal attribute.]" He answers,

> XV. One does not remember what another has seen; the body remains not one and the same from decay; there cannot be transference of impressions, and if you accept a non-momentary existence there is no other means.

If intelligence belonged to the body, there could be no remembrance in youth of things experienced in childhood, just as Maitra cannot remember what Chaitra saw; nor can you say that the body continues one and the same in childhood and youth, because of its "decay," *i. e.* destruction, since by a difference of size the thing itself becomes different, as the destruction of the former size is brought about by the destruction of the subject in which it resided. Nor may you maintain that the second body, as the effect, may still remember what had been experienced by its cause the previous body, because "there cannot be transference of impressions," otherwise we should have the child in the womb remembering the experiences of its mother. "But may there not be a transference of impressions from the material cause to the effect?" [the subsequent body being made out of the previous one.] He replies "if you accept a non-momentary existence, there is no other means." In other words, if you do not accept the Bauddha doctrine that all things are in a continual flux,—one heap of atoms the next moment producing another heap,—but allow that things do last from moment to moment, then the parts, as the hands, &c., are the material cause of the body; and, if so, then on your hypothesis, if a person's hand were cut off, the maimed body ought not to remember a former experience of that hand, as it would now no longer be a part (*i. e.* material cause) of the body. Nor can you say that "intelligence belongs to the atoms and therefore there is remembrance because these remain," because, if so, remembrance ought to be imperceptible [while yet it is perceptible by the internal organ, mind,] just as the form of the atoms is imperceptible; and also there ought to be no remembrance of anything once experienced by the atoms of the hand, if there be no longer union with those atoms, the hand being severed from the body.

XVI. "Well then, why not allow, with the Bauddhas, that all things are dissolved every successive moment, and that each previous heap of atoms, as a material cause, produces a succeeding heap as its effect? in this way there is no difficulty to account for memory." He replies,

> XVI. This could not be without difference of kind, and if this latter were true there could be no inference; and without inference even your hypothesis could not stand; nor could there be perception without ascertainment.

By "difference of kind" he means the Bauddha notion of "efficient form,"* without which " this," *i. e.* the doctrine of a continual flux, could not be established; [and this notion cannot be proved] since, on the simple hypothesis of the seed &c. continuing on from moment to moment, you can easily account for the production or non-production of the effect respectively by the presence or absence of the concurrent causes, water, &c., and thence you can account for the production of the shoot by the nature of the seed [without assuming any 'efficient form;'] so that if the individual seed be allowed to continue on, how can there be any such momentary flux?—Again, even if you assume this peculiar kind of species, 'efficient form,' to abide in the perceptible individual but to be itself beyond the cognizance of the senses, there could be no such thing as inference, as fire can only then be the cause of smoke, when its nature as fire acts as the efficient form of the first moment's smoke; but even if you suppose that one special smoke (the first moment's,) is produced by fire, you cannot thereby infer that fire is the cause of *all* smoke, because by your own hypothesis you must allow that this very smoke is the cause of its own special effect, the second moment's smoke, [and this of the third, &c.;] and hence it would follow that all inference would be abolished, as it would be impossible to establish the universal major premiss, which depends for its validity on an argument to preclude the possibility of an instance where the middle term is found disjoined from the major, which argument must be always based on the relation of cause and effect [as existing between the major and middle.†] And without inference it is impossible to establish your own hypothesis of a momentary flux, since it can only be cognized by means of inference. Nor can you say that "perception itself is the evidence of flux," because, according to your doctrine, the only perception which can really have authority is the indeterminate‡ *(nirvikalpaka)* since that alone is produced by the object;

* As the Naiyáyikas hold that the species jar *(ghaṭatwa)* resides in all jars, so the Bauddhas hold that a *quasi-játi*, called *kurvadrúpatwa*, resides in each thing when that thing is actively employed in producing its effect, as a jar in holding water, or rice in producing a plant. When there is no effect being produced this *kurvadrúpatwa* is absent. But for their assumption of this occasionally present principle, every thing would *always* produce its effect.

† Cf. S. Muktáv. p. 122. There is an interesting attempt in the Sarva Dar's. Sangraha, pp. 7, 8, to establish the authority of the universal proposition from the relation of cause and effect or of genus and species.

‡ The Hindus hold that on the contact of the organ of sense with an object, as *e. g.* a jar, there arises the idea of a jar and also the idea of the nature, i. e.

yet—since even this is only inferred from the subsequent determinate perception,—in the case of an object which only lasts one moment, there can be no such determinate perception, and consequently, with the failure of this, fails likewise the indeterminate. Again, the so-called species of efficient form in the case of seed-produced plants is not a true species, as it is obnoxious to the charge of 'confusion,' since, *a.*, it will be found present in barley without the species rice,—*b.*, it will not be found in rice stored in a granary [and therefore lying idle and not producing its effect] while the species rice *is* found present there,—and, *c.*, both species ['efficient form' and 'rice'] are found simultaneously conjoined in sown rice when it is actually producing its shoot.—Hence we Naiyáyikas (to avoid this fault of 'confusion,') assume that there are many subdivisions of the species 'jar' (and not merely one undivided)—these subdivisions being severally pervaded by [i. e. included under] 'silver' &c. [as silver jars, earthen jars, &c.] And [if you ask why we call them all by the common name jar, we reply that] the general appellation jar arises from our viewing them as all possessed of one common attribute, viz. the being composed of parts which [however different in material] possess a particular kind of arrangement [called kambugrívá in the case of jars].

XVII. "Well, then, let us consider the flux hypothesis as still undetermined, [*i. e.* it is at any rate not shewn to be impossible;] for as for any argument against it on the plea of recognition ('*i. e.* this is the jar I saw yesterday,') we overthrow it by maintaining that there is a doubt as to its being the same jar." He replies,

XVII. There can be no doubt as to things continuing, nor as to perception, nor can there be as to authority of proof from the self-contradiction,—as the same proof which establishes the oneness of the object during the moment may establish it during a longer time.

There can be no doubt as to the continuance of objects as we can perceive it by recognition; nor can there be doubt as to our recognition, as we can ascertain its correctness by our being conscious of

εἶδος of jar (both being equally objects of perception,) but the two ideas are distinct,—this is *nirvikalpaka*. Subsequently the mind combines them into one idea, 'a jar possessing the species or nature of jar,' and this is *savikalpaka*. We are however not conscious of the first step,—it is only recognised as necessary from an analysis of the subsequent compound idea.

possessing this knowledge. Nor can there be doubt as to the authority of *all* evidence "from the self-contradiction" which it involves, since if you doubt of the authority of your own consciousness of doubt the very existence of your doubt is itself unproved; and again, if you cannot establish any thing as authoritative, you cannot have any doubt even as to authority, because you will not have established your point to doubt upon [and your doubt will have no foundation]. "Well, but may we not doubt [not of all authority but] of the authority of your so-called recognition, since we can see cases of erroneous recognition, as when we say of a man whose hair has grown again after it was cut, 'this is the same hair as before,' &c. ?" To meet this he gives the second line. The same proof, viz., the absence of opposite qualities, by which we know in the case of the jar which exists only one moment, that during that moment it is the same and not a different jar,—may teach us in the case of the jar which is supposed to continue on from moment to moment, that it too is the same jar and not a different one. Since just as one cognition may be connected with many different objects [as *e. g.* a table with the things on it,] so too one object, as a jar, may, without inconsistency, be connected with many different moments, the connection with those moments being necessarily successive,* because it depends on the succession of the moments, its causes.

XVIII. "Well then let it be considered as proved that there is a cause of another world *(i. e. adṛishṭa;)* but here the doubt may arise, *a.* is causality essential or communicated by some thing else,—if the first, then it ought to act indifferently towards all things, just as blue is blue to all; if the second, then if we allow the 'communicating something' to have essential causation, *it* too will be liable to the aforementioned objection; and if, on the other hand, its causation is communicated, we shall have a *regressus in infinitum*, as we shall require an infinite series of such communicating somethings? *b.* And again if causation be essential, effects ought to be produced from the very first moment of the existence of the cause." He replies,

XVIII. Without first determining the power of the

---

* *I. e.* there must be this difference between the two connections alluded to,—one is contemporary, the other successive.

cause, even blue &c. are not actual existences; it becomes capable when associated with something else, why then should it not be allowed to be universal?

The 'power of the cause' is the cause's nature as a cause, *i. e.* causality [*i. e.* its being such a thing as a cause;] until we have ascertained this, the 'blue' of your illustration has no authority [because, if it has no cause, it must be merely an error;] and so your argument would fall to the ground, viz. " all that is real is universal in its action, as blue, &c. and therefore if causality be not universal in its action, it is not real," since your major premiss will not be universally true if you admit that there is a cause for your quoted 'blue,' as indeed there must be, since it is non-eternal,*—there being no proof of the existence of an eternal blue.—The second line overthrows the second paragraph (*b.*) "It" the cause, when "associated with something else" *i. e.* with the concurrent,† "becomes capable" of producing the effect; hence it does not result that its causality must shew itself in action from the very first moment of the cause's existence. The latter words express that the author has no objection to admit universality of action, if properly understood, "why then should it not be universal?" Even the universality of action which you ascribe to blue, &c., only means really that all men speak of and treat them as blue, &c.; and this kind of universality is equally found in the cause when associated with its concurrents [as fire &c. with fuel, or the seed with water, air, &c.] since it is an established fact, that we all do apply the term 'causality' to such cases, and treat them as such.

XIX. "But if we even accept your opinion that desert may reside in the soul, must we not still say that it is not produced by the soul as a material cause,‡ since in the case of an eternal and all-pervading substance [like soul] there can be no negative instance either in point of space or of time, and causality can only be proved by an induction from affirmative instances together with negative, a cause being defined as that the absence of which necessitates the absence of

---

* If a non-eternal thing is real, it must have a cause, and therefore your very illustration proves the fact of non-universal causation.

† Our 'condition.'

‡ The Nyáya holds that knowledge, desert, &c. reside in the soul as its qualities, and the subject is the material cause of its qualities.

something else [*scil.* the effect]. But since in this way desert will have no material [intimate] cause, of course it can have no non-intimate and instrumental causes, since they are allowed to be causes only as acting in close proximity to the other ;* and hence it will follow that desert will be eternal [as it is uncaused,] and therefore, being eternal, it cannot be conceived as producing enjoyment, limited to particular souls at particular places and times." He replies,

XIX. Surely precedence is causality, since it is proved by any argument; likewise for the eternal all-pervading; otherwise there could not be the idea of the subject.

Causality does not always imply the existence of negative instances, but its true definition is " necessary precedence without superfluous determination."† The negative instance is not the only means of proving causality, since it may be equally proved by the evidence which establishes its subject ;‡ hence the causality of the eternal and all-pervading soul " may be proved by any argument." " Otherwise there could not be the idea of the subject," [as the proof of the soul's existence is that we require a subject for pleasure, pain, &c.] and hence the subject's (*i. e.* the soul's,) being a cause is established by the same argument which establishes the subject's existence. From seeing that the component halves are always found where jars are and jars never found where these are not, we learn that substance as substance is a material cause to the effect connected with it by intimate relation; and hence, by rejecting earth, &c., we can establish by exhaustion that for the qualities knowledge, desire, &c. there must be a material cause other than earth and the rest, *i. e.* soul.

But in reality there is one kind of argument from negative instances§ which does establish material causation as follows, " that which is not a half, has no jar connected with it by intimate relation; and similarly, that which is not soul has not knowledge, &c. thus

---

* Siddhánta Muktávali, p. 12.

† For the five kinds of Superfluous determination of causation see S. Muktávali, pp. 13—16. The *anyathásiddha káraṇa* is that pseudo-cause whose absence does not directly necessitate the absence of the effect.

‡ We have a good instance of this kind of argument in the Sánkhya argument for the assumption of the internal organ mind in p. 17. Mind is assumed in order to account for the fact that two cognitions are not simultaneous,—the same proof will of course equally establish that mind is a cause of cognition.

§ This is called the *anyonyábháva vyatireka* in contradistinction to the *atyantábháva vyatireka*—the latter is in the form—" where there is no half, there is no jar."

connected with it.' So too we may argue in the case of time [although time is eternal and all-pervading] 'that which is not time cannot have a jar connected with it in that particular relation [called temporal ;'] and in this way the argument from negative instances may be applied to prove that time is a condition as the temporal site in which the jar is made.

Thus there is no contradiction between our conclusions and the declaration of S'ruti which affirms that 'the world is delusive,' since the terms Delusion, Nature, Ignorance, &c. really mean only 'desert.' And hence the existence of God is established as the superintendent of desert in producing its effects [by §. iv.]

XX. He thus sums up the substance of the chapter,

> XX. May He whose unparalleled concurrent energy *this* is,—called Máyá from its being so hard to unravel, or Nature from its being the first principle, or Ignorance from its horror of right knowledge ;
>
> May He that deity by whom is lulled the turmoil of the waves of mundane existence,—immediately, himself being the witness, the passionless, create in my mind devotion towards himself.

'This' the concurrent cause in the form of desert,—it is unparalleled since all effects depend upon it,—the word *Máyá* is used to mean 'desert' by metonymy, [as it primarily means Delusion,] 'resemblance' being the cause of the extension of meaning,* as each is alike hard to be unravelled.

* Cf. Sáhitya Darpaṇa, ii. §. 18.

Note on the term 'Avachhedaka' (p. 7.)

The term *Avachhedaka* has at least three meanings, as distinguishing, particularising and determining.

a. In the phrase 'a blue lotus' 'blue' is the distinguishing *avachhedaka (i. e. vis'eshaṇa,)* of the lotus,—it distinguishes it from others of different colours.

b. In the sentence 'the bird sits on the tree, on the branch,' वृचे शाखायां पक्षी, *s'ákháyám* particularises the exact spot,—this is the *ekades' ávachhedaka*.

c. But the third is the usual Naiyáyika use of the word, *i. e.* as determining, *niyámaka*. Wherever we find a relation which is not itself included in any one of the seven categories but is common to several, we require something to determine its different varieties; thus if we say that fire is the cause of smoke, or, vice versâ, smoke the effect of fire, we do not mean only this particular case but any fire or smoke; we therefore require, to determine this particular relation of causality, something which shall be always found present with it. This in 'fire is the cause of smoke' will be *vahnitwa*, the species or τὸ τί ἦν ἔιναι of all fires. This will always be found present wherever the causation of smoke is found, and it is therefore called the *dhúmakáraṇatávachhedaka*, as *dhúmatwa* would be the *vahnikáryatávachhedaka*. If we have several causes or effects (as *e. g.* green wood in the case of smoke,) each *káraṇatá* or *káryatá* will require its own *avachhedaka*. But we could not say that 'substance' is the *avachhedaka* of 'quality' although it does always accompany it,—because quality is a category by itself and not common to several. An *avachhedaka* is always required for such relations as *káraṇatá, káryatá, s'akyatá, jneyatá, pratiyogitá,* &c. Thus *gotwa* is the *avachhedaka* of the *go-s'abdas'akyatá*, as otherwise the word *go* might be restricted to mean only this particular cow or extended to include every animal; and in वह्निभावस्य प्रतियोगी वह्निः we have *vahnitwa* as the *avachhedaka* of the *pratiyogitá*. This determining notion need not be always a species; thus in कार्यस्य जनकः चेष्टावान् *cheshṭá* is the *avachhedaka* of *káraṇatá*, and *cheshṭá* is included in the category of 'action.'

SECOND CLUSTER.

I. The Second objection was that there is no proof of God, since the means of attaining paradise can be practised independently of any such being. That is to say, " sacrifices which are the instruments of obtaining paradise can be performed even without a God, since it is proved by the Veda that sacrifices are a means of obtaining heaven, and the Veda possesses authority from its eternity and freedom from defects, and we can also gather its authority from its having been accepted by great saints [as Manu and others;] and therefore you cannot establish the existence of God, on the ground that he is the author of the Veda; or we may suppose that the Veda was made by Sages like Kapila and others, who gained omniscience by their preeminence in concentrated devotion."—He replies,

I. Since right knowledge requires an external source, since creation and destruction take place, and since none other than He can be relied on,—there is no other way open.

The right knowledge caused by testimony is one which is produced by a quality in the speaker, viz. his knowledge of the exact meaning of the words used;* hence the existence of God is proved, as he must be the subject of such a quality in the case of the Veda. " But may we not allow that such a quality as the knowledge of the exact meaning of the words used is required in the case of an effect which implies an agent; but in the case of the uncreated Veda it is its freedom from defects which produces its authoritativeness, and we can know its authoritativeness from its having been accepted by great

---

* All right knowledge, *pramá*, is produced by some virtue in the means used, as all wrong knowledge by some defect. Thus in sense-perception the virtue required is the ἀρετή of the eye &c.; in inference it is the knowledge of a real vyápti; and in testimony the right knowledge must be produced by a speaker who knows the true meaning of the words used. The speaker's claim to this knowledge is vitiated by conscious deception as well as by unconscious ignorance; as in the former case the speaker's right knowledge is in abeyance, and it is his *assumed* erroneous cognition (*dhárya-jnána*) which is the immediate cause of the words used. (Cf. Plato, Rep. p. 382.)

saints?" He replies "because creation and destruction take place." After a mundane destruction, when the former Veda is destroyed, how can the subsequent Veda possess authority, since there will then be no possibility of its having been accepted by great saints? And again the non-eternity of sound is proved by the universal conviction 'the letter *g* is produced,' and an eternity in the form of an unbroken succession is stopped by the possibility of mundane destruction. "Well, then, let us say that at the beginning of a creation Kapila and others were its authors, who had acquired omniscience by the power of merit gained by the practice of concentrated devotion in the former æon." He replies " none other than He can be relied on." If you mean by omniscient beings, those endued with the various superhuman faculties of assuming infinitesimal size &c. and capable of creating every thing, then we reply that the law of parsimony bids us assume only one such, namely Him the adorable Lord. There can be no confidence in a non-eternal and non-omniscient being, and hence it follows that according to the system which rejects God, the tradition of the Veda is simultaneously overthrown,—'there is no other way open.'

II. "But may we not reply that your assumption of a mundane creation and destruction is unwarranted, since there is no evidence for it, and there are also several arguments against it. Thus *a.* there is a law that day and night are, from their very nature, uninterruptedly preceded by day and night; *b.* the nature of time in itself is always accompanied by the perception of the fruit of former works, for time brings to effect the various pre-existing deserts [ripening them as seeds sown;] and you cannot prove that desert can suddenly be stopped in its action; *c.* a Brahman must be born from a Brahman, but since at the beginning of a creation no one could be a Brahman [for want of previous merit] you could not establish the necessary succession of caste in the succeeding generations; *d.* as there could then be no teacher or learner, there could have been no acceptance of the conventions of language, and hence you could not establish the tradition of words; and *e.* at the beginning of a creation there could be no dexterity in the different necessary arts of life as making jars, &c., since this requires previous instruction from another, and thus the chain of the tradition of all the arts of life would be cut short." He replies,

II. As in the days of the rainy season &c., time as determining mundane existence is the condition; there is cessation of action as in deep sleep; the castes originated as herbs and scorpions; the conventions of words, &c., are like jugglery.

a. If you would prove that the days of the rainy season have been uninterruptedly preceded by similar rainy days, you must first have the condition that they have been preceded by a certain period of the sun's course defined by his entrance into certain signs of the Zodiac, [as Taurus and Gemini,]—and so here if you would prove that day and night must have been uninterruptedly preceded by day and night, you must have as the condition an uninterrupted series of previous mundane works; or in other words, the limiting condition is the nature of time as determining this mundane existence [and you cannot argue from the mere nature of time in itself.] *b.* As in time of deep sleep* there is a cessation of the desert which produces the fruit enjoyed by certain individuals, so at special times there may be a cessation of all desert for all souls, hence he says, "there is cessation of action as in deep sleep." *c.* A certain herb can be produced by the seed of that particular herb and also by the manure of rice-dust;† or again a scorpion can be produced from cow dung as well as from a scorpion; and so at special times by a special desert (or fate) acting alone a Brahman can be produced,‡ while at the present time a Brahman can only be produced from a Brahman parent;—there will be no contradiction as (by I. vi.) we allow that difference of species [though not of genus] does reside in different effects. *d.* Just as a juggler having made a puppet pulled by strings, bids it bring a jar and the jar is brought, and thus instructs a child, so likewise God, having assumed two bodies in the mutual connection of master and disciple, and thus initiated

---

* The Vedántins and Sánkhyas hold that in deep sleep there is pleasure, but the Naiyáyikas deny it, as without *jnána* there can be no *sukha*.

† The water in which rice has been washed is considered an excellent manure from the fertilising nature of the rice-dust. Besides the *tusha* or husk, there is a red covering easily pulverised adhering to the rice-berries, called in Sanskrit कण in Bengali कुँड़ and in Hindustani کُس. This is alluded to in the Atharva Veda, xi. 3, 5. अश्वाः कणा गावस्तण्डुला मशकास्तुषाः.

‡ A similar notion of spontaneous production (تولد) after a mundane renovation is found in the Akhláki Jaláli, Introd.

the tradition of words, taught their meanings to the men then newly created. *e.* In the same manner having himself originated the tradition of making jars &c., and the other useful arts, he instructed them therein.

III. The opponent's attempt to preclude any discussion being overthrown, he adds some confirmatory reasons.

III. The gradual failure of the tradition of the Veda, &c. may be inferred from the observed failure of generation, ceremonial purification, learning, &c. and the power of study and of performing ceremonial works.

The argument runs thus,—The tradition of the Veda, &c. is inferred to be subject to entire interruption from its gradually failing, just like a lamp, as it burns on. The rest of the couplet is added to establish the *fact* of the reason given. *a.* 'Failure of generation;' originally creatures were produced from the mind,* then by sexual intercourse solely for the sake of issue, but now entirely through desire of sensual gratification. *b.* ' Failure of ceremonial purification;' originally the very food of the parents† was ceremonially purified, [in the putreshṭi yága,] then afterwards the child in the womb, then the child after birth, and now hardly at all any how. *c.* ' Failure of learning;' originally they studied the whole Veda with its thousand S'ákhás and eventually one S'ákhá only, thus it has gradually decayed. By the &c. we may understand ' livelihood,' ' duty,' &c. *d.* ' Failure of livelihood;' originally they lived on gleanings, then on unsolicited alms, then on agriculture, &c., and lastly they supported themselves on the wages of servitude. *e.* ' Failure of duty,' originally duty had four legs, asceticism, knowledge, sacrifice and charity; in each subsequent age, as the Tretá &c., it lost one leg, until in the Kali it totters on a single leg, charity;‡ or again [taking *dharma* in the sense of observing the prescribed duties of caste, &c.,] once they ate the leavings of the sacrifice, then next the leavings of a guest, then food prepared by themselves, and lastly they ate even with menial servants. *f.* Then we may notice the failure of power to study one's daily portion of the Veda and to perform works as sacrifices &c.; from the failure of the power of study as the cause results failure of the power of learning as

---

* As Brahmá's mind-begotten sons. See also Indische Stud. ii. p. 97.
† Cf. Rámáyaṇa, i. 15.
‡ Cf. Manu, i. 81, 82, 86.

the effect, hence in the S'loka we have the 'power of study' mentioned separately from 'learning.' And in this way with the destruction of the universe are all included living beings destroyed. Thus do we establish the fact of these universal destructions.—The Veda is authoritative as having been received by great saints who displayed a zealous earnestness in the practice of sacrifices, &c.—which earnestness was untainted by such vicious causes as a wish to deceive, association with heretics, acting for some secret motive, addiction to eristic disputation, living as one pleases,* heedlessness of the distinction between lawful and unlawful food and drinks, &c.†

IV. He sums up the substance of the chapter.

IV. Him who in sport having repeatedly made this strangely wonderful world by his illusive power, again causes it to collapse, and having destroyed it again re-makes it as a magic show,—that Deity, S'iva, the might of whose will bursts forth unhindered into accomplishment,—him I salute, the sole ground of confidence, and may I continue to pay him homage even unto the end.

* As by unlawful trades.
† Other Pandits divide the original differently and explain it to mean " addiction to eristic disputations, desire of a livelihood, or reckless (*adwaita*) lust of food and drink.' "

THIRD CLUSTER.

I. The third objection was that there were positive arguments to prove God's non-existence. "Just as we infer a jar's absence in a given space of ground, [i. e. its non-existence there,] so we infer God's non-existence from His not being perceived. If you reply that 'the Supreme Being is not a legitimate object of perception, and, therefore, since we cannot here have a valid non-perception, we cannot assume His non-existence,'—we retort that in the same way we might prove that a hare's horn may exist since we have only to maintain that it is not a legitimate object of our perception." He answers,

I. In an illegitimate object [of perception] how can there be a valid non-perception?* and still more, how can you establish your contradiction? How can the hare's horn be precluded as absurd if it be an illegitimate object? and how can you have an inference without a subject to base it on?

In the case of the Supreme Being who is not a legitimate object, how can there be a valid non-perception? It is only *this* which precludes a thing's existence; but the absence of perception which obtains in the case of God cannot exert this precluding influence, as otherwise we should equally be forced to deny the existence of ether, merit, demerit, &c. But a horn must be a legitimate object of perception,—how then can your retort contradict our argument? If you say that a hare's horn is an illegitimate object of perception, then of course its existence is not necessarily precluded,—there is only an absence of proof to establish it; but this cannot be retorted against *us* as the fifth Cluster will fully shew that there are positive arguments to establish God's existence.† "But may we not infer God's non-

---

* A valid non-perception is when an object is not seen and yet all the usual concurrent causes of vision are present, such as the eye, light, &c.

† We infer that there *is* no jar when we do not see one, because had there been one, we should have seen it, but in the case of the Supreme Being, ghosts, &c. as they are acknowledged to be imperceptible, we could only *at most* say that their existence is '*not proven*;' and this is here not admissible in the face of the positive argument of the fifth chapter.

existence from the absence, in His case, of a body which always accompanies an agent, and also of any assignable motive for action?" He replies,—how can you have an inference where the minor term is itself controverted? while on the other hand the very proof which will establish the existence of the subject (God), is itself sufficient to debar your subsequent inference [that there is no God].

II. "Well, then, let us say that God is introduced through an error, and that the subsequent argument is to prove either the nonexistence of any agency in this wrongly assumed subject or the subject's non-existence." He replies,

> II. The very possession of the absence of some rejected attribute proves the subject's reality, since it makes it a locus. The state of a counterentity [to non-existence] *i. e.* the absence of the absence, must belong to a *something*.

"It makes it a locus"—*i. e.* it gives to the absence a 'local habitation' in the subject, and therefore an unreal thing can never properly be a subject. [If you shift your ground and say that the argument is to prove God's non-existence, we reply that] the state of a counterentity to non-existence, *i. e.* the absence of the absence, cannot belong to a *no-thing*, or, in other words, just as that subject from which a given attribute is excluded cannot be unreal, so neither can an unreal thing be the object of a negation.

III. "But why may we not learn the absence (or non-existence) of a thing by its non-perception, even though the thing itself be an illegitimate object of perception?" He replies,

> III. In the case of a hare's horn, &c. the validity of their perception would imply defective means thereof; but if these be present, perception would ensue, and if there be no perception, there can be no such means.

Non-perception can prove the non-existence of a thing only where it is the so-called 'valid non-perception;' otherwise we should have to concede the non-existence of all such things as are beyond the reach of the senses.—'Valid non-perception' means the presence of all the various means of perception, other than the thing itself [which is supposed to be absent] or the attributes [as form &c.] inseparably connected with it. Hence if we allowed that in the case of the [nonexistent] hare's horn there was valid non-perception, this non-perception must be accompanied by a set of means connected with certain defects* [like a jaundiced eye &c.; as this *is* 'the presence of the various means of perception other than the thing itself or its inseparable attributes.'] But this is unallowable, as in such cases a perception [however erroneous, as of a really white shell appearing yellow,] would ensue; and if perception does not ensue, it proves that it is not a case of valid non-perception.

IV. Here the atheistic Sánkhya will interpose, "why not say that the soul is in some respects ignorant, and that the earth, &c., do not prove creative power to reside therein from the very fact of its having the nature of soul?" He replies,

> IV. If you mean the well-known soul, our point is gained, if the unknown, your reason is unproved; the general consent brings the same result, and in the case of the class it equally holds.

If you mean by soul the well-known mundane individual soul, we are quite willing to grant what you say; but if you mean the unknown, *i. e.* the Lord, your reason is unproved [as we may dispute that 'the nature of soul' resides in God]. If you reply that all allow that the subject (soul) has the nature of soul, then, according as you decide the alternative—is this 'soul' of yours similar to our *jívátmá* or different, —we shall accept your argument as proving our own point, or meet you by denying your proposed reason [or middle term]. The last clause of the verse meets the reply "let the *species*, soul, be our subject,"— because in this case too "it equally holds." We agree with you so far as that it is not the *species* that is the maker of the world [but an individual Supreme Soul;] still as the 'nature of soul' [*i. e.* the idea or species] does not abide in the species itself [but in the individuals] we still deny your middle.

---

* To understand this, we must remember that the means of perception are twofold,—those connected with the object, *i. e.* producing right impressions, and those connected with a defect in the senses (as jaundice &c.) *i. e.* producing wrong impressions. The non-existent hare's horn cannot be a case of the former, as it is invisible; nor can it be a case of the latter as this would necessitate some perception, however erroneous.—I have followed the Pandits in taking *yogyánupalabdhi* as a *karmadháraya-samása*, but it would make this passage easier, if we could take it here as a *shashṭi-tatpurusha*, i. e. as equal to *yogyasyánupalabdhi.*

V. " But why not say [with the Vedántin] that the absence of creative agency is to be proved of that soul which is established by the S'ruti, &c. ?" He replies,

> V. If the S'ruti, &c. have authority, your negative argument is precluded; if they are fallacious, our old 'baseless inference' [of §. i.] is stronger than ever.

If you admit that the S'ruti, &c. have authority, then, as the existence of God's creative agency &c. is thereby established, your argument to prove their non-existence is already precluded. On the other hand, if they have no authority, our old difficulty of a 'baseless inference' returns in full force [as the minor term, soul, in which the middle 'the nature of soul' was to reside, is itself unproved].

VI. Here the Chárvákas step in, " why talk of such a thing as 'valid non-perception?' [§. iii.] let us lay it down as a rule that whatever is not perceived, does not exist, and hence let the mere absence of perception be a sufficient proof of a thing's non-existence. As for this rule of ours overthrowing all inference, we are perfectly content to have it so, and we grant at once that, on the perception of smoke, to conclude that fire accompanies it is mere supposition." He replies,

> VI. There is no doubt in seeing or not seeing, since the existence or non-existence of the thing is ascertained; even perception becomes impossible, if its cause is precluded by its not being seen.

a. [We reply that 'supposition' will not explain men's inferring fire from smoke, for] Supposition is " doubt;" but this does not exist in the case of seeing, as the thing seen is then ascertained; nor does it exist in the case of not seeing, as the absence of the thing is then, in your opinion, concluded. *b.* If the eye &c., the causes of perception, are precluded as causes by the fact that they are not themselves objects of perception, there will not be even such a cause of knowledge as your perception; but if you grant that these exist even at the very time when they are not perceived, your argument proves too much, and therefore the mere fact of a thing's not being seen does not necessitate its non-existence. *c.* And again a Chárváka, when he leaves his house, ought to bewail as being well assured that his wife and children have ceased to exist; and even on his return he ought not to find his family there, otherwise the mere fact of 'not seeing,' as it proves too much, would be no longer a valid reason, [and he should hold like a true philosopher 'amica uxor, magis tamen amica veritas'].

VII. "But if non-perception be not a proof of non-existence, then would it not follow that a universal proposition can never be determined, as there will always be the fear of some condition at present unseen, and hence an ever recurring fear of some instance of smoke unattended by fire? and if so, what becomes of inference?" He replies,

VII. If there be doubt, there is inference; still more if there be no doubt. Discussion is allowed by all to stop fears, since fear is limited by direct inconsistency.

If, after being assured that in the present instances before us [i. e. this smoke and fire,] there is no false assumption of connection, you go on to fear that there may be such in similar instances in another time and place, this very supposition of another time and place comes from inference; hence inference is proved. If there is no such fear, then, in the absence of any fear of the contrary, inference is all the more established. If you ask "what is to stop this fear?" it is replied that this fear is precluded by a discussion to stop any opposite instances. "But have we not here the fault of an 'in infinitum regressus,' since this discussion is itself based on an universal proposition [i. e. the major premiss in which the middle term is declared to be invariably connected with the major?]" he replies 'fear is limited by direct inconsistency;' there cannot be any doubt regarding the major premiss on which the discussion is based, when this doubt would contradict some acknowledged principle. Thus supposing that a doubt should arise as to whether the effect might not be produced without any assumed cause,—it would of course follow, if this doubt were legitimate, that we should not seek food to satisfy hunger or employ words to produce an impression on the hearer's mind, [as these and other similar effects could arise without their causes being employed;] and therefore a limiting condition which is only suggested by an unsupported doubt, is of no validity where there is no discussion to back it. This has been thus expressed by a logician, "so long as there is reason to fear even the hundredth particle of a connection between the middle term and some opposite instance [*i. e.* one which, though it contains the middle, does not contain the major term, as the redhot iron ball in the argument 'the mountain has smoke because it has fire,'] how can the middle term have any power to convince ?" Now the fear of a too general assumption of connection depends on the fear of there being some limiting condition to be supplied ; as has been said, " some reasons [*i. e.* middle terms which are too general, as ' fire' to prove the existence of smoke,] are dependent on universal connections supplied by others [as that between smoke and ' fire produced by wet fuel ;'] these too general reasons, even when seen to be present, do not establish the conviction of the major term." Thus the universal connection with the major term, which exists in a middle term that is limited by a 'condition,'* is cognized as included in the former middle term [as fire] distinguished by the determining notion necessary to define its relation as a middle term [*sc.* the species fire,†] hence it may be said to transfer its own attribute of universal connection with the major term to the old middle term which is, as it were, in juxta-position with it and abides in the same subjects ; and therefore the word *upádhi*, here used for ' the condition,' is used by us in the same sense as when it signifies [with the Vedántins] the China rose which transfers its own redness to the colourless crystal. These too general middle terms, even when they are actually perceived to exist in the subject, do not produce certainty as to the existence of the major term, since the too general attribute [the possession of fire] creates a doubt as to the desired major [smoke.]

VIII. [Thus far for Inference; the opponent, however, may still retort,] " But may we not say that Comparison (*Upamána*) precludes the existence of God ?‡" Now the Vais'eshikas reply that it does not preclude, inasmuch as they do not allow that Comparison is a distinct species of proof [as it is included under inference,

---

* As *e. g.* fire produced by wet fuel.
† See note on *Avachhedaka*, p. 26.
‡ *Upamána* is the knowledge of a resemblance, which produces an inference consisting in the knowledge of the relation of a name to something so named. Thus a man is told that a *gavaya* (bos gavæus) is like a cow, and on seeing the animal in the forest he infers that this is what was meant by the word *gavaya*. Similarly here we have the inference " whatever is like the individual soul is not omniscient nor omnipotent, and this being which is like the individual soul is what is meant by the word God."

See Nyáya Sútras, ii. 46-48]. Here the Mímánsakas come in and maintain, that Comparison is that proof which gives us the knowledge of a separate category called Likeness. They reason as follows, —*a*. Likeness cannot be a *substance* or a *quality* or an *action*, because it is found residing by intimate relation in qualities [and substance cannot thus reside in qualities, nor can a quality or action thus reside in another quality or action.*] *b*. It cannot be *community* [or genus,] because it depends on its correlative [*i. e*. the other thing with which the first is compared,]† and also because it may reside in genera,‡ &c. [as we may say 'the genus of cow is, like that of horse, eternal.] *c*. Nor can it be *non-existence*, since it is not cognized in its relation to the counterentity.§ *d*. Moreover, likeness is not known through *perception*, since it is not cognized by a simple exercise of our senses [but requires some thought and consideration ;] nor can you say that the senses may give us the knowledge of it, when there is the contemporary knowledge of the correlative,—because, after the cognition that the bos gavæus is like a cow, we may also have the cognition that that cow is like a bos gavæus, but this latter cognition cannot be produced by perception as the cow is supposed to be out of sight. *e*. Nor can the knowledge of Likeness be produced by *inference*, since it is produced even in the absence of any sign [or middle term].‖ *f*. Nor can it be produced by *testimony*, since this is not present everywhere¶—To meet this theory (of Likeness being a separate category,) he replies in this and the following couplets *in the character of a Vais'eshika.*

* Cf. Bháshá Parichchheda, s'l. 13. and Siddhánta Mukt. p. 4.

† Likeness is not identity—it implies the existence of points of difference.

‡ Community or genus resides in the first three categories only. I may add here that the Nyáya does not recognize our subordination of genera and species. The genus is not superior to, but co-ordinate with, the species. Thus *a'swatwa* and *sattá* both abide in *as'wa*, but *sattá* also abides with *ghaṭatwa* in *ghaṭa* and with *s'uklatwa* in *s'ukla*. Hence *sattá* is called *para*, and the others *apara*.

§ Resemblance implies the correlative, but not the opposite, as absence does, *e. g*. 'the absence of a jar,' where the knowledge of the absence depends on the knowledge of a jar.

‖ The supposed inference would be "That cow is like the bos gavæus, because the former is the correlative to the likeness residing in this latter." But the knowledge called *upamiti* may be found when this middle term is not explicitly recognized.

¶ The information was to the effect that the bos gavæus is something like a cow; and the man's subsequent inference is in a different form, viz. 'that cow is like a gavaya.'

VIII. In the case of contradictories, there can be no middle course; nor can you assume the two contradictories to be identical, because the fact of their contradiction is directly asserted.

"There can be no middle course,*" *i. e.* you cannot make some third supposition different from either, from the very fact that they *are* contradictories [and therefore the one or the other must be true]; nor can you assume them to be identical. The word 'contradictories' in the second line is an instance of the so-called *hetu-garbha-vis'eshaṇa*, or attribute which contains an implicit reason,† [*i. e.* this very word shows why you cannot assume them to be identical.] When you say 'it is not non-existence,' we know that it must be existence, and when you say 'it is not existence,' we know that it must be 'non-existence.' The whole purport of this is as follows,—Likeness must be either existence or non-existence,‡ since no one knows of any third alternative. If the latter, then it at once falls under *non-existence*, the seventh category [of the Vais'eshikas] If the former, then, *a.* if it possess qualities, it must be under the category of *substance*; *b.* should it not possess them, but possess genus, and be other than a quality, it must be under *action*; and *c.* should it be other than an action, it must be under *quality*. *d.* Should it be without qualities and genus, but not itself reside by intimate relation, it must be under the category of *intimate relation*; *e.* should it be found residing in intimate relation and that too in many subjects, it must be under the category of *genus*; *f.* but if found residing in only one subject, it must be the (vais'eshika) category of *particularity*.— In the same way we may refute the supposition of such additional categories as Capacity, Number, &c.

IX. "But why should not Likeness be only a common property, and Comparison be that proof which produces the cognition thereof?"§ He replies,

* We have here our 'excluded middle.'

† In this it differs from the *swarúpa vis'eshaṇa*, which is simply descriptive and nothing more. Cf. the *kávyalinga* in Rhetoric (Sahitya Darp. X. §. 710).

‡ What follows can only be understood by a reader acquainted with the seven Categories of the Vais'eshikas (Cf. Dr. Roer's translation of the Bháshá Parichchheda, pp. 1—8.)

§ This was the view of the Vedántins (see Vedánta paribháshá, iii.) according to which the *instrument*, in knowledge derived from comparison, was the cognition that 'this animal is like a cow,' and the *conclusion* was that 'the cow is like this bos gavæus.' It is refuted by the supposed Vais'eshika.

IX. As Likeness, so too Unlikeness; and so a new proof would be required. If you answer, 'the latter is only a case of Presumption,' then why not say the same of the former?

After the cognition, 'this (camel) is unlike a cow,' you must suppose another cognition, 'that cow is unlike this (camel,') which must, on your view, be produced by a new proof [*i. e.* a fifth].—" No, this clearly arises from the process called Presumption,* as you cannot have in *this* thing unlikeness to *that* without also having in *that* thing unlikeness to *this*." But the same process will equally apply in the former case, as you cannot have in the bos gavæus likeness to the cow without also having in the cow likeness to the bos gavæus. So that there is no need to accept a new proof (Comparison) which is to produce a knowledge of Likeness.

X. [Thus far the Vais'eshikas, whose opinion we Naiya'yikas accept so far as it overthrows our common antagonists, the Mím'ansakas; but as they have gone further and have attempted to overthrow the existence of this assumed proof,] the Naiy'ayikas here step forward in defence of the impugned proof, Comparison.

X. They hold that the knowledge of the connection of a name with the thing named is the result of Comparison,† since it cannot arise from Perception, &c.

The 'knowledge' or ascertainment of the 'connection'—*i. e.* power or meaning,—of the 'name,' as bos gavæus, with the 'thing named' *i. e.* the animal distinguished by the species bos gavæus, is the result of the particular kind of proof called Comparison; 'since it cannot arise from Perception, &c.' as the several causes of those other proofs, *i. e.* the senses, sign (or middle term,) and testimony have no power to produce it.

XI. "But why may there not be a knowledge of the word's

---

* "Presumption is deduction of a matter from that which could not else be. It is assumption of a thing not itself perceived but necessarily implied by another which is seen, heard or proved." (Colebrooke)—See Siddhánta Muktávali, p. 128. The Mímánsakas make this a separate proof, but the Naiyáyakas make it only a particular kind of inference, corresponding to our disjunctive Hypothetical Syllogism (see Bháshá P. s'l. 143.)

† This is the Naiyáyika view of Upamána, cf. Nyáya sútrás, i. 6, and Tarka Sangraha, §. 68.

meaning from* the information previously given, that an animal like a cow is what is meant by the word *gavaya;* or from the inference drawn therefrom, that an animal distinguished by the species *gavayatwa* is what is meant by the word *gavaya* from the very fact of likeness to a cow?" He replies,

> XI. Since mere Likeness cannot be the determining attribute, and since *the* determining attribute is not then known, the definite meaning [fixed by the will of God or by human convention,] cannot be made known by testimony or inference previously [to seeing the *gavaya* itself.]

The 'definite meaning' means here the connection [between the name and the thing named] in the form of the word's power as determined by the species *gavayatwa*.† This cannot be obtained from testimony or inference, as the man previously [to seeing the actual *gavaya* in the forest] had not any idea of the true species of the animal.‡ Nor can you assume that the mere idea of likeness can be the determining notion to fix the word's meaning, as it is too vague to possess such an authority.

XII. "But why not say that even although, on first hearing the information given, there is no knowledge of the species bos gavæus, yet when the species is known by perception, then from the information 'a thing like a cow is what is meant by bos gavæus,'—which by metonymy comes to mean the species,—we may gain the knowledge of the meaning of the word in that form [by testimony and not by comparison?"] He replies,

> XII. The sentence, having already logical connection, is complete and seeks nothing further; we only need connection with an implied meaning, where the existing connection of the meanings of the words is incomplete.

When the verbal testimony has produced the knowledge of what is

---

* The opponent endeavours to shew that this knowledge can be accounted for by testimony or inference, without assuming such a new proof as Comparison.

† The Nyáya holds that a word does not properly mean a species or an individual, but an individual as distinguished by such and such a species; thus the species is the determining notion by which the word can mean any individual of the species. See S. Muktávali, pp. 82, 83.

‡ At first he only knew vaguely that the word *gavaya* meant a something like a cow; but he did not know the actual species of the animal, its peculiar attributes, form, &c., until he had positively seen it.

meant by the word *gavaya*, from its being applicable wherever the attribute 'likeness to a cow is found,'—it has no further tendency [or *nisus*] to produce any verbal knowledge of the species, because its logical connection is already complete. For it is only where the primary meanings of the words are deficient in their logical connection,—*i. e.* are in any way incompatible with one another,—that we have to search for a connection with some other meaning produced by metonymy, as in the stock example 'a herd station on the Ganges,' [where the word Ganges, primarily meaning a 'river,' by metonymy means the 'bank].'

"But may we not say that the generic argument* "the word *gavaya* is possessed of that which causes direct significance, because it is a word properly formed according to the rules of grammar,"—as we can disprove any other assumed cause of direct significance,—will ultimately, by exhaustion, necessitate our accepting the species *gavayatwa* as the cause of the word's direct significance?" We reply, no, because your major term in the conclusion cannot have any other form than that which it had in the major premiss.† Nor can you say that "the word *gavaya* is possessed of *gavayatwa* as the cause of its direct significance, because it *has* some such cause and all other causes are severally precluded," because such a negative argument is not valid, as your proposed major term is not current, [*i. e.* your major term "possessed of gavayatwa &c." is only applicable to this one word, and is therefore not a '*major*' term at all.] And again, the cognition that "the abode of *gavayatwa* is what is meant by the word *gavaya*" is established by consciousness as actually experienced, even in the absence of any negative inference; and hence we are compelled to assume a special proof for it, viz., *upamána* or Comparison. [As for any attempt, as in § ix., to establish a separate proof from unlikeness, we reply,—] After understanding the meaning of such a sentence as 'Shame on the camel with its extraordinarily long neck and eating the hardest thorns, the outcast of beasts,'‡ the cognizing, on seeing such an animal, that this was what

---

* For this and the other two kinds of *anumána* see Nyáya Sútras I. 5. It is defined by the Commentator as "that which is recognised from generic properties, its own specific ones being unnoticed."

† If from premisses which established that wherever smoke was, fire was, and that the mountain had smoke, we inferred by exhaustion that the mountain had the fire peculiar to mountains and not culinary or digestive fire, this would be an improper inference; and, similarly, here we cannot infer that, because the word *gavaya* is possessed of that which causes direct significance, it therefore must be possessed of *gavayatwa* as that cause.

‡ Cf. Nyáya Sútra Vritti, i. 6.

was meant by the word 'camel' is also produced by Comparison, [which is equally the recognition of likeness or unlikeness.]—Our conclusion is that Comparison, which properly only ascertains the direct significance of a word [and has nothing to do with establishing the object's existence or non-existence,] cannot preclude the existence of God.

XIII. [We now proceed to examine the fourth proof, *i. e.* Testimony;—and here] the Vais'eshikas at once assert that there is no need to fear lest Testimony should preclude the existence of a Supreme Being, as this supposed proof is not different from Inference, [and has therefore been already discussed.] On hearing the words spoken and consequently recollecting their meanings, an inference arises, [they say,] to establish a logical connection between these meanings,*—this inference being in the one or the other of the two following forms,—*a.* "These meanings of words are mutually connected from the very fact that they are brought to recollection by the aid of words which possess expectancy, compatibility, and juxtaposition,† just as in the special case of the meanings brought to our recollection by the aid of the words, 'drive the cow with the stick';" or *b.* "these words must have been preceded by the speaker's right cognition of the connection between the several meanings which these words respectively call to our recollection,—from the very fact that they are words possessing expectancy, &c.;"—the latter inference establishing the hearer's knowledge of the connection, from the general rule that 'the cognition of a cognition must have the same object as the original cognition,' [and therefore when I know that such and such was the speaker's meaning, my knowledge must have the same object as his, and consequently no such *pramáṇa* as 'testimony' or *s'abda* is needed.]—He replies,

XIII. If your alleged inference implies certainty, it involves too much; if only possibility, there is no ascertain-

---

* *S'ábda-bodha* is often called *anvaya-bodha, sc.* the knowledge of a logical connection between the meanings of the words. There is a current definition, एकपदार्थेऽपरपदार्थस्यान्वयबोधः शाब्दबोधः ।

† "Expectancy means a word's incapacity to convey a complete meaning without some other word to complete the construction. Compatibility consists in a word's not having a meaning incompatible with that of other words in the sentence. Juxtaposition consists in the enunciation of the words without a long pause between them." Dr. Ballantyne's Tarka Sangraha, § 71.

ment; expectancy is a cause [of Verbal knowledge] by its very presence; juxtaposition, if accompanied by compatibility alone, is unrestricted.

a. In the case of the former inference where the subject is the 'meanings of words,'—we must mean the conclusion to be either that they are *certainly* mutually connected or that they are *possibly* connected, *i. e.* possess a capability of being connected.*

The former alternative involves too much, as it would apply in such phrases as ' he sprinkles with water,' [which would not hold in the case of water in the form of ice;]—under the second, there is no ascertainment of connection at all, and there is also the fault of superfluous inference, as your conclusion, *i. e.* ' possessing capability of being mutually connected,' is already included in your alleged reason ' from the very fact that they are brought to recollection by the aid of words which possess compatibility, &c.'—as the ' compatibility' there mentioned only means that they indirectly possess a character† which necessitates a logical connection between their meanings.

b. As for the second inference, ' Expectancy' is properly the mind's inquiry after certain additional meanings, which are supplied by words suggested by the construction,—as, e. g. on hearing the word *cyathum* the mind goes in search of a fresh meaning supplied by a suggested *affer* or *vide*, and on hearing the word *affer*, it similarly supplies *cyathum* or *vestem*; Expectancy is therefore a cause of verbal knowledge by its very presence, [i. e. whether it is definitely known or not; but if it were to be included in the middle term of your inference, it must be actually known in order to be so included].

c. " But why may we not say that the cause of verbal knowledge is juxtaposition together with compatibility, [thus excluding expectancy?]"—He replies that they are ' unrestricted,' i. e. they are not limited by any ' universal connection' with verbal knowledge‡ [and are therefore useless to produce a conclusion.] Thus in such a sentence as *hic adest filius regis homines summoveantur*,' the words *regis* and *homines* possess compatibility and juxtaposition, and would therefore,

---

* Similarly a cause *(Kárana)* is said to be *swarúpa-yogya* and *phalopadháyaka*, —in the former case it exists δυνάμει, in the latter ἐνεργείᾳ.

† *Payastwa* resides directly in the *padártha* but indirectly in the *pada*.

‡ *Scil.* they may be found present where *it* is absent, as fire is found without smoke.

according to your view, possess a logical connection and produce verbal knowledge, although there is no expectancy, [as the sense is already satisfied by the logical connection between *filius* and *regis*].

XIV. But here the Prábhákaras* come in and say, " Testimony can be a source of right knowledge in the case of the Veda, as the Veda is not made by man and consequently there can be no inference to establish the speaker's knowledge; but in secular matters there is required a previous knowledge, viz., that the testimony is given by a reliable [*i. e.* worthy, *ápta,*] speaker. And thus we have first such an argument as ' this speaker possesses a correct knowledge of the meaning of the sentence which he uses, because he uses a sentence produced by a knowledge of its meaning which knowledge does not arise from mistake, &c.,' [sc. he himself knows, and speaks to inform *me ;*] and this argument will establish the sentence's meaning *indirectly*, as being the distinguishing characteristic of the speaker's knowledge. We may next proceed to use a second argument, [having previously by the former one established that the speaker's knowledge *is* correct,] viz., ' these meanings of the separate words are mutually connected, because they are the object of the speaker's correct knowledge,' and thus *directly* establish the meaning of the sentence. In this way, *i. e.* only after these two arguments, does the knowledge of the connection of words [*i. e.* the knowledge produced by testimony,] arise from words whose meaning is previously fixed by compact; and hence testimony in secular matters is only a repetition [of what is previously known,] and consequently not itself a source of right knowledge at all.† To meet this, he replies,

XIV. Since the meaning is already ascertained, before the inference, from the words whose signification has been ascertained, it is the middle term of your inference which will be a repetition, since the recollection of a universal proposition implies delay.

Even in secular cases the meaning of the sentence is ascertained previously to any supposed inference, since the meaning of the words has

---

* The Prábhákaras are the followers of the great Mímánsaka doctor, Prabhákara. He is also called the Guru in contradistinction to the Bhatta, i. e. Bhatta Kumárila.

† The Prábhákaras define right knowledge as *agrihíta-gráhakatwam* ' the apprehending something previously not apprehended'—see the fourth chapter.

been already determined in the Veda [as you yourselves admit ;] and therefore it is your middle term which is obnoxious to the charge of superfluous repetition, since inference must always produce a slower cognition than testimony, as the former is unavoidably impeded through the delay involved in recollecting the necessary universal connection (*vyápti*).

XV. " But since knowledge produced by testimony is out of the question, where there is any doubt as to the speaker's being reliable and still more where it is certain that he is *not*,—why should we not hold that the ascertainment of this point is the real cause of such knowledge,—and a thing's being spoken by a reliable speaker will mean that it is produced by an accurate knowledge, in the speaker, of the original meaning of the sentence ?—thus the knowledge of the meaning of the sentence must originally be derived from inference." He replies,

> XV. . Since even *there* we must establish our point by an inference,—' these Vaidic meanings are mutually connected from their being brought to our remembrance by words which are themselves free from any imputation of defects incident to a human being',—how can even the Veda itself be cleared from *that* ?

There is no evidence to prove that the ascertainment of the speaker's being reliable is a cause of verbal knowledge ; [a truer cause is the one generally admitted to be a concurrent to S'abda, viz., the ascertainment of compatibility between the words used,] since in an incompatible sentence we see the knowledge of the connection [*i. e.* the so-called verbal knowledge,] stopped in consequence of the knowledge of the compatibility—*i. e.* the absence of any manifest contradiction,—being retarded [and hence the two seem related as cause and effect.]* If not, then, in the case of the Veda, let the knowledge of its being unproduced by a person, be the cause of verbal knowledge; and as we shall thus have the connection between even the Vaidic meanings established by an inference such as this,—'these

---

* This will no doubt require an inference, but this inference will not establish the S'ábdabodha but only clear away any apprehended contradictions and leave the way open to the proper cause *S'abda-jnána*. The inference is only a negative, the *S'abda-jnána* is the positive, cause.—I may add that this discussion on S'abda is one of the obscurest parts of the book. The old printed text was here very corrupt, and that now given is from the two old MSS. mentioned in the preface.

Vaidic meanings are mutually connected from their being brought to our remembrance by words which are themselves free from any imputation of defects incident to a human being,'—how can we clear the Veda itself from 'that,' *i. e.* the old charge of superfluous repetition?

Some, however, have said that "it is not the *word* but the *word's meaning* which is the instrumental cause of verbal knowledge,—hence we can understand written poetry, &c., because the knowledge of the meaning of the sentence is produced by the meanings of the words [although the words are here not spoken*]. [It might be said in objection that, if this were true, the accusative *dwáram* 'januam' ought to produce verbal knowledge by itself; but to this we should reply that] even though we grant the knowledge of 'janua,' there can be no knowledge of connection, *i. e.* verbal knowledge, in the absence of the quality of 'expectancy'† which necessarily resides in the word's meaning,‡ according to the rule 'verbal expectancy is fulfilled by words alone.'§ In this way we should refute the opinion of the Guru Mímánsakas, viz., that 'the meanings of words are [not the cause of verbal knowledge but] only the distinguishing mark of the phrase 'knowledge of *the meaning of the word*,' since without the knowledge produced by words there cannot be the knowledge of the connection of the meanings of words,‖ as has been said, "from their coming first, from their power of conveying a meaning, and from their conveying the speaker's intention, the power of causation must pre-eminently be held to reside in words."' This opinion we repeat, is overthrown,—because, if we only substitute 'reliable speakers' *(áptánám)* in the s'loka quoted, for 'words' *(padánám)*, we see directly that the 'being spoken by a reliable speaker' is only a distinguishing mark of the phrase, 'the knowledge of its being spoken by a reliable speaker;'¶ and since the knowledge of the word's meaning must be granted, the word *per se* is a superfluous, and not a true, cause."—This

* *Pada* means a word spoken, cf. S. Muktávalí, p. 78.
† See Ballantyne's transl. Sáhitya Darpaṇa, p. 14.
‡ In written poetry none of the words are properly *padas* and therefore there can be *anvaya* and *ákánkshá* between them; but not so between one spoken word as *januam* and another not spoken as the understood *claude*.
§ In written poetry it is *árthikákánkshá*.
‖ That is, according to the Guru, there is a series, 1, the *pada*, 2, the *padárthopasthiti*, 3, *S'ábdabodha*, but the first is the true cause of the third.
¶ That is, the supposed series will be, 1, *ápta*, 2, *áptoktatwajnána*, 3, *S'ábdabodha*; but all allow that *ápta* is not the cause of verbal knowledge but only of the spoken words. Similarly *pada* cannot be the true cause in the former series.

laboured exposition is, however, mistaken, since the meanings of words cannot be the cause of verbal knowledge, from the very fact that they may apply to past or future as well as to what is actually present; nor can we say that the recollection of the word's meaning is an instrumental cause, since it has no operation (*vyápára*).* The true instrumental cause is the knowledge of the word [produced by hearing,] and its accompanying operation is the recollection of the word's meaning—[these directly and indirectly producing verbal knowledge.] In the objected case of written poetry, &c., the instrumental cause of verbal knowledge is a mental knowledge of the word, [its corresponding operation remaining still the same, *i. e.* the recollection of the word's meaning].

XVI. [Having thus established the fact that testimony is a separate proof against the Vais'eshikas in § xiii. and having overthrown the wrong notions of the proof as held by the Mímánsakas in §§ xiv. and xv., he now proceeds to shew that this proof cannot preclude the existence of a Supreme Being.]

"Well, then, let us concede that Testimony is a distinct kind of Proof; but why should it not preclude God's agency as a Maker?† Thus we read in the Bhagavad Gítá "Though actions are ever done by the qualities of Nature, the soul, blinded by egoism, thinks 'I am the doer.'" 'Nature' means here the principle, Intellect,—the 'qualities' goodness, &c.; the soul thinks through delusion that itself does the actions done by these. Hence agency is imaginary, not real. But in the case of an omniscient Being there could be no such imagination, since He would see every thing as it really is.—For the grammar of the couplet quoted, we make *Kartá* govern the accusative instead of the genitive, in accordance with the rule in Pániṇi (ii. 3. 69.)" He replies,

XVI. The testimony of an unworthy person has no force of proof; there can be no 'worthiness' in the case of a thing not seen [by the speaker]. We must have an omniscient Being to see the invisible, and an eternal Veda is untenable.

---

* The Naiyáyikas maintain, against the Vedántins, that every *Karaṇa* must have a *vyápára*,—for the latter's definition, see supra p. 13, note.

† In which case it would preclude his existence, as the Naiyáyikas only accept a Supreme Being as a Creator, and not as an Epicurean deity.

If this testimony of the 'Sruti, which you bring forward to establish that God is not the Maker of all things, is the testimony of an unworthy person, it has no authority; if it is the testimony of a worthy person, then one who possesses the knowledge of such transcendental facts *must* possess an eternal and all-embracing knowledge, since all allow that He has no organs, &c.* The eternity of the Veda has been already disproved [in the second cluster;] and therefore the existence of an eternal and omniscient Author of the Veda is established.

XVII. "But if so, then what becomes of those passages of 'Sruti† which declare that there is no such Maker?" He replies,

> XVII. Such passages have more than one meaning, since the S'ruti also declares His existence; they may merely mean that He is unstained [by attributes;] and if the S'ruti declares His existence, it cannot imply the opposite.

These passages, to which you refer, do not necessarily bear only one meaning, *i. e.* His non-existence,—since there are many other passages which establish His existence, as *e. g.* that from the Gítá, "from me all proceeds;" and the two meanings cannot be equally valid, since they are mutually contradictory. If we examine them more closely to decide which alternative is the true one, we shall find that the [apparently] opposing passages really mean only that God is to be contemplated as the Soul void of all special qualities; while the confirmatory passages become the properly authoritative, inasmuch as they are supported by the inference, based on the discussion of the relation of cause and effect, &c., [which will be given in Chapter V.].

XVIII. [Having thus shown that Testimony cannot preclude the existence of God, he next proceeds to examine the supposed fifth Proof of the Vedántins and Púrva Mímánsakas, *i. e.* Presumption or *Arthápatti.*] "But if this Being were omniscient, would He not cause us to act, even without giving us definite instructions [as in the Veda?] —and hence the uselessness of Vaidic instructions, thus involved in your hypothesis, is of itself sufficient to preclude the existence of God.

---

* The &c. includes body, middle term in inference, &c. These causes of knowledge being thus excluded, God's knowledge must be uncaused, and therefore eternal. If any should be inclined to attribute them to God, on him must lie the *onus probandi.*

† E. g. the Rig Veda, *ko addhá veda, &c.*

You cannot say that He does not know how to make men act in a certain way unless He gives them definite instructions,—since this would overthrow His supposed omniscience. This is a case of Presumption,* and Presumption we hold to be a fifth kind of Proof." He replies,

XVIII. Since the absence of the cause involves the absence of the effect, there can be no knowledge without proof; and in the absence of knowledge there can be no action. The same rule will hold even on an atheistic theory of sacrifice.

If there be no cause of knowledge, *(pramána)* there can be no knowledge, *(pramá.)*† since the absence of the cause necessitates that of the effect; and if knowledge be wanting, there can be no action, since action is caused by knowledge. Now, in the present instance, the only cause of knowledge is such a Vaidic injunction as " let him who desires heaven offer the Agnishṭoma sacrifice," &c.,—hence Vaidic instructions are by no means useless. Otherwise [i. e. if you allow the possibility of ceremonial works without an authoritative command (*vidhi*,)] " the same rule will hold even on an atheistic theory of sacrifice" [like that of the Mímánsá ;] as we can similarly prove that the Veda is still useless, since destiny can set men in action without it. But the true view is that Presumption is not a separate kind of Proof.

XIX. This latter view he now proceeds to establish,

XIX. If there were no limitation, there could be no inconsistency,—that which does not limit cannot establish [any absurdity ;] there can be no real contradiction between two equally trustworthy proofs ; and if Presumption were admitted, it would equally apply to the commonest cases of Inference.

a. The well known example of Presumption is—that on ascertaining that the living Devadatta is not in the house, there arises the knowledge that he is out of doors. But in this very instance, if there were no limitation or understood ' universal affirmative connec-

---

* For Colebrooke's definition, see *supra*, p. 40, note.
† *Pramá* here means only *jnána*,—it simply implies a conviction in the agent's mind, whether right or wrong.

tion' *(anvaya-vyápti,)* there could not arise that conviction of absurdity or inconsistency with the premisses which any other conclusion would involve, [which forms the very essence of Presumption; since it is only valid by adding as a suppressed major premiss that the living Devadatta must be either within or out of doors.] " That which does not limit,"—i. e. that which does not invariably accompany the middle term—cannot establish your presumed inconsistency, since this inconsistency is only valid where the absence of the including major term necessarily involves the absence of the included middle.* Hence the recognition of such a threatened inconsistency [as you maintain in this proof of Presumption] can really be resolved into the recognition of a general negative proposition *(vyatireka-vyápti,)* which would necessitate a negative conclusion contrary to the facts.†

b. It has also been maintained that " after the cognition that 'he is somewhere but he is not in the house,' there arises the idea of contradiction, and our proof of Presumption comes in to resolve this apparent contradiction by shewing that the words ' he is somewhere' really mean that he is somewhere *else* than in the house." But this is untenable. For two equally trustworthy evidences‡ cannot be contradictory, because, in such a case, one would necessarily have to give way; but wherever we have such an apparent contradiction, inference will serve to establish that they must relate to different subject matters, as we may reason that an [apparent] contradiction must relate to different subjects from the very fact that it is established by certain proof, for if it did relate to the same subject it would involve an absurdity. If this were not so, you might have such a Presumption as ' smoke will establish the existence of fire,' since without fire it would be absurd, and thus there would be no such proof as the Inference which our opponents allow as well as we. Again, we might have such an apparent contradiction as ' fire is not perceived at the foot of the hill, and yet the seen smoke is a proof that there is fire somewhere,' and we should have to call in the assistance of your Presumption to establish the existence of fire in some other part of the hill. [Nor can

* I. e. The absence of fire (the *vyápaka* in an *anvaya-vyápti*,) necessarily involves the absence of smoke (*vyápya*).

† I. e. His not being out of doors (when he is not within,) is always accompanied by his non-existence.

‡ As *e. g.* the sense-perception that he is not in the house, and the testimony that he is somewhere, drawn from the infallible dictum of astrology that our friend will live a hundred years.

the opponent object to this that "inference *must* still always be granted, as without it the proof that establishes the constant accompaniment of smoke by fire could not establish the conclusion that fire exists in the present case,—because we reply that] even if there were no such thing as inference at all, the proof that establishes* the constant accompaniment of the middle term by the major would still establish the existence of the major term in the present case [i. e. that there is fire in this mountain] by Presumption. Hence the admission of Presumption as a proof would only abolish Inference.

XX. That *Non-perception (Anupalabdhi,)* [which the Vedántins and Púrva Mímánsakas add as a sixth proof or source of right knowledge,] cannot preclude the existence of God, has been already shewn in the first couplet of this chapter; but in reality this is not a distinct kind of proof at all. This he now proceeds to shew,

> XX. From the cognition of non-existence not being mediate—from the senses not being then engrossed in other objects—from its instrumental cause not being cognized,—and from the internal sense having to do with actual entities.

a. All must allow that *that* knowledge is a case of '*perception*,' the cause of which is a non-perception whereof we are ourselves unconscious,†—since that knowledge of an object's non-existence which was produced by a conscious non-perception would be a case of '*inference*,'‡ and all knowledge is produced by the senses which is non-eternal§ and immediate. By its 'not being mediate' we mean that it is 'not caused by knowledge,' [which is the distinctive mark of perception, as contrasted with inference, comparison and testimony.] *b.* The senses are the instrument in the perception of a jar's absence as of its presence, since there is no preferable object to engross their energy,—for assuredly we cannot say that their energy is then engrossed in the perception of the *site*, since the ear can detect the cessation of sound (i. e. its *dwans'ábháva,)* even where there is no

---

* See Bháshá parichchheda, 'sl. 136, o.

† A common definition of perception is 'that knowledge whose cause is not cognized', *ajnáta-káranakam jnánam*, e. g. the sight does not perceive the eye, &c.

‡ The inference is that a jar is not here from the fact that it is not perceived.

§ I. e. *janya*. The Divine *pratyaksha* is of course eternal.

perception of its site, ether,—and the eye can similarly detect the absence of form in the air. *c.* We can also conclude by inference that the knowledge of a thing's absence is produced by the senses,—from its being a knowledge produced by an instrumental cause which is itself not recognized. *d.* Our perception of external objects is universally produced by the mind (or internal sense,) assisted by instrumental causes [as the senses] which are themselves actual entities [and not, like Non-perception, a mere negation]. For these four reasons we conclude that the senses, and not the so-called Non-perception, are the true instrumental cause in the perception of a thing's absence from a given spot.*

XXI. He now adds other reasons for this opinion, as follows.

XXI. It must be the senses, from their power of perceiving the counterentity; from the inseparability of the operation from the cause; from the fact that defects reside in the senses; and from determinate perception.

Our intended conclusion is that the senses are the true instrumental cause in the perception of a thing's absence.

a. "From their power of perceiving the counterentity" to the absence, [*i. e.* the thing said to be absent]. Just as Inference can make known to us a thing's absence as well as its presence, so also can the senses. *b.* "But may we not say that the power of perceiving the counterentity is not a proper reason for your inference, since all causes are of course subject to the condition of 'being free from superfluous causation?'† and in the present case, the senses perceive the site, and are therefore 'superfluous causes' for perceiving the absence in that site,‡ [the perception of the site being the true cause of the perception of the absence]. To this he replies, "from the inseparability of the operation [from the cause]." Thus the senses are not a 'superfluous cause,'—because the perception of the site [which you erroneously take to be the cause] is only the operation *(vyápára)* which invariably accompanies an instrumental cause.§ If this were not so,

---

* Both parties allow that non-existence is an object of perception, but the Vedántins hold that *anupalabdhi* is its proper cause, while the Naiyáyikas hold that the senses are the true instrumental cause and *anupalabdhi* only a concurrent.

† For *upádhi* and *anyathásiddhatwa,* see p. 37, and note, p. 24.

‡ Just as the father of the potter is a superfluous cause for making the jar.

§ The *vyápára* is the *causa causata (taj-janyatwe sati taj-janya-janakah.)*

the eye, &c., would be superfluous instrumental causes in the perception of a thing's existence, in consequence of such an operation as the conjunction of the eye with the object. *c.* We must all allow that an erroneous perception of a thing's absence, [when it is really present,*] arises from a defect in the instrumental cause, and defects reside only in the senses, &c., for non-perception in itself admits of no defect, and the true faults of the senses are such as jaundice, &c. Hence he adds "from the fact that defects reside in the senses." *d.* A determinate perception of the spot of ground and the absence† cannot [according to your opinion] be produced by the senses, because it is a perception of absence or non-existence,—nor can it, on the other hand, be produced by Non-perception, as it partly includes existence [so far as the spot of ground is concerned;]—hence we must accept the senses as the cause of determinate cognition.‡

XXII. [The opponent may, however, raise an objection to our last argument,] *a.* "Why may we not say that Non-perception, [although it does not produce the determinate cognition,] produces the [indeterminate] cognition of the absence of the jar, and then follows the cognition of the spot of ground as possessing the absence of the jar, [which latter cognition is produced by the senses, acting by a transcendental relation called *jnánalakshana*,] just as the transcendental perception by the eye that 'sandal wood is sweet'§ is said to follow the perception of its sweetness by the proper sense, *i. e.* that of smell; and in this way non-perception may be called an instrumental cause as producing the cognition of absence. By examining a determinate perception we are compelled to infer that the object must be first perceived indeterminately and is then subsequently perceived determinately by the senses. *b.* Again, how can we be said to have any proper 'sense-

---

* As when a jaundiced eye does not see a white shell but a yellow one. See *supra*, p. 27, note.

† *I. e.* this spot of ground has the absence of a jar,—see *supra*, p. 20, note.

‡ By the opponent's opinion this particular determinate perception can be produced neither by *indriya* nor by *anupalabdhi*; but according to ours there is no difficulty, as *indriya* is equally the instrumental cause in cases of *bháva* and *abháva*, the difference being that in the former *indriya-sanyoga*, in the latter *anupalabdhi*, is the concurrent.

§ This is the so-called *jnána-lakshaná* which takes place where one sense supplies a perception which is properly given by another. (Cf. Bháshá-parichheda, śl. 64.) It is said to cognize the object (as *sawrabha*,) *per se*, apart from any thing connected with it, and is thus distinguished from the *sámánya-lakshaná* which cognizes all the cognate objects under the form of the species, as definitely perceived in the individual object, *e. g.* all jars past, present, and future, as possessing the species of this jar. Both are transcendental (*alaukika*) perceptions.

perception' of non-existence since it has no direct connection with the senses ? for the only relation which absence could be said to be capable of, i. e. that called the *vis'eshaṇatá sambandha*,* cannot but involve another relation simultaneously existing with it. Hence we must allow that the instrument [in the cognition of *abháva*] cannot but be our unavoidably assumed Non-perception, and not any one of the senses." He replies,

XXII. From the cognition of the distinguishing mark, if such is accepted,—from the superfluousness of the assumed proof, if such is not accepted,—from the 'in infinitum regressus' if we assume another relation; and if you do not accept my view, any other explanation is untenable.

a. Those who hold that the cognition of the 'distinguishing mark,'— i. e. the cognition of the counterentity,†—is the cause of the perception of *abháva*, must also hold that there can never be an indeterminate cognition of *abháva* at all, since we find in this case the means for producing determinate cognition only ;‡ but in the perception of a real object, as a jar, there must be first the indeterminate cognition alone, since at that moment there can be no cognition of the distinguishing mark as distinguishing, [i. e. *ghaṭatwa*] which is the cause of the subsequent determinate cognition. b. But those who hold that we can perceive *abháva* apart from its counterentity, [i. e. without bringing in the idea of any relation between them,] can also allow that we have an indeterminate perception of *abháva*; and as this can be easily derived from the senses like any other case of indeterminate perception, it follows that the supposition of Non-perception as a distinct proof is superfluous.

c. "From the 'in infinitum regressus,' if we assume another relation." The relation called 'the nature of the thing' and not any new

* *Vis'eshaṇatá* means 'the state of being a *vi'seshaṇa* or distinguishing mark or property ;' thus the jar on a given spot is the distinguishing peculiarity of that spot, and there are thus two relations which the jar holds to its site, that of ' distinguishing' (*vis'eshaṇatá*) and that of 'contact' (*sanyoga*). But since in *abháva* there is no such second relation, we have no right to suppose the first. The Naiyáyikas, however, hold that this is really included in the *swarúpa sambandha*, see *supra*, p. 13, note.

† The *avachchheda* or *vis'eshaṇa*, in the phrase *ghaṭábháva*, is of course the counterentity or *pratiyogi*, i. e. *ghaṭa*.

‡ In the indeterminate, you have not as yet the idea of the relation of 'distinguishing' and ' distinguished,'—see p. 21, note.

category, is really the only relation existing between the *abháva* and its site,—since the assumption of such a relation here as a special *vis'eshanatá*,* would certainly lead to an endless succession of relations ;† and hence we must accept such a relation as that called 'the nature of the thing,' [and this being *sui generis* requires no second relation]. [If you ask " how can *abháva* be an object of sense perception at all," we reply,] that its sense-perception is possible because the relation between the eye and its object, which is necessary in every act of perception, is here fulfilled (in the case of an absent jar,) at second hand by the relation between the spot of ground and the said absence, which we call the distinguishing relation.‡

d. If you do not accept my explanation of this *swarúpa* relation between the jar's absence and its site, then it will be extremely difficult to establish any other principle, even on your hypothesis that a proof called Non-perception is an instrumental cause. For to explain more fully,—all allow that no proof or source of right knowledge [and therefore not even your own Non-perception,] can apprehend any thing subsequently which was not originally an object of indeterminate cognition,§ and thus even in inference, &c., we all admit that there must have been some previous indeterminate cognition of fire, &c.,‖ [and therefore there must be an indeterminate cognition of *abháva*, and this can only be caused by the senses alone.] Again, the very phrase, ' a site of ground possessing the jar's *abháva*' compels our opponents to admit some relation between the *abháva* and the site [and this can only be that called *swarúpa*, which we have previously established.]

---

* Understanding by it a separate relation from *swarúpa*.

† I. e. just as the relation of contact requires another relation, i. e. that of intimate relation, so this relation would require a relation to connect it with its related subjects, and so on. The Nyáya holds that *samaváya* and *abháva* abide in their subjects by the *swarúpa sambandha* only.

‡ The spot being distinguished by the absence of the jar, *ghaṭábhávavad bhútalaṃ*. This will be clearer to the reader if he will compare the description in the Siddhánta Muktávali, p. 51, how the eye sees the jar by direct contact, its form by the intimate relation existing between the jar and its qualities, and the form's species (*rúpatwa*) by the intimate relation between that species and the *rúpa*. It may be illustrated algebraically $\left\{ (a+b) + c \right\} + d$.

§ The indeterminate knowledge is neither *pramá* nor *bhrama*, and therefore there is no *pramáṇa* for its production.

‖ Similarly in testimony, before we can understand the sentence *Devadatto gachchhati*, (*i. e. Devadatto gamanakartá asti*), we must have had an indeterminate cognition of *Devadatta* and *gamana*.

XXIII. He thus sums up the substance of the chapter.

XXIII. Paralysed in their power by necessarily looking to His countenance,* the various proofs,—Perception and the rest,—fail even to attain their proper nature,† and the threatened rise of contradiction is utterly crushed down; to Him, then, the one to whom all are subject, who delights in the sportive exercise, unrivalled and independent, of His almighty power,—to Him, the god even of gods, we betake ourselves with our highest faith aroused.

" Paralysed in their power by necessarily looking to His countenance," *i. e.* their force precluded by positive arguments which prove the subject's actual existence. 'He delights in the sportive exercise of his power,' since He is the one primary cause of the absence of pain.‡

---

* They depend on God, as otherwise, by § 2, the inference would be baseless without a subject; and this defect is only removed by the inference itself being overthrown—in other words the *ás'rayásiddhi* is only avoided by *bádha*.

† They cease to be 'proofs' at all.

‡ Cf. the definition of Final Liberation in the Nyáya Sútras, I. 22 as 'absolute deliverance from pain.'

FOURTH CLUSTER.

I. The fourth objection was that even if God did exist, he could not be a cause of right knowledge to us. "God cannot be an authority to us, because he has no right knowledge, as his knowledge lacks the indispensable characteristic of cognizing an object uncognized before;* hence he neither possesses right knowledge himself nor can produce it in us, and who would trust the words of a being who cannot be a cause of right knowledge?" He replies,

> I. Cognizing for the first time is no true mark, as it is both too narrow and too wide; we hold right knowledge to be an independent impression which corresponds to the reality.

Your 'cognizing an object uncognized before' is not an indispensable characteristic mark of right knowledge, as it fails to apply in such an affirmative instance as repeated knowledge [*i. e.* seeing a thing a second or third time], and wrongly applies to such a negative instance as the erroneous judgment that 'this [nacre before me] is silver.' He then gives his own definition in the second line. The ancient Pandits did not apply the term 'right knowledge' to remembrance, because it is necessarily 'dependent,' as it has the same object as the original impression which produced it, and therefore its authoritativeness must stand or fall with that of its originator. Hence he adds the epithet 'independent.'

'II. "*a.* But" (reply the opponents) we may deny that our definition is too narrow as not applying to repeated knowledge. We maintain that cognition must produce a particular quality, [*i. e.* cognizedness,] residing in the object,†—otherwise there would not be

---

* The P. Mímánsá concludes that as God must *always* know, his knowledge would not fall under the definition of 'right knowledge.' They deny that remembrance can be right knowledge; the other schools generally allow that it is a kind of pramá but not independent.

† The Sanskrit reader will observe that this is the opinion of the Bhaṭṭa Mímánsakas in the S. Muktávali, p. 118. They hold that all cognition is super-

in cognition the definite distinguishing of the object, [*i. e.* that this thing is cloth and not a jar;] and hence, even in repeated cognition, we have 'the cognizing of a thing before uncognized,' [since each separate act of cognition on our part produces *anew* this particular influence or quality in the object, and this therefore is ever cognized anew.] *b.* [Again, you would prove the existence of God by the argument that the creation of the world must imply a previous knowledge of the material cause,—*i. e.* the atoms, out of which it was made,—from the very nature of effects, since all effects, as jars, &c., imply such a knowledge; and as this knowledge is not found in individual souls, it must belong to the Supreme Soul. But we would meet this by proposing a dilemma.] When you talk of 'God's knowledge of the world's material cause,' do you allow that this knowledge produces this particular quality of cognizedness in its object or not? If you allow it, then you must also concede a second similar quality of cognizedness, residing in the knowledge itself, in order to distinguish definitely that it *is* the knowledge of the material cause, [*i. e.* to know that he knows it,] and this again will necessitate a third and so on,—thus we have a regressus in infinitum. If you do not allow it, then your alleged reason (or middle term) 'the very nature of effects' fails from being too general,—since in this very instance 'cognizedness' is an effect and yet you own that *it* is not produced by a previous knowledge of the material cause. Hence we cannot admit that the existence of God is proved as the Maker of the world." He replies,

> II. In the absence of the object's real nature to distinguish it, it would be useless to seek help [from cognizedness;] and even supposing that, without this (nature), you might succeed in an existing object, yet what could you do in a non-existing?

The especial nature of the thing is that which definitely distin-

---

sensuous; but after the cognition of a jar there is produced in the jar a quality called cognizedness,—this cognizedness becomes an object of perception in the form 'this jar is cognized by me;' hence I infer the existence of the cognition from its effect, and I also at the same time infer the correctness of the cognition. The Nyáya holds that the three steps, 1, knowledge, 2, consciousness or knowing the knowledge (*anuvyavasáya*,) and 3, the knowledge of its correctness are successive; the Mímánsá holds that the two last are simultaneous and in fact identical.

guishes the object [so that we determine it to be not a jar but cloth;] otherwise there would be no definite distinction, even though your quality of 'cognizedness' had been communicated to it. And again, even although we granted that 'cognizedness' is produced in the case of an existing object, yet it could not arise in the case of a non-existing object, [as *e. g.* a jar now destroyed,] since its material cause, [*i. e.* that object,] would be non-existent; and hence it would follow that here, at any rate, there would be nothing definite to distinguish the object. We therefore conclude that a thing's special nature is that which alone definitely distinguishes it.

III. "But may we not apply the general rule, 'an action must produce some effect on its object,' and hold that the action of cognition similarly produces a quality residing in its object?" He replies,

> III. 'Action' cannot serve you as a reason to prove any new quality [such as 'cognizedness,'] since it is either too general or falsely assumed; nor will perception prove it, since it shews that cognition is itself the distinguishing connection.

a. If you mean by 'action' the signification of the verbal root, then, as in such an instance as 'he unites his arrow to the sky' there is no effect produced by the action on its object the [impassive] sky, your assumed reason is too general. *b.* If you mean by 'action' the operation of the instrumental cause,* then again also your reason will be too general, as no effect is produced on the jars by the contact of the organs of perception therewith. *c.* If you say that 'action' means motion, then, as cognition is not a motion at all, your reason is falsely assumed in the subject.† *d.* "But may we not say that such phrases as 'the jar is cognized,' 'the jar is intuitively known,' &c., shew that perception is the proof of this very quality of cognizedness?" [as 'cognized,' &c., really mean 'possessed of cognizedness,' &c.] He replies by the second line of the s'loka. Wherever you have a de-

---

* Cf. Bháshá P. 'sl. 58. and *supra*, p. 13, note.

† *Swarúpásiddhi* is that fallacy where the assumed middle term is not present in the subject or minor term, as 'the lake has fire, because it has smoke.' In the present case the argument is 'cognition produces an effect on its object from the very fact that it belongs to the class action,' action being defined to mean 'motion.'

finitely distinguished cognition, you have as its object the distinguishing attribute, the thing distinguished, and the connection which exists between them; and this connection may sometimes be that of contact [as in such cases as 'the spot of ground possessing a jar on it;'] in others it may be the connection constituted by the nature of the things connected.* Now just as we see in such [reversed] phrases as 'the cognition of the jar'† [where the jar is that which distinguishes the cognition, and the Mímánsakas allow that their cognizedness only resides in an object and not in the cognition,] that the latter kind of connection is that which exists between the cognition and the jar, so the same connection appears to be found in such phrases as 'the jar is cognized' [where the cognition is that which distinguishes the jar‡]. Otherwise, if this were not the connection, you would have to assume in such cases as 'the jar is desired,' 'the jar is produced,' novel connections such as 'desiredness' and 'producedness.'

IV. [If the opponent reply, "why should we assume these novel connections? The well known *swarúpa-sambandha, i. e.* the connection constituted by the nature of the things, will suffice in these cases;" to meet this] he now proceeds to shew that the *swarúpa-sambandha* will equally serve in the original case of dispute, [*i. e.* the same connection which holds in such cases as 'the jar is made,' 'the jar is desired,' &c., will equally hold in 'the jar is cognized.']

> IV. The cognition is distinguished by its object alone, since the cognitions themselves have no definite form to distinguish them from each other; and in the common phrases about the objects of actions it is the verb which distinguishes.

Just as [in such phrases as 'a cognition of the jar'] we have the knowledge distinguished by its object the jar, [*i. e.* it is *that* which

---

* See note, p. 13.

† Here all agree that the cognition does not reside by intimate connection (as the genus in its individuals,) nor by contact (as the jar on the ground;) and therefore by exhaustion it must be the *vishayatá-sambandha. Ghaṭa-jnánam* therefore means *vishayatayá ghaṭavad jnánam,* and similarly *jnáto ghaṭaḥ* means *vishayatayá jnána-vis'ishṭo ghaṭaḥ.*

‡ The Mímansá holds that *jnátatá* is a quality in the object, the Nyáya that it is a *swarúpa-sambandha* between the *jnána* and the object.

makes this cognition different from other cognitions;] and just as in common phrases about the objects of actions, as jars, &c., we have the particular meaning of the verbal root as that which distinguishes the particular phrase [and thus makes it differ from other similar phrases,]* so too in such alleged cases as 'the jar is cognized,' it is the cognition alone which distinguishes this particular knowledge in regard to the jar, and it is not from any other supposed attribute [as your 'cognizedness'].

V. "May we not, however, still maintain that God's knowledge is not properly 'right knowledge' *(pramá)* since it is not produced by proof *(pramáṇa;)* and therefore God can neither be a right knower *(pramátá)* Himself nor be a cause of right knowledge to us, since the essential conditions for both are absent in Him?" He replies,

> V. Right knowledge is accurate comprehension and right knowing is the possession thereof; authoritativeness is, according to Gotama's school, the being separated from all absence thereof.†

Right knowledge is a notion corresponding to the object; and this is not inconsistent with God's knowledge, even though His knowledge be not produced [but eternal]. 'Right knowing' [*i. e.* the being a right knower,] means the being connected with right knowledge by intimate relation, [*i. e.* that relation which connects a substance and its qualities;‡] and this can be established of God, even though He be not a cause of right knowledge to us. In the same way God is an authority as being Himself ever connected with right knowledge, *i. e.* as being ever 'separated from all absence thereof.' There is no need to include as absolutely necessary in your definition that He must be an instrument of right knowledge to others, since God's authoritativeness is thus declared in the Nyáya Sútras, (II. 68.) "The fact of the Veda being an authority, [*i. e.* an instrument of right knowledge,] like the spells [against poison, &c.,]

---

* Thus in 'a jar is made,' 'a jar is broken, &c.,'—it is the verb which distinguishes the several sentences.

† *I. e.* there may be a partial *pramá* even in a case of error, (thus the jaundiced perception is right as to the *shell*, though wrong as to its colour;) but *prámáṇya* can never be found where there is any, even only a *partial*, absence of *pramá*.

‡ God is *pramáṇa-kartá*, *i. e. pramátá*, but *kartá* must not be taken in its usual meaning (as his knowledge is eternal,) but in that of *ás'raya*.

and the medical science, follows from the authoritativeness of the fit person [who gave it"]. Nor need you object that this will lead to God's being a fifth cause of right knowledge, *(pramána)* and thus our old division of four *pramánas* will be violated,—because our old division will still hold as applying to *instrumental* causes of right knowledge, [and the Veda, our fourth *pramána*, is God's instrument]. Nor need you object that " God's knowledge [if He be omniscient] will embrace error [as well as truth,] and apprehend the objects of error [as well as those of truth,] and therefore will itself be liable to the imputation of error,"—since the nature of right knowledge is not violated so long as the knowledge is not associated with a contradictory object, [*i. e.* so long as I do not apprehend silver in what is not silver but nacre]. Now it is an actual fact that in error there is a definite object, as nacre, and also that it is viewed under the notion of silver; and God's right knowledge cannot be impaired by his apprehending this fact.

VI. He now gives a s'loka recapitulating the purport of the Chapter.

> VI. He, in whose intuitive unerring perception, inseparably united to Him and dependent on no foreign inlets, the succession of all the various existing objects is contained,—all the chaff of our suspicion being swept away by the removal of all possible faults as caused by the slightest want of observation in Him,—He, 'Siva, is my authority; what have I to do with others, darkened as their authority must ever be with rising doubts?

" The succession of all the various existing objects"—*i. e.* all the world is the object of God's perception. " All possible faults," as partiality, aversion, &c. " All the chaff of our suspicion is swept away,"—all our suspicion as to the Veda's want of authority. " Others," *i. e.* heretics.

FIFTH CLUSTER.

I. The fifth objection was 'from the absence of positive proof.' "May we not say that there are no proofs to establish God's existence?" He replies,

    I. From effects, combination, support, &c., traditional arts, authoritativeness, 'Sruti, the sentences thereof, and particular numbers,—an everlasting omniscient Being is to be established.

a. The earth, &c., must have had a maker because they have the nature of 'effects,'* like a jar; by a thing's having a maker we mean that it is produced by some agent who possesses the wish to make, and has also a perceptive knowledge of the material cause out of which it is to be made.† *b.* 'Combination' is an action, and therefore the action which produced the conjunction of two atoms, initiating the binary compound, at the beginning of a creation, must have been accompanied by the volition of an intelligent being, because it has the nature of an action, like the actions of bodies such as ours. *c.* 'Support, &c.' The world depends upon some being who possesses a volition which hinders it from falling, because it has the nature of being supported, like a stick supported by a bird in the air; by being supported we mean the absence of falling in the case of bodies possessing weight. By the '&c.,' we include destruction. Thus the world can be destroyed by a being possessed of volition, because it is destructible, like cloth which is rent. *d.* 'From traditional arts.' *Pada* [which is not used here in its usual sense of 'word,' see *infra* § v.] is derived from the root *pada, i. e.* 'that by

---

* This is proved because the world consists of parts which are arranged in a certain way and are severally produced and destroyed, (see Sarva D. Sangraha, p. 81, last line).

The argument from *Káryatwa* is really the same as that employed by Chalmers (in his Natural Theology,) to rebut Hume's objection to the à posteriori argument on the ground that the world is only a singular effect.

† Cf. Bháshá Parichchheda, § 149.

which something is known,' *i. e.* the traditional arts of mankind. The traditional arts now current, as that of making cloth, &c., must have been originated by an independent being,* from the very fact that they are traditional usages like the tradition of modern modes of writing† [invented by men independently, as systems of short-hand, &c.] *e.* 'From authoritativeness.' The knowledge produced by the Veda is produced by a virtue residing in its cause,‡ because it is right knowledge, just as is the case in the right knowledge produced by perception &c.§ *f.* 'From S'ruti,' *i. e.* the Veda. The Veda must have been produced by a person from its having the nature of a Veda‖ like the Áyur-veda (*i. e.* the *upaveda* so called, treating of medical science) *g.* Again, the Veda must have been produced by a person because it has the nature of 'sentences,' like the Mahábhárata; or, in other words, the sentences of the Veda were produced by a person because they have the nature of sentences, just as the sentences of beings like ourselves. *h.* 'From particular numbers.' The measure of a binary compound is produced by number since it is a derived [*i. e.* not eternal] measure and at the same time is not produced by measure or aggregation,¶ like the measure of a jar composed of three *kapálas* which is larger than that of one composed of two such *kapálas* [and this increase can only be due to *number*, as the *kapálas* in themselves are all equal;] for the

---

* *Swatantratwam* is defined as *asmadíya-vyavaháránádhína-vyavahára-kartritwam*.

† The Hindus hold that the Devanágarí alphabet is of divine, while Bengali, Persian, &c. are of human, origin.—There is a current s'loka of Brihaspati,

वाक्षासिकेऽपि विषये भ्रान्तिः सञ्जायते यतः ।
धानाऽक्षराणि हृष्टानि पञ्चाऋढान्यतः पुरा ॥

‡ See Bháshá P. §§ 130-3. Wrong knowledge or error is produced by a fault in its cause, as jaundice, &c. in the eye; and right knowledge is produced by a guṇa or virtue, (like Aristotle's ὀφθαλμοῦ ἀρετή or βελτίστη ἕξις). This virtue in the case of the Veda is its quality of being uttered by a fit person, *i. e.* one possessing a true knowledge of words and meanings.

§ Some say that the guṇa here is the absence of jaundice, &c., others the direct contact of the organ with a true object.

‖ By Nyáya Sút. ii. 68, we learn that ' that is Veda where the fact of being a cause of right knowledge is admitted.'

¶ Cf. Bháshá P. § 110. The infinitesimality of atoms is eternal.

measure of an atom* does not produce measure because its measure is eternal [and therefore incapable of change] or because it *is* the measure of an atom. Hence at the beginning of a creation there must be the number of duality abiding in the atoms, which is the cause of the measure of the binary compound, but this number cannot be produced at that time by the distinguishing perception of beings like ourselves. Therefore we can only assume this distinguishing faculty as then existing in God.†—By the last words of the text it is meant that it is the Being, possessed of this attribute [of omniscience,] who is everlasting,‡ and hence is established his eternal omniscience.

II. "*a*. But may we not say that inasmuch as only one possessed of a body can be a maker, the existence of God is precluded as the distinguishing attribute of a maker is precluded ? *b*. We have also the contrary syllogism, that we cannot allow the earth, &c. to have been produced by a maker, as there is the absence of the being produced by a body which invariably accompanies the being produced by a maker. *c*. There is also an opposing universal proposition, viz. that only one possessed of a body can be a maker. *d*. By the induction

---

* Ibid. § 14. The atoms of Hindu philosophy, being infinitesimal, would only produce still smaller totalities (like multiplied fractions or added negative quantities) as measure can only produce a further result homogenous with itself. It is the tertiary compound, which, as having finite magnitude (*mahattwa,*) produces measure, just as the jar's measure is caused by that of its two halves.

† To understand this argument, we must remember that the Nyáya holds that all number beyond unity is produced in things by an effort of our mind,—in nature all things exist *singly*, and it is we who combine them into sets of two, three, or more at our pleasure. The first operation is that distinguishing perception called *apekshábuddhi*, by which we say of each thing, ' this is one,' ' this is one,' &c. This produces duality, &c. in the objects, as e. g. in two jars, which duality resides by intimate relation in each of the objects, but resides in *both* by a peculiar connection called *paryápti*—it is this last which gives the idea of "two pots," and not merely that of one pot possessing duality here and another possessing it there. As the binary compound only differs from the atom by number and not by measure or size, (as both are, as far as we are concerned, alike infinitesimal, however one may be really larger than the other,) we must have recourse to the Supreme Being's *apekshábuddhi* to account for the existence of number in the binary compound at the time of creation. The smallest perceptible size is the tertiary compound, consisting of three binary ones. See Colebrooke, i. p. 278. It is singular that the Nyáya should adopt such a conceptualistic view of number, while it yet holds such realistic notions of genus.

‡ There are two kinds of *anvaya* or logical connection, *vis'ishta-vidhayá* and *upalakshaṇa vidhayá*. The former is where the epithet is emphatic and is therefore never disjoined from the subject; the latter is where the emphasis is laid on the subject and the epithet or predicate may be sometimes separated. (Thus Phidias the sculptor is not always actually sculpturing.) In the present case the epithet ' everlasting' belongs to the former class and can never be separated from its subject the Supreme Being as distinguished by the attribute of omniscience, and this attribute is therefore everlasting.

which extends over every case presented by experience [as jars, &c.,] we infer that a maker must have a body, but by the relation existing in the present argument between the minor term earth, &c. and the major term it would appear that the maker is incorporeal [as no maker is in this case perceptible]—hence the possibility of the alleged major term is unproved, and there is also a mutual contradiction between the subject, [maker,] and the attribute ascribed to it, [incorporeal.] *e.* We may also establish the fallacy of a too general middle term by inserting the condition§ " from being produced by a corporeal agent" instead of the old middle " from being an effect." Thus there are five separate fallacies involved by the alleged middle term." He replies,

II. There is no precluding, as this, [our middle term,] is indispensable ; nor are there any valid counterarguments, as those alleged are too weak ; whether our assumed connection be established or overthrown, there is no mutual contradiction ; nor can you have a too general middle term, without any reason for it.

a. Because the possession of a body is precluded in the case of the subject [sc. the Supreme Being,] it does not follow that his possession of the attribute of being a maker is precluded, since ' this,' *i. e.* our middle term (—" having the nature of an effect"—) which necessarily establishes the existence of the subject [as every effect implies a cause] is too powerful to be set aside, as it is this which must undoubtedly be looked to as producing the knowledge of the subject at all, and without the knowledge of the subject, as we have previously proved, [in III. § ii.] it is impossible to establish the knowledge of non-existence. And thus there is no such pretended perception as would preclude the existence of God because his distinguishing attribute as maker is precluded. Nor again is there any such precluding inference as " God cannot be a maker because he has no body," [since in your opinion the very existence of God is unproved, and how then can you discuss his attributes ?]

b. We cannot admit as a valid opposing argument " the earth,

* For *Upádhi,* the condition which must be supplied to restrict a too general middle term, see *supra,* p. 37.

&c. are destitute of a maker because they were not produced by a body," because your middle term is fallacious as assuming too much, since the words 'by a body' are superfluous.*

c. The middle term in our argument, " having the nature of an effect," is more valid than that of the opposite argument [" the earth, &c., are not produced by a maker from their not being produced by a body,"] because ours is supported by its being actually found as an attribute of the minor term [earth, &c.], and there is also an argument to stop any certain negative instance ;† while on the other hand your alleged universal proposition "only one possessed of a body can be a maker," is too weak to stop us [as it is not found as an actual attribute of the minor term and there is moreover no such acknowledged principle.]

d. If by the connection existing between the minor and major terms it be established that the maker is incorporeal, then there is no contradiction, since in that case it is understood that being a maker may coexist with incorporeality ; and, again, if it be not established, then, even in this case, there is no contradiction, [i. e. your alleged fault falls to the ground,] from the want of any subject in which it is to abide.

e. Since there is an argument on our side by which to preclude any certain negative instance, there cannot be here such an inconclusiveness as a mistake as to the major premiss caused by the absence of any such precluding argument, i. e. the fallacy of a too general middle term ; and moreover your pretended ' condition,' "produced by a body"—is itself overthrown by the absence of any argument on *your* side to preclude a negative instance.‡

III. " But may we not bring forward the opposing argument, that ' if God were a maker he would have a body ?' while at the same time there is no argument of equal weight to support your view." He replies,

* The older Naiyáyikas maintained that the argument "the mountain has fire because it has blue smoke" involved the fallacy of vyápyatwásiddhi, because the alleged middle term was unnecessarily restricted. See Siddhánta Muktáv. p. 77. The moderns however more wisely consider it as a harmless error, and they would rather meet b. in the text by asserting that there is no proof to establish the validity of the assumed middle term.

† I. e. wherever you have an effect, you must have a producing cause,—therefore you cannot have an effect without a maker.

‡ There are two readings here विपक्षबाधकाभावेन and विपक्षबाधकावतारेण. If we adopt the latter, it means " by the presence of an argument on our side to preclude a negative instance."

III. Our opponents' arguments, being defective, cannot invalidate our reasoning by their fallaciousness,—while the favourable argument from the abolition of effects tells on our side.

These opposing arguments are 'fallacious' because they are subjectless, so long as the existence of their subject, God, is itself unproved. But the argument "there could not be an effect without a causer," is ' on our side.' There is also S'ruti to prove it, " I am the origin of all, from me all proceeds."* And that S'ruti has pre-eminent force which is supported by reasoning, according to the verse, [of Manu,] " He, and none else, knows religion, who investigates the Veda and the religious teaching of the Ṛishis by means of such reasoning, as is not contrary to the Veda and the S'ástras."

IV. " But how does the fact of a thing's being an effect necessitate that it should have been produced by volition ?" He replies,

IV. If it [the atom] acts independently, it ceases to be brute matter,—desert does not abolish visible causes; if there be no cause there is no effect; a particular effect has a particular cause.

There cannot be an effect without a causer. If the atom were endued with volition it would follow that the atom was intelligent, since an unintelligent thing can produce an effect only when impelled by an intelligent being ; and desert [or fate] can only produce effects by the concurrence of visible causes.† Nor may you say that " the volition of the conscious agent is the cause in effort‡ only and not in all action generally," because even though a particular kind of volition may be the cause in the case of effort, this does not preclude volition generally as the cause of action generally ; otherwise, because a particular seed is the cause of a particular shoot, it would follow that seeds in general [*i. e.* the class, seed] could not be the causes of shoots in general.§

* Bhagavad Gítá, x. 8.
† Otherwise all things would be produced by desert alone, and all other causes would be superfluous.
‡ There is a memorial verse, ज्ञानजन्या भवेदिच्छा इच्छाजन्या भवेत् कृतिः । कृतिजन्या भवेच्चेष्टा चेष्टाजन्या भवेत् क्रिया ॥ *Ichchhá* is *chakírshá*, *kṛiti* is *yatna* or 'volition.'
§ This argument depends on two principles,—*a.* the same relation of cause

V. " But what is the proof that support, &c. (§ i.) are produced by volition ?" He replies,

> V. In this way 'support' and 'destruction' require no limiting condition because they are effects ; and the same thing holds of 'traditional arts' and 'authoritativeness, &c.' through an interruption [of the tradition].

'Support' and 'destruction' do not require any limiting condition [*i. e.* they are not too general middle terms,] because they are produced by volition [*i. e.* inasmuch as they are effects, they involve volition by § iv.]   Since, through the interruption of the tradition,— *i. e.* through a partial destruction of the world [as of one loka,]— there is an absence of all patterns, &c. the succeeding copier cannot himself be the origin of the tradition since he does not know the tradition ; hence is established the existence of some being who, at the beginning of a creation, originated the various traditional arts, as of making jars, &c.* In the same way we may prove that the authoritativeness of the ideas produced by the Veda, &c. are not too general middle terms, [Cf. § xvi. *infra.*]

VI. Or we may interpret the first couplet of this Chapter in the following manner.

a. 'Effect' may mean 'purport' [*i. e.* the 'effect' to be produced on the hearer's mind ;] it has been said that words are authoritative only in reference to their purport, and therefore he is God whose purport is declared in the Veda.

b. 'Combination' may mean 'explanation ;' the Vedas must have been explained by some one who knew their meaning, since their sentences have been received by great saints ; and, if they had not been explained, these saints, not knowing their meaning, would not have fulfilled their injunctions by sacrifice, &c., and if a finite being had explained them, his explanation could not have been relied on.

and effect which exists between particulars exists likewise between their respective classes यद् विशेषयोः कार्यकारणभावस्तत् सामान्ययोरपि and *b.* the general causes only produce their effects when conjoined with the particular causes, सामान्यसामग्रो विशेषसामग्रीसच्चिनैव कार्यं जनयति. Thus Archbishop Whately has made a book on Logic,—man can therefore make logical books ; only in each particular case we require the concurrents, education, leisure, &c.

* See *supra,* p. 28. It is interesting to compare this with Isaiah xxviii. 26. Cf. also the Greek legend of Triptolemus, and Whately's Lectures on Pol. Economy, pp. 79, 84.

c. 'Support' may mean 'preserving the tradition.' The &c. may include 'performance.'

d. The existence of God is also established by the meaning of the 'words' I's'wara, &c.,* as has been said, "Denomination† is purport, the explanation of an all-seeing one is valid; the words I's'wara, &c. must have a meaning in accordance with the custom of mankind." 'Denomination' here implies a particular kind of wish. In the same way in such verses as " I am the origin of all" the word " I" means an independent utterer, since even in secular matters that word alone has authoritativeness which possesses a definite meaning; and in accordance with the rule, "he who knows secular things knows Vaidic also," the same rule holds in a transcendental subject which holds in the case of a secular 'I,' &c.

e. The word *pratyaya* which we formerly rendered 'authoritativeness' may also mean 'affix,' *i. e.* the affix of the imperative implying 'let' [as in 'let him sacrifice;'] the meaning of the command has been defined as 'the will of a fit person;' and *He* whose will it is, is God.‡

VI. Activity is really volition, *(yatna,)* and this springs from the desire to act, and this from knowledge, and the object of this knowledge is a command, or [as we would hold] it is rather that which causes a command to be inferred.

After the knowledge produced by a command arises 'activity;'§ and this activity springs directly from a certain wish, *i. e.* 'the desire to act;' and this desire arises from the 'knowledge' that the thing is to be accomplished by action and that it is the means to obtain the desired end [happiness]; and the object of this knowledge is the fact that the thing is to be done and is a means to our obtaining the desired end, *i. e.* the fact of its being a command. This was the opinion of the ancient Naiyáyikas; but he expresses his

* The &c. includes Om, &c.
† Colebrooke translates *uddes'a* by 'enunciation,'—" the mention of a thing by its name,—that is, by a term signifying it, as taught by revelation; for language is considered to have been revealed to man."
‡ This interpretation of *pratyaya* leads to a long and intricate discussion on *vidhi* which lasts to the end of § xiv. He goes on with his explanation of § i. in § xv.—The first question is, since *vidhi* is *pravartaka vákya*, what is *pravritti*?
§ *Prayatna* is divided into three kinds (Bháshá P. § 148,)—*pravritti, nivritti* and *jivana-káraṇa*, i. e. activity, cessation from activity, and vitality.

own in the last words of the couplet ' or rather it is that which causes a command to be inferred,' *i. e.* the real meaning of the tense affix expressing command is ' the will of a fit person,' which causes the hearer to infer that to act accordingly will be the means to obtain the desired end.

VII. He now proceeds to prove by exhaustion what is the object of that knowledge which causes that wish which produces activity, [*i. e.* he here shews what it is *not*, his own view will be given in § xiv.]

> VII. [The various current notions of the meaning of 'command' are wrong; thus] it cannot be an attribute in the agent, either from improper exclusion and inclusion,—or because activity does not always ensue, —or from the ensuing inconsistency,—or from the non-existence of the action-producing wish,—or from the involved uselessness [as a cause] of the knowledge that such an action is a means,—or from confusion.

a. If you say that an attribute in the agent,—muscular action,—produces 'activity,' [and is therefore the meaning of 'command,'] then it would follow that in such a command as 'let him know the soul' we should properly have no activity at all, while, on the other hand, on hearing such an indicative sentence as 'he goes to the village' we should have activity produced in the hearer. *b.* If you say that the real meaning of 'command' is 'volition,' then follows the fault that activity does not always ensue; since, although volition is also implied by other tense signs than those of the potential and imperative, yet no activity follows if we do not ascertain that it is a means to a desired end, or if we know that it is a means to an undesired end.

c. If you say that 'wish' [*i. e.* the agent's, as in 'let him who desires swarga offer such a sacrifice'] is the proper meaning of 'command,' then you incur the fault of 'inconsistency.' If 'wish' be the meaning of 'command,' then on the one hand the knowledge of the wish [*i. e.* the knowledge of the command] can only be produced by the previously existing wish [as all knowledge depends on the prior existence of its object,]—while on the other hand the wish must be produced by the knowledge of the wish,*—hence you reason in a circle,—which is called in the couplet, 'inconsistency.'

d. But an opponent may reply that 'the abovementioned knowledge of the wish [*i. e.* the mere knowledge of the wish itself as implied in the terms of the command '*swargakámo yajeta*,' this knowledge of the meaning not being accompanied by any *conscious wish* in the person's own mind,] is produced by the tense affix,'†—to this he replies, 'from the non-existence of the action-producing wish.' Even if the knowledge of such a wish be produced, yet no activity will ensue, as there is no such wish present as we defined in § vi. to be the cause of activity, since only such a wish can produce activity as is a cause by its own nature (and not simply from its being *known*),‡ and even on your own shewing there cannot be *such a wish* at the time of hearing the tense affix of the command, but only that knowledge of a wish which is produced by the spoken word. *e.* But it may be replied " is not this very wish produced by the tense affix of the command '*let* him, &c. ?' " he replies, that the universally acknowledged cause, knowledge, will be overthrown. The knowledge that the action enjoined is a means to the desired end, which all accept as the cause of the wish, will be in danger of being overthrown, as the effect will be sometimes produced by the tense affix, even where this acknowledged cause is not found.

f. But some may say that 'the meaning of the command is a wish [for the end] produced in the mind of the agent by a knowledge determined by happiness, &c.§ (as the ultimate fruit to be desired) at the time of hearing the command,'—he replies, 'this will cause confusion.' All allow necessarily that the knowledge that the action is a means to the desired end is the cause of the wish for the means [*i. e.* the required action of sacrifice,] and as there is no other cause for

* I. e. you will have a consecutive series, 1, *ichchhá*; 2, *ichchhá-jnána* or *vidhi-jnána*; 3, *ichchhá*. The second *ichchhá* is 'the desire to act' of § vi. which arose from the knowledge that such an action is commanded.—The true order is, 1. *ishṭa-sádhanatá-jnána*; 2. *ichchhá, (upáyechchhá;)* 3. *pravṛitti*. He here proves that *vidhi* cannot mean the second; he subsequently shews that it cannot be the third. Udayana and the old Nyáya differ as to the *first*, see § xiii.

† I. e. by *S'abda*, not by *ichchhá*.

‡ There are two kinds of causes *swarúpa sat* and *jnáta*; an example of the former is 'eating is the cause of satisfying hunger,' of the latter 'smoke is a cause of fire (being inferred').

§ The &c., includes 'absence of pain.' The former fault will not apply here as this knowledge of the desire for the fruit *will* cause action,—if a man does not desire heaven, the command *Swargakámo yajeta* is not a command *to him*.

L

this knowledge that the action is the means to the desired end, the tense sign of the command must be its cause;—hence the knowledge of the wish for the end is not a cause of activity, as activity can be found where it does not exist [if only the knowledge of the action's being a means to a desired end exist;] and hence there would be confusion of the two causes, because *your* cause 'the knowledge of the desire for the fruit' is always found accompanied by *my* cause, 'the knowledge that the action is a means to a desired end' [and as in certain cases mine is found where yours is not found, mine will be sufficient by itself and why then need we bring in yours at all?] The commentator adds another objection in the fact that as there is no proof that the knowledge of the wish for the fruit produces the wish for the means, [this being produced by the knowledge that the means will produce a desired end] it follows that the former cannot be the meaning conveyed by the tense affix of the command [because this meaning whatever it be, must necessitate action].

VIII. "Well, but why not say that the knowledge of volition [as implied in the potential used imperatively] is alone that which sets men in action, but that no tense-sign besides this does express volition, since all the other tense-signs express only an operation in accordance with the meaning of the root? For we find this the case in such instances as 'the chariot goes' [where we have an operation but no volition."] He replies,

> VIII. In consequence of the fixed rule about applying the term 'maker' drawn from the distinction between the use of the phrases 'made' and 'not made,' making or action means volition only; and that action which is causative in reference to a subsequent thing is the meaning of the tense-sign.

In accordance with such phrases as 'the pot is made,' 'the shoot is not made,' we may say that the potter, &c., are makers but not the other instrumental causes [as the wheel, &c.,] hence we may say that the meaning of the root *Kṛi* is making or action, [*i. e. kṛiti*, or volition.]—" But if so, would not the words 'volition' and 'tense-sign,' be synonyms? [as all tense signs can be resolved into *kṛiti, i. e. yatna.*"] He replies by the last paragraph. That making or action, which is the means in reference to an actual subsequent end, is the meaning of the tense-sign,—*i. e.* the meaning of the tense-sign is only a volition in accordance with the end. Or (according to another view) the meaning of the tense-sign is a volition which produces a repetition of the meaning of the root, in the form of successively repeated operations in accordance with the desired end, one following the other. In this way the tense-sign will have three meanings, volition, accordance with the root and successive repetition [while under the first view it will have only the two first; under either view, however, the tense-sign will involve more than simple volition and therefore cannot be its synonym].

IX. "But may we not allow that the root *Kṛi* may mean volition, and yet maintain that the tense-sign only means an operation in accordance with the root, the volition being only understood by an inference?"* He replies,

IX. The meaning of the tense-sign is a volition and this applies to all tense-signs equally; since by it all can be clearly developed, and since the alleged inference cannot be established.

As by 'it,'—*i. e.* making, or the word which expresses making (*karoti*) the meaning of the tense-sign is developed at length, as in *pákam karoti,* ' he makes cooking' for *pachati,* ' he cooks,'—we must have ' making,' *i. e.* volition, as the meaning of the tense-sign; [and again your supposed inference fails] since an operation in accordance with the root does not always imply a volition, as an operation in accordance with the root 'cook' in the present case can be found even in an unintelligent thing [as in the wood, fire, pot, &c., where of course there can be no volition.]

"But, if so, why on hearing the objective case 'boiled rice,' do we naturally require the sentence to be be filled up by ' he cooks' or ' he eats?' [On *my* hypothesis it is easily explained, as I maintain that all tense-signs imply an operation in accordance with the root's meaning, and from this we can infer volition in this instance; but on your hypothesis, it is not so obvious."] This can be explained, in our view, by the fact that an objective case is invariably accompanied by a volition [expressed by the tense-sign,] just as on the other hand

* The inference will be in this form—wherever there is no volition there is no operation in accordance with the root.

on hearing the verb 'he cooks,' we naturally require the sentence to be filled up by some object.

X. "But since by developing the full meaning we do obtain an agent (as in 'he makes cooking' for 'he cooks') why should we not say that the tense-sign signifies also an agent?" He replies,

> X. We must not suppose that the tense-sign directly signifies [an agent,] as this which is connected with number can be obtained by inference; and in the obtaining of that which is connected with number, the rule holds for that only which has expectancy.

We must not suppose that the tense-sign signifies an agent, since this 'agent' is gained by an inference from the number expressed by the tense-sign. What we mean by 'being gained by an inference' is that something is qualified by the meaning of the tense-sign, while at the same time it is expressed by a word ending in the nominative case. We use the former phrase 'qualified by the meaning of the tense-sign' to exclude such ambiguous cases as 'having eaten Devadatta goes away,' &c.,* and we use the latter phrase 'while at the same time, it is expressed by a word ending in the nominative case,' because in such instances as 'it is slept by Devadatta,' &c., it is the meaning of the root, 'sleep,' which is qualified by present time, as implied in the tense-sign [and verbal roots have no cases.] [Nor may we say that the object is connected with the tense-sign as well as the subject,—because] in such phrases as 'Chaitra cooks rice,' &c. since the meaning 'rice' is already connected with the idea of object as implied in the objective case, we are not to suppose that there is any further dependence (as of expectancy) on the volition expressed by the tense-sign; hence the tense-sign is connected with the meaning of the crude form as expressed in the unmodified† 'casus rectus.' Hence in accordance with the rule that 'the number [of the tense] is connect-

---

* Here Devadatta is qualified by number and volition through the meaning of the tense-sign, *i. e. Devadatta ekatwaván kritimánscha ;* but *bhuktwá* is not thus qualified,—it itself is an adverb and qualifies the verb. According to Hindu grammar the adverbial suffix *twá* involves the elision of the nominative affix (cf. Pán. 2, 4, 82) and therefore the second part of the definition would apply, but not the former.

† I. e. Non-oblique case, *i. e.* not a *káraka*. सुड् means here *rectus ;* there is a Sútra उक्तात् सु औ जस्; । 'The signs of the Nominative case are used after a word which is the subject of a verb.'—The 'casus rectus' will be *Chaitras* in the *Kartriváchya* sentence, and *taṇḍulam* in the *Karmaváchya.*

ed with that with which the volition implied by the tense-sign is connected,'—since this follows because this volition and number are expressed by the same tense sign,—the nominative case is employed only where the number of the agent, &c.,* are already signified by the tense-sign. And in the same way the object cannot be said to be directly signified by the tense-sign.†

XI. "Well, but," say the Mimánsakas, "may not the command be the attribute of the object?" He replies,

> XI. The object cannot be the meaning of the command because it would apply too far; nor can the produced desert (*apúrva*) since it would lose its very nature; nor can an especial effect, since it is not always found present; nor, also, can the act, since men do not necessarily engage in the performance.

a. If you say that the objects [of the sacrifice] are heaven, &c.,‡ and the meaning of the command is an attribute in *them*, *i. e.* the fact of their having to be produced,—it is answered 'the object cannot be the meaning of the command because it would apply too far,'—since, if, as you say, the attribute of their having to be produced resides in heaven, &c., it would follow that a person possessing this knowledge might engage in any other action than sacrifice [as eating, &c., since 'the having to be produced or accomplished' resides, according to your opinion, in the *object* and not in the *act*.]

---

* I. e. the agent *Kartá* in most sentences, and the object *Karma* in such as 'the prize is gained by Devadatta.' As in the sentence 'Devadatta goes' the tense-sign signifies the volition *(kriti)* and not the agent, but by the connection we gain the latter, so in the sentence "the prize is gained by Devadatta" the tense-sign equally signifies the volition, and by the connection we gain the object.

† In the sentence *Chaitras taṇḍulam pachati*, *taṇḍula* means simply 'rice' and is connected with the affix *am* which signifies that *taṇḍula* in the singular number is the object; this *am* is connected with the root *pacha* which means ' cooking ;' *pacha* is connected with the affix *tip* which means 1, *vartamána-kála*, 2, *yatna*. 3, *sankhyá*. The present time as implied by *tip* is connected with *yatna*, and *yatna* and *sankhyá* are connected with the *kartá Chaitra*. In the sentence *Chaitreṇa taṇḍulam pachyate*, the same process can be traced; *chaitra* is connected with the affix *tá*, *tá* with the root *pacha*, *pacha* with the affix *te*, and *te* as before with *taṇḍulam*. The grammarians maintain that in the former case the real meaning of the verbal affix is directly *Kartá*, in the latter *Karma;* the Nyáya maintains that in both cases it is *yatna* (sc. *Kriti*), but indirectly by *anvaya* it may be respectively *Kartá* or *Karma*.

‡ As in such commands as "let him who desires heaven offer the *jyotishṭoma* sacrifice," &c.—The opponent maintains that their real meaning is, "heaven is to be produced," *swargah káryah*, but not 'the sacrifice is to be performed.'

b. If you say that the 'object' means *apúrva*,* and that the meaning of the command is an attribute in *it*, *i. e.* the fact of its having to be produced,† then it is answered, 'it would lose its very nature;' for the very word *apúrva* [as compounded of *a* 'not' and *púrva* 'previously existing'] implies that it was not known before the verbal knowledge was produced by hearing the command; and if it is known before [as it must be, if the words of the command are to imply it,]‡ then it would cease to be *apúrva* at all; and, on the other hand, if it is not known before, then how can you have any knowledge of the meaning of the tense-sign in the command, and consequently how can you have any verbal knowledge of *apúrva* produced by this tense-sign?

c. If the Mímánsaka replies, 'why should there not be a previous knowledge that *apúrva* is the meaning of the command, so far as regards its *general* character as a thing to be produced,—but when the verbal knowledge is gained, then in consequence of the compatibility§ there arises a knowledge of *apúrva* as an *especial* thing to be produced,' to this it is answered, 'because we do not always find this especial *apúrva* present,' *i. e.* it would follow that there is no *apúrva*|| in necessary observances [as the morning and evening prayer, &c.,] or in absolute prohibitions [as that from injuring living creatures,] since we find no persons enjoined to perform them as they desire certain fruit to ensue [which fruit is to be attained by the produced *apúrva* as the means,—and consequently the tense-sign as in *má hinsyát* becomes meaningless.]

d. Or we may take this third sentence of the original in a different sense as follows. An objector might say, "but why might we not hold that we recognise that the word means a particular *apúrva*

---

* The unseen efficacy which arises from the sacrifice cf. p. 10.

† In this view the meaning of the command will be 'by him who desires heaven, the merit which is the cause of its attainment, is to be produced by the jyotishṭoma sacrifice.'

‡ 'The knowledge of the power of a word is necessary, for if the power of a word be not apprehended previously, there could not be any recollection,—since this depends upon that relation called 'power' (*i. e.* the connection between a word and its meaning),—even though the word might be heard' (Siddh. Mukt. p. 79.) The knowledge of the connection between a word and its meaning is the cause of the meaning's being recollected when the word is heard, and from this recollection ensues verbal knowledge.

§ Expectancy, compatibility and juxtaposition are the three causes, or rather necessary conditions, of verbal knowledge, see *supra*, p. 43.

|| See Dr. Hall's Refutation of Hindu Philosophy, pp. 22—24.

*accompanied (though not necessarily so) by being an effect, just as the word 'earth' means a something necessarily distinguished by possessing a certain nature but not necessarily accompanied by the attribute of smell?" To this it is answered " because we do not find it so," *i. e.* because we cannot so know an *apúrva* distinguished by the character of *apúrvatwa*. It is possible for the substance possessed of the special nature of earth to be known to possess smell, by means of memory or inference from a previous perception; but such a supposition is precluded in the present case by the very name *apúrva*, which implies an absence of any previous perception, and which would therefore be rendered nugatory.

e. " Well, why not take the sacrifice as the 'object,'† and then the meaning of the command will be an attribute of *it*, *i. e.* the fact of its having to be performed?" To this it is answered in the last words of the original verse. Your view cannot hold, since we do not see that men engage in the performance of the sacrifice, if there be present in their minds the idea that it will be only a means of trouble and expense, [while on your view the simple fact of their knowing it to be a command that 'by him who desires heaven the *jyotishṭoma* sacrifice is to be performed' should impel them irresistibly to the performance thereof.]—The word '*also*' implies that the object cannot mean '*apúrva*,' since the very same objection will hold as in the previous supposition of ' the sacrifice.'

XII. "But may we not say that words are the instrument of verbal knowledge, and that the enforcing power is an attribute residing in *them*,‡ and that the knowledge thereof incites men to engage in the enjoined rites;—hence it is said, ' the tense-signs such as the imperative, &c., express a *special* signification *i. e.* an enjoining power, while the common signification of all the tense-signs is an effort of the agent in accordance with the meaning of the root.' There arises from the tense affix of the imperative the idea of an enforcing power, setting a man to perform the enjoined sacrifice;

---

* For *upalakshita* see note ‡ in p. 66.

† Under this view the real meaning of the command will be ' by him who desires heaven the *jyotishṭoma* sacrifice is to be performed..'

‡ According to the Mímánsá, *bhávaná* resides in the agent as a volition *(yatna)* to perform some act to attain a desired end, and it may be expressed by any tense-sign; but it resides in the eternal Veda as an enjoining power *(preroṇa)*, the end of which is the production of the former volition of the hearer,—this is only expressed by the imperative or potential.

while the general meaning of all the tense-signs is an effort tending to the production of a certain action [thus *Devadatto gachchhati* means that 'Devadatta is possessed of a volition tending to produce going.'"] He replies,

XII. This enforcing power of the imperative, &c., is not to be maintained, since it cannot be proved, and since men do not engage in the performance, even though they know of the existence of this presumed enforcing power, [*i. e.* unless they have also the knowledge that it will be a means of procuring their wishes;] and again exhaustion is difficult to rest upon, as contradiction equally applies to this view, as well as to the others.

If you object that as every other meaning of the imperative tense-sign is excluded, it follows by exhaustion that this enforcing power must be its meaning, he replies that the contradiction equally applies to this opinion, as well as to the others, [as action does not necessarily follow from the knowledge of it.]

XIII. "But," says the Naiyáyika, " why should not the meaning of the command be the fact that the rite is a means to a desired end,—this residing as an attribute in the instrument, the sacrifice?"* He replies,

XIII. [This cannot be] because it is sometimes given as the reason for the command; because the command may be inferred therefrom; from the absence of this meaning in the second and third persons [of the imperative]; from its recognition in other meanings; and because on this view prohibition could not be established.

a. Because the fact of its being the means to the attainment of a desired object is often alleged by the speaker as proving the meaning of the command; and as a thing cannot be *its own* proof [it follows that the fact of its being a means to a desired object cannot be the meaning of the command]. Thus when it is said as a secu-

---

* The old Nyáya maintained the meaning of *vidhi* to be इष्टसाधनत्वं कार्यत्वञ्च. Udayana maintains it to be आप्तवक्त्रभिप्राय: The modern Nyáya (*i. e.* Siddhánta Mukt.) gives बलवदनिष्टाननुबन्धीष्टसाधनत्वं

lar command, 'let him who desires fire rub two pieces of *aruṇi* wood together,' if you ask 'why?' the utterer of the command replies, 'because the rubbing two pieces of wood together is a means of producing fire.'

b. Another reason against your view is—because a command may be inferred even *after* the knowledge that the action is a means to the desired end has been produced by the *arthavāda* [or supplementary passage explaining the purpose of the command];—but if by the command which is thus inferred we were only to understand the fact that the action in question is a means to the desired end, then this inference would be wholly superfluous. Thus on hearing the S'ruti 'he crosses over death, he crosses over Brahmanicide [who offers the As'wamedha'], all the systems allow that there arises the inference of a command in such a form as 'let him who desires to cross over death and Brahmanicide, offer the As'wamedha.'

c. "From the absence of this meaning [*i. e.* its being a means to the desired end,] in the second and third* persons of the potential used imperatively;" in such phrases as 'you should do it' and 'let me do it' an injunction, or wish is implied [but not the fact of its being a means to a desired end,]—injunction means here the wish of the speaker; and consequently we may conclude that the first person also only means the wish of the speaker [and not the fact of the action being a means to the desired end.]

d. "From the fact that this meaning of 'wish' is acknowledged in the other meanings of the potential," as for instance in its meaning of 'respectful solicitation.'†

e. "Because on this view prohibition could not be established." Thus in the injunction "let him not eat the Kalanja,"‡ you cannot maintain that it is *not* the means to a desired end [as of course the eating will produce its proper pleasure.] Nor can you say [with the modern school,] that the meaning of the command is that the action is not accompanied by a predominant undesirable result, because this will not apply to such cases as 'let him who desires

---

* In Hindu grammar the third person corresponds to our first.

† अध्येषणा is the चघीष् of Pāṇini (3, 3, 161). The Saṅkshipta Sāra explains it by भक्तारपूर्वकं गरोर्निर्योजनं as भवान् पुचसध्यापयेत्।

‡ Some hold the *Kalanja* to be the flesh of a deer killed by a poisoned arrow—others hemp or bhang,—others a kind of garlic. See Raghunandana's Ekādas'i tattwa.

to kill his enemy by incantation offer a hawk' [because this rite produces hell as its fruit]. And [if you say that in the case of the offerer, hell is not considered by *him* as a predominant undesirable result, since he still performs the ceremony, I reply that this does not hold, as] you cannot maintain that the sacrifice *generally* does not produce a result which the mass of mankind regard with predominant aversion, because the man who does *not* perform the sacrifice certainly has this predominant aversion which restrains him from yielding to the temptation of the gratification of a present revenge at the risk of a future torment in hell.

XIV. [After this lengthened discussion of the various current opinions on the nature of *vidhi* or command,] the author now proceeds to deliver his own.

> XIV. The primary meaning of the potential used imperatively, &c., is the will of the speaker in the form of a command enjoining activity or cessation therefrom; while we conclude by inference that it is the means to a desired end for the doer.

The will of a fit person, *i. e.* God, having for its object engagement in the performance of an act [*i. e.* as in command] or refraining therefrom, [*i. e.* as in prohibition,] is the primary meaning of the affixes of the potential, &c.; and from these is to be inferred [see § vi.) that it is the means to obtain a desired end, [and hence the existence of 'command' proves the existence of a commander, God].

But the commentator here adds as a remark, that this view of Udayanáchárya is untenable, as by it you could not properly have prohibition at all, since every action of every kind is in one sense the object of God's will, [*i. e.* nothing, whether good or evil, takes place without his will]. If you reply that 'command' is 'God's will,' meaning by 'will' such a will as is unaccompanied by any predominant undesirable result, we object that the definition becomes needlessly complicated; and the old Naiyáyika opinion of § xiii. is after all the best.*

---

* Udayana gives as his definition of 'command' the 'will of a fit person,' *i. e.* God. It is replied that this will include too much as even evil actions are in one sense done with God's will. The definition is then corrected to 'such a will as is unproductive of any predominant undesirable result,'—in this view we may allow God's will in the case of an evil action, but here we shall not have *vidhi*, 'command,'—as it is such a will of God as produces hell to the doer.—The com-

XV. He now [resumes the interpretation of the first S'loka, interrupted by the late discussion on *vidhi* §§ vi.—xiv. and] proceeds to give the second meaning of 'S'ruti.'

XV. All the Veda refers to the Supreme Being as its object; only, by means of its own primary meaning, like the words 'heaven,' &c., can it refer to a command.

In every part of the Veda is God's existence established, as for instance in such passages as, 'Vishṇu verily is the sacrifice' *(passim)*, 'he sees without eyes,' (Swet. Up. iii. 19) 'by the command of this (previously mentioned) indestructible being, O Gárgí, heaven and earth stay upheld in their places, (Bṛihadár. Up. iii. 8, 9.) Nor may you say with the Mímánsá, that 'these passages, being declaratory or indicative* [and not expressed in the potential or imperative, as commands are,] refer to something else, *i. e.* a command elsewhere expressed,' [or in other words they are the *artharáda* of a previous *vidhi*],—because even according to your own opinion, these passages about God do possess an authority to establish the existence of their primary meaning, from their agreeing with such positive commands as 'let him adore God,' just as the passages declarative of heaven, hell, &c., [establish the objects which they primarily mean, because they are connected with such positive commands, as 'let him who desires heaven offer such a sacrifice,']—otherwise the very words 'heaven,' 'hell,' &c., would have no authority to establish their own primary significations. Hence he adds the latter line of the ꞌSloka, since it is only by establishing its own primary meaning that a declaratory passage can be said to agree with a command.

[The commentator now proceeds to give a second explanation of 'the sentences thereof' in § i.] The 'sentences thereof,'—*i. e.* the sentences of the Veda, expressing praise and blame,—must have been preceded, in the speaker's mind, by the knowledge of praise and blame, from the very fact that they are sentences which express

mentator objects to this as needlessly complicated; but it is not uninteresting to find the same thought in Anselm's 'cur Deus homo?' "although man or an evil angel be unwilling to submit to the will and ordinance of God, yet he cannot escape from it, because if he will flee from the will of God commanding him, he comes under the will of God punishing him."

* According to the Mímánsá those passages which are not *vidhi* are *siddha* as opposed to *sádhya*; they describe something past or present *(swarúpakathanam)*, while the *vidhi* relates to something future which is to be performed.

praise and blame, like such a secular sentence as 'the mango fruit is very sweet when ripe,' [as none could say this with authority unless he possessed previous knowledge thereof].

XVI. He now gives a second explanation of 'particular number' in § i.

> XVI. In such phrases as 'let me be,' 'I was,' 'I will be,' &c., the number belongs to a speaker; nor could there be the current names of the 'Sákhás, without a primal utterance.

a. The first person singular as used in the Veda declares the 'number' of an independent speaker,—there being many such instances, as in the passage* "It reflected, 'let me, the one, become many,'" &c.

b. He now gives a third meaning of the word *sankhyá*, as making it the same as another derivative from the same root, *samákhyá*, 'name, fame,'—"nor could there be &c." There are traditional names, in the Veda, of all the various 'Sákhás (or current recensions,) as Káṭhaka or that belonging to Kaṭha, Kálápa or that belonging to Kalápa, &c.; nor can we explain this on the hypothesis† that these men first read that particular recension only, [others having before then read many or all,] since the number of readers is endless and in the eternal succession others besides these mentioned may well be supposed to have read those 'Sákhás only, [and why then were not the 'Sákhás called by their names?] Therefore we are driven to the belief that the adorable Supreme Being, seeing all supersensuous objects and possessed of boundless compassion, did at the beginning of each creation assume a particular body belonging to Kaṭha, Kalápa, &c. which body was moved by the merit of beings like ourselves,‡ and the 'Sákhás which He thus uttered were severally called by these particular names.

---

* The two old MSS. read this quotation as I have printed it. Some copies read स for तत् but none have the usual reading found in Chhánd. Up. vi. 2.

† Cf. 'Sabara's Comm. on Jaimini, i. 1, 30.

‡ The final cause of God's assuming these bodies was to render possible the happiness due to the merit of men like ourselves,—*adrishṭa* is an impelling cause of every thing down to the junction of two atoms, see Muktávali, pp. 104, 105.

Thus have we established that it is the contemplation of God, which is the true means of liberation, (see I. ii.)

XVII. He now adds a couplet in reference to those who believe not in God.

> XVII. Iron-souled are they in whose hearts Thou canst find no place, though thus washed by the repeated inundations of ethics and Vaidic texts; yet still in time, Oh merciful one, Thou in thy goodness canst save even those who oppose our proposition, and make them undoubting in their conviction of Thy existence.
>
> XVIII. But as for us, O Thou essentially Fair, though our minds have been long plunged in Thee, the ocean of joy,* yet are they verily restless still and unsatisfied; therefore, oh Lord, haste to display Thy mercy, that our minds fixed only on Thee, we may no more be subject to Yama's continual inflictions.
>
> XIX. This garland of flowers of ethics, radiant in its beauty,—what matters it, whether it perfumes the right and left hand† or not?—only may the Guru of Indra's Guru‡ be pleased by my presenting it as an offering at his footstool.

---

* For *addhá* explained as *tattwam*, see 'Sis'upála-badha, iii. 42, schol.
† Or 'the sapaksha and vipaksha of my argument.'
‡ 'Siva, as the guru of Brihaspati. Brihaspati is represented as the guru of Indra in the Aitareya Bráhmaṇa, VII. 28.

www.ingramcontent.com/pod-product-compliance
Lightning Source LLC
Chambersburg PA
CBHW031453160426
43195CB00010BB/961